From
Brother Lovell
"Steven Lovell"

BENJAMIN BONNEVILLE

Soldier of the American Frontier

EDITH HAROLDSEN LOVELL

First Printing: March, 1992

International Standard Book Number
0-88290-438-8

Horizon Publishers' Catalog and Order Number
1951

Printed and distributed
in the United States of America by

Horizon Publishers
& Distributors, Incorporated
P.O. Box 490 Bountiful, Utah 84011-0490

Contents

Introduction

Meet Bonneville, soldier of the American frontier. He was short, stocky, bald-headed and black-eyed. He wasn't a trapper, but always appears in that chapter of western history. He wasn't exactly an explorer, for others had preceded him in most of his travels. A native of France, he served in the United States Army for over fifty years. Mountains, streets, products, schools, a salt desert, a prehistoric lake and a power dam have been named for him.

Most of Bonneville's tasks were obscure, unnotable. One assignment which he conceived and asked for in the early 1830s was not run-of-the-mill, though not unique in Army annals. From the journal of that project, Washington Irving produced *The Adventures of Captain Bonneville*, the account of an expedition to the Rocky Mountains. It was a best-seller, and brought spiralling dividends of popular appreciation for the vast western country and the value—even the necessity—of its belonging to the United States.

The nation profited well from Bonneville's travels, though the Army was testy that he overstayed his leave. For an outlay of only a captain's pay, the government received the first comprehensive report of the intermountain country. Bonneville described the geographical features, resources, climate, the names, numbers, locations and attitudes of the Indian tribes and the extent of British domination of the area, all from first-hand observation and from information gleaned in the field. He reported also conditions in Spainsh California as seen by a party he sent there.

Maps which Bonneville personally and painstakingly drew were the first to show correctly the mountains and plains and the intricate river drainage systems. Map historian Carl I. Wheat has called Bonneville's maps "of real import," pointing out the accurate placement of the heads of Wind River, the Green, Sweetwater, Salmon and Gallatin's fork of the Missouri, as well as the course of the Snake and Salmon rivers to the Columbia and of the Bear river to the Great Salt Lake.

Map chronicler G. K. Warren has added "The existence of the great interior basins without outlets to the ocean, of Mary's or Ogden's river (Humbolt) . . . and of the Sevier river and lake was determined by Captain Bonneville's maps . . . the map of the sources of the Yellowstone is the best original one of that region."

Even modest fame has its price. To Bonneville, success of his expedition was a mixed blessing. He was dropped from Army rolls for overstaying his leave; his months-long battle for reinstatement was complicated by the War Department's loss of his original reports—one was found years later. Some fellow officers resented him, and he was by-passed for a number of choice assignments. After Bonneville died, H. H. Bancroft maligned him with utterly untrue accusations of Indian cruelty and of fortune-hunting; a few careless later writers have echoed Bancroft's false assessment.

In his half-century of Army service, Bonneville tramped from one outpost to another, witnessing and living the drama of a burgeoning and blossoming young United States laying claim to a continent. Like many citizens, native and adopted, he cherished a vision of a fair, free and magnificient nation. He was an eager American.

A notion lingers of campfires and comradery, of enterprise and daring somehow related to national pride. Bonneville is the inquisitive adventurer probing into remote places. He is the brash enterpreneur of the fur trade, the emissary of friendship to the Indians, the watchful sentinel eyeing covetous foreign countries. He is the statesmen's tool of force to settle differences, to maintain—sometimes to expand—national boundaries. He is the dusty anonymous infantryman who trudged the prairies and valleys with musket and saber, who shaped cottonwood logs into a show of law and order called a fort so that homeseekers might feel secure. He is the tough, proud, faithful soldier of the old west. This last fancy might have pleased him most.

Acknowledgments

More good people than I can begin to count—and thank— have helped me in this project. I must especially acknowlege Karen Grover, Kathryn Jenson, Jessie Barzee and David Lovell, as well as Dena Norman and Cathleen Lovell. Above all, I appreciate the enduring support of my good companion, George Everett Lovell.

Appreciation is also expressed to Duane Crowther for his final editing of the book, and to the staff of Horizon Publishers for their design and book production efforts.

In the friendly world of history, record-keepers and hobbyists go to great lengths to supply requested information. Librarians ferret out books and articles and extend one's reach with interlibrary loans. Historical Societies preserve—and share—letters, clippings, bits and pieces to complete the mosaic. Families encourage and show approval even when wisdom demurs.

For the writer of biography remain the intriguing pursuit of fading footsteps and the fearsome responsibility of producing an honest likeness of a fellow man. Deep appreciation is expressed to all who have assisted me in meeting these challenges.

Chronological Time Line

Benjamin Louis Eulalie Bonneville

1796—Born in Evreux, France.

1803-1813—Grew up in New York City; ward of Thomas Paine.

1813—Cadet, United States Military Academy.

1815—Commissioned Bvt. 2nd Lieutenant. Served at Fort Wolcott, Rhode Island, Fort Independence, Massachusetts, Fort George, Maine, in Light Artillery.

1819—Second Lieutenant, Eighth Infantry. Served in construction of Jackson Military Road, and Bay St. Louis, Mississippi.

1820—First Lieutenant. Seventh Infantry. Served at Fort Smith, Arkansas Territory, and Fort Gibson, Indian Territory.

1825—Captain, Seventh Infantry. Granted year's leave to travel to France with LaFayette. Served, Fort Gibson to 1830.

1831—Granted leave to explore Rocky Mountains. Made preparations at Washington D.C., West Point and St. Louis.

1832—Traveled with wagons across continental divide. Trapped, observed and mapped area which became Wyoming, Idaho, Oregon and Washington. Sent Joseph Walker and men to California. Reported dead; dropped from Army rolls, 1834.

1835—Returned to New York and to Washington to fight for reinstatement.

1836—Traveled to Powder River (Wyoming). Reinstated, April. Served at Fort Gibson, Fort Towson, Fort Smith.

1839—Served with regiment in Second Seminole War in Florida to its conclusion in 1842. Recruiting, Baltimore, 1842.

1842—Married Ann Callender Lewis at Carlisle, Pennsylvania.

1842-1845—Served at Fort Brooke, Florida, Baton Rouge, Fort Smith.

1845—Major, Sixth Infantry. In Mexican War served in Wool's march to Monclova, Parras and Saltillo; marched with Worth through Carmargo to join Winfield Scott, by sea to Vera Cruz; march to Mexico City and battles of Cerro Gordo, Churubusco, Molino del Rey and Mexico City, 1847. Wounded at Churubusco.

1848—Commanding, Fort Gibson; 1849, Fort Kearney, Nebraska.

1849—Lieutenant Colonel, Fourth Infantry. Commanded at Madison Barracks Lake Ontario. Traveled by Great Lakes steamer to command at Fort Howard, Wisconsin. Regiment ordered to Oregon.

1852—Commanded Fourth Infantry in sea journeys and Isthmus march to San Francisco and Benicia, California, and to Vancouver Barracks. Washington. Commanded three years there.

1855—Colonel, Third Infantry, Commanded 700 soldiers by sea to Corpus Cristi, and march across Texas to New Mexico. Served at Fort Fillmore, Santa Fe and Albuquerque. Commanded Department of New Mexico in 1857 Apache War, and again in 1858-59 Navaho campaigns.

1860—Marched Third Infantry down entire length of the Pecos to Fort Clarke, Texas.

1860-1861—Sick leave, Carlisle, Pennsylvania and St. Louis.

1862, Served St. Louis in Civil War as Superintendent of Recruiting, Chief Mustering and Disbursing Officer of Missouri, and commanding Benton Barracks. Wife and daughter died at Benton Barracks, 1862.

1865—Brevet Brigadier General, March 13, 1865, for long and faithful service in the Army. Commanded at Jefferson Barracks. St. Louis, to retirement, October, 1866.

1866-1870—Lived in St. Louis.

1871—Married Susan Neiss. Lived in St. Louis and Fort Smith.

1878—Died, June 12, in Fort Smith. Buried in St. Louis.

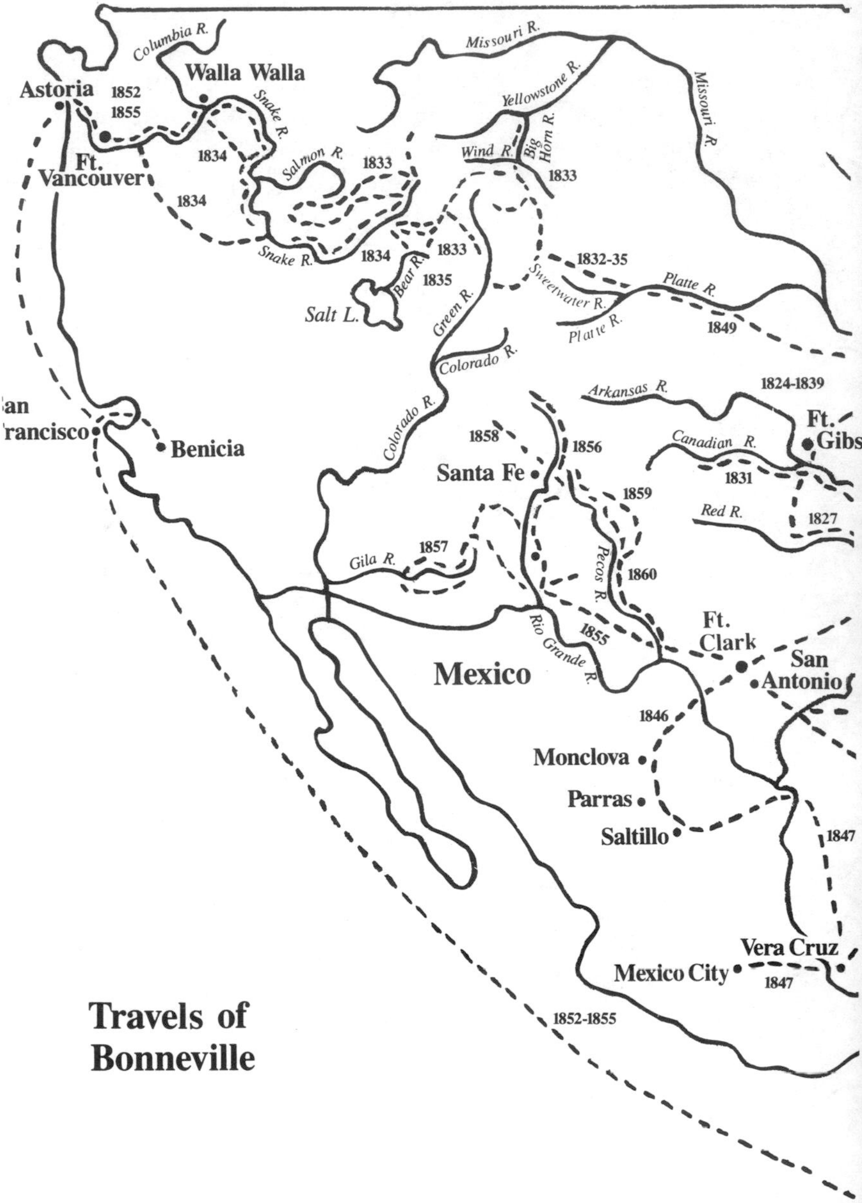
Columbia R.
Walla Walla
Astoria
1852
1855
Snake R.
Ft. Vancouver
1834
Salmon R.
1833
1834
Snake R.
1834
1833
Bear R.
1835
Salt L.
Missouri R.
Yellowstone R.
Missouri R.
Wind R.
Big Horn R.
1833
1832-35
Sweetwater R.
Platte R.
Platte R.
1849
Green R.
Colorado R.
Colorado R.
Arkansas R.
1824-1839
Ft. Gibs
Canadian R.
1831
Red R.
1827
an Francisco
Benicia
1858
1856
Santa Fe
1859
Gila R.
1857
Pecos R.
1860
Rio Grande R.
1855
Ft. Clark
San Antonio
Mexico
1846
Monclova
Parras
Saltillo
1847
Vera Cruz
Mexico City
1847
1852-1855

Travels of Bonneville

Ft. Howard
1851
Missis sipi R.
1829
1832
1836
1870
St. Louis
1829
Ohio R.
1826
Ft. Smith
1822
1822
Baton Rouge
1820
1821
New Orleans
Ft. Brooke
1839-1842
1855
1847
Sweet Springs, VA
1848
Washington
1860
Baltimore
1842
Carlisle
1842
1850
Madison Barracks
Ft. George
1817
1818
Ft. Independence
Boston
Paris
1826
Ft. Columbus
New York City
Philadelphia
1825
Paris
Norfolk
Paris
1802
1819
1842
Colon
Panama

Photo courtesy of U. S. Army Military History Institute (Carlisle, PA).

Chapter One
1796-1819

Birth, Youth and the Army

Washington Irving has already written about Bonneville. Is there any more to be said? Well, yes. Talented Irving spotlighted one endeavor with wit and verve, but thirty-eight months do not a man's life story tell, nor lend dimension to a personable immigrant whose years and efforts spanned the blossoming of America.

Birth in Normandy, France

If the inscription chiseled on his tombstone is correct, Benjamin Louis Eulalie de Bonneville was born April 11, 1796. This date disagrees with some printed versions of his age, and also disposes of the legend that he was the son of the Marquis de Lafayette, for that flamboyant Frenchman was in prison in Austria from 1792 to 1797.

It may be indicative of the muddled loyalties of the times that the son of Nicolas and Marguerite Eulalie Brazier de Bonneville was given the royal name Louis, along with Benjamin, by tradition in honor of Benjamin Franklin, the late American minister to France. Benjamin was born sixty miles west by northwest of Paris in Evreux, Normandy, a cathedral town which had sheltered the Bonneville family for centuries. Nicolas and Marguerite were the parents of Louis, Thomas, Benjamin and Marie, according to a family record book. This is the only mention of the children Louis and Marie in first-hand information, and it may be that these two died in infancy.

Father's Background and Early Association with Thomas Paine

Benjamin Bonneville's father, Nicolas, was born in 1760 in Evreux, the son of an attorney, Pierre-Jean de Bonneville. Ancestors in Normandy included an archbishop, Pierre, and Nicolas, Lord of Chamelac.

As a young man Nicolas went to Paris where he gloried in the world of words. With a talent for languages, he translated Shakespeare and German works into French. Still in his twenties, he was a man of stature in the world of letters.[1] At this time his thoughts turned to his country's problems. A poem in his 1786 book of verse "has, at an earlier date, the fine sonority of the Marseillaise."[2] He was awarded the "Decoration of Mt. Carmel" and was elected a Depute in the National Assembly. He married Marguerite Eulalie Brazier in the early 1790's.[3]

Nicolas wrote and published a history of Europe. Joining the clamor for a more-representative government, he edited small journals reflecting citizen resentment at government indifference to want. He translated and published Thomas Paine's "Rights of Man." Paine, erstwhile English corsetmaker, tax collector and free-thinker, had achieved fame in America in the 1770s with his essays "Common Sense" and the "Crisis" series, urging the colonies to put off the shackles of the mother country. Paine counted as friends most of the signers of the Declaration of Independence, and with Lafayette, shared George Washington's campfire during many campaigns. Indicted in England for high treason, he came to Paris and was given a seat in the French Assembly by the Girondins, the political party of Nicolas de Bonneville and the Marquis de Lafayette.

When radicals precipitated the Reign of Terror, cathedrals and public buildings were pillaged. The guillotine claimed hundreds. Besides Louis Sixteenth and Marie Antoinette, twenty-one Girondist members of the National Assembly were executed, including many of Nicolas de Bonneville's friends. Lafayette was leading an army in Austria and surrendered—disgracefully, some said—but lived to serve his country another day, for the Austrians kept him locked up for five years. Thomas Paine, enraged at being arrested, turned his venom on Christianity, and wrote his caustic "Age of Reason." James Monroe rescued him from prison; among his loyal friends were two other Americans, poet Joel Barlow and aspiring painter Robert Fulton. Another close associate was his French translator and publisher, Nicolas Bonneville. Paine is said by his biographers to have stood as godfather for Thomas Nicolas de Bonneville, born in 1794. Twice married, but now alone, Paine had no children.

Denounced as an "aristocrate" and imprisoned with other Girondists, Nicolas escaped execution by the "9 Thermidor" upheaval in power. After his release from prison, he "remained in Evreux under strict surveillance." During this time, Marguerite was a "merchant of novelties" in Evreux.[4] Described as a great lady noted for her manners, Marguerite had some facility of pen, and like Adrienne de Lafayette, remained loyal to her Catholic heritage in spite of her husband's dallying with modern philosophies. Though Evreux is described as within sight of the smoke of Paris, it was by temperament and tradition a world apart. Normandy had been invaded by Vikings hence the name but centuries of amiable mixing of Norse independence and Latin mellowness had produced a stable, pleasant way of life. Norman cathedrals' stained-glass windows filtered a warm glow over fine wood-carved interiors. Tall poplars guarded thatched houses, and wooden-wheeled carts rumbled along country roads. Here, as they waited out the aftermath of the French Revolution, Marguerite and Nicolas welcomed their son, Benjamin Louis Eulalie de Bonneville.

Back again in Paris, Nicolas edited a daily newspaper and frequently dissented from the policies of the ruling Directoire. Thomas Paine came to live at the Bonneville home in the fall of 1796 or spring of 1797.

"Our house was at No. 4 Rue de Theatre Francois," Marguerite wrote. "All the first floor was occupied as a printing office . . . Mr. Bonneville gave up his study and a bed-chamber to Thomas Paine."

"During the six years he lived at our house, he frequently pressed us to go to America, offering us all that he should be able to do for us, saying he would bequeath his property to our children."[5] Nicolas continued as Paine's mouthpiece, translating his essays and printing his comments. He also maintained his own independent editorial stance. When he criticized Napoleon he was arrested and his press confiscated. After his release he was penniless. Paine, disillusioned, made plans to go to America where his friend Thomas Jefferson was now president. He sailed for the United States in early autumn, 1802.

Benjamin's Move to America

"Seeing a new revolution that would strike, personally, many of the republicans, it was resolved soon after the departure of Mr. Paine for America that I should go thither with my children, relying fully on the good offices of Mr. Paine, whose conduct in America justified that reliance," Marguerite wrote. "Some affairs of great consequence made it impracticable for Mr. Bonneville to quit France," she added, leaving unanswered questions. Was Nicolas planning to participate in a new movement to establish a republic? Did he hope to retrieve his lost property? Most accounts say that Nicolas was under surveillance, a parole of sorts, an ambiguous condition in which the victim never knew what misstep would lead him back to prison. Marguerite's departure was of some emergency, for she sailed with her small boys on a vessel bound for Norfolk, Virginia, far away from Paine's homes in New York and New Jersey.

Like many immigrants to America, the Bonnevilles arrived in debt for their passage. From Norfolk, the French mother wrote to Thomas Paine in Washington. In his reply dated November 15, 1802, Paine wrote that he was happy she had arrived safely and that he would send the 22:10 sterling due. He directed her to Bordentown, New Jersey, to the home he had been given for his services in the War for Independence.[6]

The United States had not greeted Thomas Paine with open arms. His criticism of religion in "The Age of Reason" had robbed him of his fame. Thomas Jefferson remained his friend, as did Albert Gallatin, whose wife was Hannah Nicholson, daughter of an old comrade of Paine's war years. But Thomas Paine had become an embarrassment and no government appointment could be expected. Paine busied himself writing letters for publication on such issues as the purchase of the "vacant backlands" of the continent. He moved on to Bordentown in February, 1803.

Life in Thomas Paine's New Jersey and New York Homes

Marguerite de Bonneville, as her name appears in French sources, was now Margaret Bonneville, living in Paine's cottage but not happy, according to Paine biographers. Paine had lived with the Bonnevilles for six years, yet Margaret was now a beggar, having but promises to advance for food and shelter for her boys. Her sponsor, in the eyes of the small town, was an infidel who would tear down the very foundations of religion.

In March, 1803, Paine went to New York City, where he was honored by James Cheetham, editor of the "American Citizen." In return, Paine wrote for Cheetham's paper. By early spring, 1804, he was living at 16 Gold Street, where Margaret Bonneville and her sons joined him. Possibly he summoned Margaret, for he suffered partial paralysis in his hands during the winter. Paine grumbled about Margaret's past board bill, but paid it. He was finding responsibility of a family difficult, and though he acknowledged his debt, he fretted that the husband and father was still absent. In a letter to the American Consul in Paris dated March 1, 1804, Paine complained that he had not received a line from Bonneville.[7]

Some Paine biographers write that Margaret's son Louis was sent back to his father in Paris in 1804. But "Louis" is never mentioned in the written accounts of Paine or Margaret. Paine writes of "the boys" and of "Thomas and Bebia."—Bebia was Benjamin's nickname. Margaret writes of "my sons" and "Thomas and Benjamin." It is unlikely that a son named Louis came to America. The children Louis and Marie, listed in the family record book, remain unaccounted for and may have died at birth.

Late in the spring, Thomas Paine went to his farm in New Rochelle, and Margaret and her sons joined him there, but soon returned to New York. Paine spent a lonely winter in the farmhouse. In the spring he wrote to his friend John Fellows in New York asking him to put Bebia and Thomas on board the New Rochelle boat.[8]

Thomas and Benjamin were to spend many pleasant hours at the farm. The Devoe family who had owned the meadows and woodlots, were of Tory persuasion and had moved to Canada in 1776; the New York Assembly presented the farm to Thomas Paine. The New Rochelle boat landed in the very bay where Hessian mercenaries had put to shore to chase George Washington's small army northward, Paine would surely have told his young wards, and regaled them as well with stories of the campaigns of three decades past. Thomas and Benjamin attended boarding school in New Rochelle and were also taught by the Rev. John Foster of Stonington, Connecticut.

Thomas Paine bombarded the newspapers with abrasive opinions on topics of the day, for he thrived on controversy. Disenchanted with editor Cheetham, he lampooned him in rival journals. There was little that pleased him during these years, though he applauded Thomas Jefferson's negotiations for the "vacant backlands" of the country and claimed some credit, for he had told Jefferson that Napoleon needed money and might sell.

Thomas Paine tried to contact Nicolas in France, in April, 1807. "My dear Bonneville. Why don't you come to America. Your wife and two boys . . . are in good health. They all speak English very well. I intend to provide for the boys, but I wish to see you here . . . Mrs. Bonneville and Mrs. Thomas, an Englishwoman, keep an academy for young ladies. I send you this by a friend, Mrs. Champlin, who will call on Mercier at the Institute to know where you are. Your affectionate friend, Thomas Paine."[9]

Nicolas may have been trying in vain to leave France. A passport dated 25 October 1805, issued to Nicolas at Evreux, permitted him to travel to the seaport town Boulougne. If he planned to embark there, he failed, and it would be years before he arrived in America. The passport describes him as 45 years old, portly, black-eyed, short of stature, and perhaps significant of his frustration and heartbreak, with "hair, greywhite."[10]

The good Mrs. Champlin contacted Nicolas and brought a reply when she returned. Paine was delighted. He wrote "My dear Bonneville: I received your letter by Mrs. Champlin, and also the letter for Mrs. Bonneville. I have written to the American minister in Paris . . . to have your surveillance taken off . . . When you come I intend publishing all my works, and those I have yet in manuscript, by subscription. They will make four or five volumes . . ."[11]

Paine's flare of hope for a new start flickered out. He lived for a time with William Carver. He quarreled with Carver and moved to 309 Bleeker Street, near the residence of Margaret Bonneville. His best friend at this time was Col. John Fellows, who had published some of his work. These two old veterans relived the stirring days of the War for Independence for Thomas and Benjamin. There had been skirmishes very near the streets where they lived and citizens had destroyed the downtown statue of King George III and molded the wreckage into bullets. The British jammed thousands of Americans into Sugar House prison off Cedar Street, where many died of cold and hunger. But in retrospect, even the defeats were touched with glory, in view of the victory that finally crowned rebel efforts.

New York City, in the early 1800s, caught up with and surpassed Philadelphia as a melting pot of adventurers and dreamers who came to the new world. Along Pearl Street were old Dutch houses, their steep-roofed, squared gables rising from white-washed walls, sturdy reminders that this spot had once been New Amsterdam. Only a few windmills remained, and the canals had mostly been filled in, but Peter Stuyvesant's old spice pear tree, bedraggled and aging, still stood at Third Avenue and Thirteenth Street.

Superimposed on the old Dutch city was the English colonial town, with shops on the ground floor and living quarters upstairs for the ambitious tradesmen who crowded busy Manhattan Island—grocers, chairmakers, bookbinders, candlers, silversmiths and tailors. On poplar-lined Bowery Lane, a Hessian mercenary had stayed on to thrive in the butcher business. His younger brother had arrived a few years later and parlayed a suitcase full of flutes into a substantial fortune as John Jacob Astor, fur merchant. Duncan Phyfe's cabinet shop was near by. Most of the streets were cobbled, and many were crooked and narrow, though Broadway was straight and lined with trees. Paintings of the city show buildings of grace and symmetry, of solid construction and lasting beauty, fit to endure for centuries, as some few have.

Undoubtedly the young Bonnevilles obtained additional schooling in New York. Somewhere along the line, Benjamin became an avid reader and an alert observer of unfolding events. By nature he was eager and friendly and would remain so throughout his life, and Paine's world of ideas may have honed his own originality of thought. Paine's friends had thinned in number, but their talents were many and varied. Artist John Wesley Jarvis, with whom Paine lived for a time, painted Thomas Paine, but not, so far as can be learned, Paine's young wards. Benjamin Bonneville apparently had no likeness made until the years had left him jowled and weary. Robert Fulton was home from Paris, leaving his career as an artist to work with the notion that boats could be propelled by the power of steam. Thomas Paine and the young Bonnevilles were most certain to have been on the banks of Hudson River on August 17, 1807, along with throngs of skeptics amazed at the "Clermont" going up the river like a teakettle, as some said.

Paine's friend Joel Barlow was putting finishing touches on an epic poem, "The Columbiad," and journeyed to Washington for a dinner honoring Captain Meriwether Lewis. President Jefferson's erstwhile secretary had returned from an exploration of the newly-purchased vacant backlands, and in a rhymed tribute, Barlow proposed that the name of the Columbia River be changed to Lewis River. Some map-makers agreed, but English cartographers did not; there appeared to be a growing disdain on the part of the British for American aspirations. Spain, too, bristled at American pushiness on the frontier. Captain Zebulon Pike explored the sources of the Arkansas River and Spanish officials arrested him for trespassing.

The Death of Thomas Paine

Death began to stalk Thomas Paine early in 1809. Margaret Bonneville wrote that he complained of loneliness. When he wanted to move into Margaret's house, she hesitated because of his many visitors, some abrasive.

"I at last consented, and hired a house in the neighborhood in May, 1809, to which he was carried in an arm chair, after which he seemed calm." Paine asked if it would be possible for him to have a Quaker burial; the request was refused. Margaret promised to bury him on the farm at New Rochelle. "The farm will be sold and they will dig up my bones," Paine prophesied.

Thomas Paine died at the Bonneville house in Greenwich. "He was, according to American custom, deposited in a mahogany coffin with his name and age on a silver plate," Margaret wrote. The casket was loaded on a wagon for the twenty-two mile journey to New Rochelle; Quaker Willet Hicks, Margaret Bonneville and her son Benjamin followed in a carriage out the Boston Post Road, across Harlem River at Kingsbridge to the farm Paine had described as "green and always peaceful."

"Contemplating who it was; what man it was that we were committing to an obscure grave . . . I could not help feeling most acutely," Margaret wrote. "Before the earth was thrown down upon the coffin, I placing myself at the east end of the grave said to my son Benjamin 'Stand you there at the other end' . . . I exclaimed as the earth was tumbling into the grave 'Oh Mr. Paine, my son stands here as testimony of the gratitude of America and I for France.' " True to her promise, Margaret installed a headstone marked "Thomas Paine, author of 'Common Sense' Died 8 June, 1809, aged 72 years."[12]

"The south part of the farm, over 100 acres, to Margaret Bonneville in trust for her children, Benjamin and Thomas, their education and maintenance until they come to the age of 21 years, in order that she may bring them up well, give them good and useful learning and instruct them in the their duty to God and the practice of morality," Paine directed in his will. The north part of the farm went to Nicolas Bonneville and to Paine's London publisher. Margaret received Paine's letters, manuscripts and personal effects. Paine asked that a wall twelve feet square be built around his grave, and that willows and cypresses be planted.[13]

A Libel Suit to Protect Name and Reputation

Paine had told some of this friends that he would leave his holdings to them; later, he said that he had changed his mind. Most shrugged it off, but William Carver attempted blackmail by accusing him of improper conduct with Margaret Bonneville. Paine scorned him. After Paine's will was read, Carver took his shabby vengeance to the alienated editor Cheetham, who was assembling a smear edition of Paine's life. Cheetham's published book included the insinuations of Carver concerning Margaret Bonneville. Cheetham asserted that Paine brought "Mrs. Bournville" with him from Paris and that Thomas had the features, countenance and temper of Paine.

Margaret was stunned. Catharine Nicholson Few, sister-in-law of Albert Gallatin, wrote to a friend for help, suggesting that ex-Chancellor Robert Livingston and others might be able to assist in righting this insulting injury.[14]

Margaret Bonneville sued for libel, not a civil suit asking for monetary damages, but a criminal suit, for this was a matter of honor. A parade of witnesses testified to Margaret's integrity; many were mothers of Margaret's pupils. The prestige of witnesses Robert Fulton and John Wesley Jarvis added weight. A Mrs. Dean was called to verify the allegation that Margaret had duped Thomas Paine into signing a bond, pretending it was an order for clothing for her children. Mrs. Dean, under oath, denied ever telling Cheetham such a story, or having ever seen his face before. At this point, William Carver deserted Cheetham and refuted the accusations he had made in his blackmail letters to Paine.

Cheetham's counsel fell back on a second position. Cheetham, he asserted, had no responsibility for errors in his sources of information. The judge agreed. The jury was instructed that if Mr. Cheetham had been informed of what he wrote, and believed it, he was justified, and that though Madame Bonneville might be an innocent woman, they were authorized to acquit Mr. Cheetham. The jury, however, took only a few minutes to return a verdict that Cheetham was guilty of libel. Nevertheless, when the convicted libeller appeared for sentencing, the judge commended him for "serving the cause of religion" and fined him only nominal court costs.[15]

For Margaret Bonneville the cloud never completely lifted, though the whispers varied. Sometimes it was Benjamin who was said to resemble craggy, beak-nosed Paine. Some had it that Paine was to have been guillotined in France, but sent Margaret's husband to take his place, then absconded with the family.[16] Always reticent about her personal affairs, Margaret became more close-mouthed than ever. Her son Benjamin shared this trait, for though he grew to be outwardly voluble, he retained an inner reserve, a point beyond which no information emerged.

Teen Years in New York City

Benjamin Bonneville lived his early teen years in wondrously busy New York City. He had young friends, among them W. E. Woodruff and Alfred Seton. The city was mushrooming northward; some thought it might cover the whole of Manhattan Island. New churches rose all over town: single-spired St. Johns, spacious St. Patricks, and others. Elgin Botanical Gardens flourished on a spot owned by Columbia College (in the twentieth century, Rockefeller Center). Scudder's American Museum adjoined the Park Theatre which John Jacob Astor had bought at auction. Astor's ambition was boundless; he planned a fur-hunting expedition to the very edge of the continent, where no Americans had ventured except the Lewis and Clark people. Besides an overland expedition, men would journey around Cape Horn with a shipload of supplies for a trading post at the mouth of the Columbia. Astor recruited partners and crew in Canada and in the summer of 1810, canoe-loads of Canadians paddled down the Hudson and docked at the New York waterfront, delighting onlookers with French boating songs. This crew was to sail around the Horn and included young Thomas McKay and also a lad of French parentage, Francois Benjamin Payette. These two Benjamin Bonneville would meet another day.

Over one hundred buildings went up in flames in the "great fire of 1811" and only valiant efforts kept it from sweeping through the whole town. New Yorkers were proud of their fire brigades; water for the fire-engines ran through a system of bored-out logs with wooden stoppers called fire-plugs. Col. John Fellows became supervisor of the city waterworks. Other friends of Thomas Paine were prospering too. Joel Barlow went to France as President Madison's emissary to Napoleon. Robert Fulton won a government monopoly in the steam-powered shipping business. Artist John Wesley Jarvis's circle included sassy and whimsical writer Washington Irving.

To carry out Thomas Paine's wishes, Margaret Bonneville published his "Origin of Free-Masonry" and through the good offices of Albert Gallatin sent it to Nicolas for translation into French.

"This consignment also resulted in obtaining letters from his wife and sons," Nicolas's biographer wrote. "It is by these letters that he learned that his friend had kept his promise to be protector and adoptive father of his family in the United States, where he himself intended to go."[17]

Thomas Bonneville Enlists in the Navy

Eighteen-year-old Thomas Bonneville chose a naval career. He received a warrant of appointment as midshipman in the United States Navy on January 1, 1812. The Navy promised action at this time, for the newspapers were filled with talk of possible war with England involving disputes at sea. Statesmen wavered, because to break with England would disrupt American sea commerce and ally the United States with Napoleon. Some argued that it was land, not sea, which was important and thought it would be easy to conquer the vast northern treasure, Canada, disposing once and for all the threat of the arrogant ex-mother country. Maybe young America was spoiling for a fight. In June, 1812, with some dissenting votes Congress declared war on Great Britain.

Entering West Point

Benjamin Bonneville was appointed to the United States Military Academy on April 14, 1813. If he had a sponsor, it is not recorded. The Army was his choice, and it would be a lifetime commitment. On Academy rolls, he was fifteen years old; family records show he had just turned seventeen.

At West Point in 1813, the young men in brass-buttoned blue coats studied mathematics, engineering, French, philosophy, drawing and map-making. The disputes of Acting Superintendent Alden Partridge with his staff spice West Point annals of the era. Called "Old Pewt," Partridge administered rigid discipline—early-morning tin-soldier drills and a black-hole dungeon for serious offenses. Intensive classroom schedules alternated with long hours of field drills. It was a Spartan existence, and many dropped out of the harsh routine. Of Benjamin's classmates, few made the Army their life's work, and only he and two others completed the long march to retirement.

West Point bluffs overlook a sharp bend in the river—Henry Hudson had anchored there. At this vital site where enemy ships might bisect the colonies, George Washington established fortifications, and devised a heavy chain to be installed across the Hudson. After the war, Washington recommended a school there to train officers in tactics. Citizens frowned on such duplication of old-world military practice, and since its inception in 1802, the Military Academy had been derided as a waste of money. Now the country was at war again, and a military training school seemed not so frivolous.

Cadets at West Point cheered the tidings of worthy actions in the war. General Zebulon Pike led his men to victory at York—later called Toronto—though he lost his life in the battle. At sea, the Royal Navy captured the United States "Wasp" and the "Chesapeake," but Captain Oliver Hazard Perry's naval squadron won control of Lake Erie. Along the east coast, New Englanders sat sourly behind a British blockade, wishing for "Mr. Madison's War" to end; there was talk of secession, for commerce was hurting. Now and then an American warship slipped out to open waters. A new "Wasp" was fitted out and sailed in May, 1814. Midshipman Thomas N. Bonneville was a member of the crew.

During July, 1814, Cadet Bonneville and the entire corps of the Academy enjoyed a trip down the Hudson on a sloop. They encamped for a month on Governor's Island off the tip of Manhattan, taking part in drills, parades, and on one occasion the execution of a deserter. Governor's Island—originally set aside for the pleasurable pursuits of English colonial governors—guarded New York City. Fort Columbus, a star-shaped masonry stronghold, stood atop a knoll. It bristled with one hundred guns, and was approached by a drawbridge over a moat.

Events During the War of 1812

Back again in the classrooms at West Point, the young men learning the arts of war found discussion material in the dramatic events of the times.

Far away, the British had temporarily conquered the great Napoleon, and his mistakes as an officer could be pointed out: primarily, he did not take care of his men. In his disastrous retreat from Russia, the story went, Napoleon complained of the bumpy road and was told that his carriage wheels were thudding on the frozen bodies of his own men. Poet Joel Barlow, on a futile diplomatic mission to Napoleon, died with the French soldiers there. Closer at hand, the cadets learned the humiliating news that the British, on August 24, 1814, made a brief surprise raid on Washington D.C. and set fire to the Capitol and other public buildings.

News elsewhere was better. Majors Winfield Scott and Henry Leavenworth won victories. General Alexander Macomb prevailed over strong British forces at Plattsburg; he was aided by the Navy's trouncing of a British flotilla in the bay. The Royal Navy bombed and shelled Baltimore's harbor defenses to no avail, and American witness Francis Scott Key triumphantly wrote "The Defense of Fort McHenry." Set to music, Key's poem became "The Star Spangled Banner."

The war was winding down, but the Army savored one more triumph. Andrew Jackson, believing the British were operating from Spanish Pensacola, Florida, wiped it out, leaving embarrassed diplomats to explain. He moved to New Orleans and put to rout the invading British, a vast expedition fresh from victories with the Duke of Wellington. The nation cheered. Later, it was found that the battle had been fought after an armistice agreement, but that sequence detracted not at all from the popularity of the new national hero, Andrew Jackson. The cease-fire, which evolved into the Treaty of Ghent, designated the 49th parallel the dividing line between the United States and Canada as far as the "Stony Mountains" and declared the Pacific Northwest open to joint occupancy.

The Navy was still counting gains and losses. The new "Wasp" had captured a number of enemy ships, and in the English channel won a bloody close-quarters battle with the British "Reindeer." For this action, Congress awarded the Wasp's Captain Blakeley a gold medal, and each of his officers a ceremonial sword. Thomas N. Bonneville's sword, with his name engraved, eventually became the property of his brother. The "Wasp" put to sea again, but Thomas was not on it. Instead, due to personal trouble, he sailed home on the "Atalanta." The "Wasp" was "spoken" south of the Madeira Islands in October and was never heard from again. Navy records show that Thomas was ordered from New York to the ship "Washington" in April, 1815, and that he resigned in March, 1816. No further mention of Thomas Bonneville, in either official or the scant family records, has been found.[18]

The War of 1812 taught the country's leaders the value of capable officers and the necessity of expanding the Military Academy. Sylvanus Thayer went to Europe to assemble books, maps, charts, ideas and tools of the military profession. New York businessmen donated funds for several buildings.

Captain Partridge continued at odds with faculty and cadets. He was accused, among other things, of granting promotions to his favorites without regard to merit. Whether or not Benjamin Bonneville enjoyed "Old Pewt's" favor is questionable. He is listed thirty-fifth in his class of forty-five, but in those early years, cadets were numbered in the order they entered. This was a sore spot to perfectionists like Bonneville's classmate Ethan Allen Hitchcock, for later graduates were listed by academic standing.

Graduation and Assignment as an Army Officer

Benjamin Louis Eulalie Bonneville was graduated from the Academy on December 11, 1815 and assigned to the Corps of Light Artillery. It was a choice berth, for the Light Artillery manned seacoast stations. Officers could count on comfortable living quarters and good rapport with local society. And of all the uniforms in an age of ornate military dress, those of the artillery officers were the most flamboyant. Jefferson boots rose high over snug trousers. A cummerbund—called a sash in the Army—cinched in the waist, but was almost hidden by a blue coat faced with scarlet. Wide-frogged buttons mounted to a stiff scarlet collar, which rose to the tip of the ear. The artillery hat was the crowning elegance: black, visored, sometimes described as "cocked," and was seven inches high. Waving atop was a red-tipped blue-and-white plume. Some of the young men may have fancied the inches-advantage the hat gave them. How tall was the young Bonneville? It has not been recorded. After he had trudged untold miles the length and breadth of the continent, after a half-century of military responsibility had burdened his shoulders, the Army measured him five-foot-five.

First Assignment: Fort Wolcott, Rhode Island

In his first assignment, Fort Wolcott on Goat Island, Rhode Island, fortune smiled on Brevet Second Lieutenant Bonneville. He commanded both the post and the single company stationed there for the reason that the captain was on furlough and the first lieutenant was "present in arrest," for an infraction not named. Thus the January 1816 Fort Wolcott Post Returns listing eight artificers, four sergeants, four corporals, three musicians and seventy-four privates was signed with a flourish by "B. L. E. Bonneville, Lieutenant, Commanding." The new lieutenant could well have viewed himself as firmly placed at the base of the ladder of success. What he did not know, perhaps, was that some of the rungs would prove to be far, far apart. Rank reigned supreme in the Army. "Lineage" lists designated seniority of officers as determined by the date of their commissions. But the practice of granting "brevets" bestowed for a job well done or from simple favoritism circumvented the process of advancement. It was ever a bone of contention in officer circles.

Fort Wolcott was a small work, with breastworks of earth and a small magazine. Captain John Smith had visited this Narragansett Bay, and Chief Massasoit, and later, rebel preacher Roger Williams, ousted from strait-laced Salem. Rhode Islanders claimed to have fought the first battle of the Revolution when they scuttled a British revenue cutter in 1772. With peace, the ship business flourished, though some said the biggest fortunes came from related pursuits, slave trade and privateering. Tales of that commerce were tall and lusty; there was a spot near Fort Wolcott where twenty-six pirates had been hanged.

Duty in Boston

In June, on orders, Bonneville marched with his company to Boston for duty. The soldiers carried smooth-bore flint-lock muskets mounted with swords. Teamsters moved the six- and twelve-pound cannon. At Boston Col. Abram Eustis commanded regimental headquarters at massive Fort Independence where forty cannon guarded the area. Fort Warren, on an island in the harbor, was similarly armed.

Frosts, floods, wind and hail almost wiped out the bounties of the earth in 1816; it was called "the year without a summer." The blight was worldwide. In France, according to the newspapers, Lafayette opened the doors to his estate and fed hundreds from the stores of his cellars. The weather upheavals stirred desperate families in Europe to leave the old countries seeking better times in the new. Waves of immigrants began to pour into the United States. In America the real victory of the War of 1812 was emerging: a growing feeling of national importance, a self-reliance that fostered industries to produce goods formerly imported, and a reaching out to far frontiers. It was as if a raw youth had tried on a man's shoes, and finding himself as tall as his elders, chafed to grow as broad as well.

Promotion to Second Lieutenant and Assignment in Maine

In March, 1817, the Army list of promotions and assignments arrived. From "Cadet Brevet Second Lieutenant" Bonneville was promoted to Second Lieutenant and his salary stipulated at twenty-five dollars per month. His company was assigned to Fort George at Castine, Maine.

Castine, on Penobscot Bay, had twice shared its hospitality with English invaders in the last half century. Baron Castine had build a trading post behind the sheltering islands to catch Pilgrim business in the 1600's. When France's claims in the new world faded, most French names were lost, though Castine's remained, as did Maine, from the French province, which was given in the new world to the whole mountain wonderland of glacier valleys and rocky coastal inlets. The English had named Fort George, and there were tales of the wars; one story described Yankee landlubbers taking a British ship by firing on it with muskets, infantry-style. In 1817 the town sat securely within earthworks so old few knew which nation had built them.

In the spring of 1818, Lt. Bonneville was ordered back to Fort Independence. There in command of F Company, he was also listed as "Conductor of Artillery," directing practice maneuvers of scores of newly-arrived recruits. It is likely that his warm relationship with the regimental commander, Col. Abram Eustis, developed at this time. Late in the fall, Bonneville was summoned to attend a court martial at Portsmouth where he was introduced to other facets of his profession. The Army disciplines its own. Officers accused of violating rules and practice are judged by a panel of peers, with punishment meted out for conviction. Though the military courts sometimes dealt with serious charges, records of many early proceedings reveal such dire accusations on one side and injured dignity on the other the reader may surmise that some of the affairs were staged as diversions from routine, or weapons in the infighting for prestige and advancement in officer circles. When his judging duties at the Portsmouth court were completed, Lt. Bonneville traveled to New York City, for he had received a three-month furlough.

Benjamin's Father Comes to America

Nicolas Bonneville had finally arrived in America. Albert Gallatin had arranged safe passage of manuscripts for the Bonnevilles, and he may have expedited Nicolas's departure, for it was said that Gallatin knew everybody in Europe. He had represented the United States in negotiating the Treaty of Ghent, and returned in the autumn of 1815.

Washington Irving has pictured Nicolas reading Voltaire in the shade of the trees at the Battery. Irving left in the spring of 1815 for a long stay in Europe; it is doubtful if he knew Nicolas well for the "happy temperament" he ascribed to the broken writer agrees not at all with accounts of his later years. A changed world greeted Nicolas in the United States. His little boys were grown and gone. His Marguerite, a young woman when they parted, now was middle-aged Margaret. If, as Irving wrote, Nicolas sat with an open book, there were regrets to cloud his reveries: the frustrations of wasted years, of inspirations not molded into words, and of watching his splendid dreams of "liberty, fraternity, equality" slip away like sands in a bottomless hourglass. Nicolas's talent had withered; his fires were cold. Whatever plans he may have had for a new beginning, he could not set them in motion. Nicolas and Margaret decided to return to France.

Most of the Thomas Paine farm at New Rochelle was sold. Nicolas received $1,000. Thomas's portion brought $1,425; it is not recorded whether Thomas received this in person, or whether, as has been written in some accounts, he was lost at sea. Before he returned to duty, Benjamin executed a power of attorney to his mother. She sold eight acres of his land to Jonathan Bayless and thirteen acres to Nathan Seacord, at a price not specified.[19] "I gave $50 to keep apart and to myself the place where on the grave was," Margaret wrote.

Benjamin's Parents Move to Paris

But a new chapter unfolded in the story of Thomas Paine. As essayist "Peter Porcupine," William Cobbett had achieved fame by denouncing the liberals of his day, particularly Thomas Paine. After a sojourn in England, Cobbett returned to the United States and announced that he wanted to make amends. This "led to his negotiations with Mme. Bonneville . . . who had been preparing, with her husband's assistance notes for a biography," according to Paine biographer Moncure Conway, who quoted Margaret: "Because of unjust efforts to tarnish the memory of Mr. Paine, indignation has made me take the pen." Cobbett is said to have agreed to give Margaret $1,000 for her manuscript, which was to contain important letters from and to eminent men. Margaret was chary of the changeling Cobbett. She stipulated that the work should be published without any addition and separate from any other writings. Soon after Margaret and Nicolas left for France, William Cobbett went to the cypress-and-willow-planted plot, dug up the remains of Thomas Paine and shipped them to England. He intended to rebury Paine there, he announced, and erect a fitting memorial to a great man. His efforts came to nothing.[20]

In Paris, Nicolas Bonneville "became a second-hand bookseller . . . his poor store was situated on Rue des Pres Saint-Jacques."[21] Few nineteenth century immigrants to the United States returned to Europe. For those whose options had run out, like Nicolas Bonneville, the old ties beckoned. But over one hundred thousand newcomers crowded American ports from 1815 to 1820, and for many it was as if the Atlantic Ocean baptized them, and they emerged clean of their past handicaps, virile, aspiring and eager.

The pull of new horizons enticed the young and the daring, and on land as well as sea, the tides surged westward. If, during his 1819 furlough, Benjamin Bonneville renewed friendships, he learned that his New York schoolmate Alfred Seton had already lived a great adventure. Seton had sailed around the Horn on John Jacob Astor's second supply ship "Pedlar." On the return trip, the "Pedlar" sailed first to the Russian post which would become Sitka, Alaska, then south past the Hawaiian Islands to San Blas, Mexico. There Seton put ashore to carry messages to Astor, and in spite of illness on the Isthmus of Darien, he was able to reach New York City.

Assigned to the Eighth Infantry

Back in the monotony of his task as "Conductor of Artillery" at Fort Independence, Lt. Bonneville found food for thought. Other regiments were drawing more exciting assignments. The Sixth Infantry had left on a journey from New York to far away St. Louis. In the South, General Andrew Jackson's campaigns against Spanish intruders, Indians and runaway slaves were the envy of soldiers safe in stodgy garrisons.

"Finding promotions slow, I transferred, or rather resigned for an appointment in the Eighth Infantry," Bonneville wrote.[22]

Chapter Two
1820-1831
Service in Mississippi and Arkansas

Journey to New Orleans

The Eighth Infantry's challenge lay far away. In late November, 1819, Lt. Bonneville with other officers and a large number of recruits—including prisoners released to serve out their terms in the Army—embarked on a sailing vessel bound for New Orleans. They were assigned to join the regiments hacking out a shortcut from Nashville to New Orleans under the command of the nation's best-known general, Andrew Jackson. Newspapers of the day had delighted in stories of Jackson. A Tennessee roughneck, he had been a saddler, teacher, race-horse buff, lawyer and plantation owner before becoming the nation's military idol for consistently outracing his orders. With the United States swaggering for having won a second war with England, Jackson's sweeps of the South to "keep order" seemed fitting. The hero of the Battle of New Orleans had captured land pirates and runaway slaves, and slaughtered Creek warriors—and their families. He had detached Florida from Spain, leaving the Monroe administration no choice but to put together a treaty and pay Spain five million dollars.

Bonneville's troop ship rode out North Atlantic weather and sailed with warmer winds past the Bahamas and into the Gulf of Mexico. It took a month to reach the hundred-year-old beacon that marked the mouth of the Mississippi. The channel led between Fort St. Philip and Fort Jackson, and into the "English turn" where crew and passengers sometimes had to tow their vessel around sharp curves. On shores, marshes and weeds merged into palms and tangled vines. Upriver were sugar plantations with porticoed mansions flanked by rows of Negro cabins.

An American city for less than two decades, New Orleans was exotic and foreign to the soldiers from New England. From the market place came the babble of strange tongues, for ships of many nations touched this focal point of the continent to be met by river boats loaded with produce from the awakening valleys. There were old-family French and old-family Spanish, and a mixture of the two, plus invading American businessmen and planters. There were Negroes, slave and free, and Greeks and Italians and the ever-present English; there were numbers of the original owners of the warm wilderness land, the Indians. New Orleans was said to be a wicked city, with gambling halls and cockfights and lively Sunday evening balls. The infantry from Boston was not allowed to linger.

Trudging northeastward to their assignment, the soldiers passed shimmering Lake Pontchartrain, and great estates in settings of moss-draped oaks. Toward Pearl River, the road passed mirror lagoons alive with herons and trumpeter swan. Dragonflies drank nectar from pink water hyacinths, and in sunny meadows were purple finches and bluebirds.

Building the Jackson Military Road

Deep in the Choctaw Nation in the two-year-old state of Mississippi, the troops from Boston made a harsh transition from walking tourists to an Army work detail. The road from there they had to build themselves, over boulders and through tangled trees and muddy hollows, until they met the crews from Nashville building southward. The Jackson Military Road was behind schedule. Andrew Jackson blamed the southern command and sent his protege, Lt. Col. Zachary Taylor to take charge. Taylor drove the crews forward at the rate of a mile or two a day.[1] The laboring crews were allowed a bonus of fifteen cents a day, plus an extra gill of whiskey. The soldiers' medical supplies ran out, their uniforms were soon in tatters and their rations were scanty. Col. Taylor's loud complaints brought a measure of improvement.

The converging Army road-building crews met during the summer. Newspapers acclaimed the finished road as one of the finest in the nation. The soldiers had bridged miles of swamps with sapling-based causeways rising above side drainage ditches. Thirty-five bridges spanned creeks and rivers "through delightful and romantic country" as one report said.[2]

Determined to shape up his regiment, Zachary Taylor built quarters at Bay St. Louis on the Gulf coast between Biloxi and New Orleans. He growled that the road work had precluded proper military training, a lack he now proposed to remedy. He may have seemed extra gruff to the tired officers and men of the Eighth; personal sorrow pursued him that summer. He had left his wife and family at Bayou Sara north of Baton Rouge, and two of his daughters died there of "bilious fever."

Promotion to First Lieutenant

Bonneville was promoted to First Lieutenant on July 9, 1820, and spent the next fifteen months in the garrison at Bay St. Louis. Sheltered by a line of islands, this area had been a favorite refuge of pirates; French explorer Bienville named the blue inlet for Louis Ninth in 1699. Pass Christian village guarded the entrance. In 1820, French-Spanish-Indian fishermen lived there. Though Zachary Taylor demanded drills and practice, men of the Eighth could ask no better than a station where the breezes were warm and the hills and bayous abounded with game and fish. It was too good to last.

Critics were in full cry against the military. Now that no enemy was in sight, orators proclaimed that a large standing army was dangerous to the liberty of the nation. Many immigrants had come to America expressly to avoid conscription into European armies. Remembering the old world's constant wars, citizens feared and distrusted military institutions. The total strength of the Army was cut to six thousand men. The Eighth Infantry was disbanded. The cutback meant that promotions would be at a standstill for years. It took a large measure of devotion to remain in the profession. Even Andrew Jackson felt the axe; Old Hickory was offered the governorship of the Territory of Florida.

Assignment to the Seventh Infantry at New Orleans

Lt. Bonneville managed to stay on officer rolls with his commission intact and was assigned to the Seventh Infantry under Col. Matthew Arbuckle. Lt. Col. Taylor was designated second in command after he sputtered in anger at another assignment which would have reduced him to Major. In October, 1821, Bonneville moved with Zachary Taylor's companies to New Orleans. Col. Arbuckle arrived, and the Seventh totalled ten companies. The faded script of the Post Returns from "Camp near New Orleans" accounts for over five hundred men and officers including one soldier in arrest for "pulling down the jail in Mobile" and another who "did not intend being absent without leave but got in a frolic." Lt. Richard Wash is listed "present in arrest;" the names Lt. E. A. Hitchcock and Lt. B. L. E. Bonneville follow, with ditto marks under "present" and possibly under "in arrest," an interesting situation if true, for Ethan Allen Hitchcock then and later considered himself a paragon of virtue. He scoffed at the frivolous pastimes of fellow officers and wrote in his diary that he used his leisure to study the classics.

Downtown New Orleans beckoned the less strait-laced. France and Spain had alternated in ownership and both had left traces. The streets were narrow; ironlace balconies formed overhead bowers and there were graceful masonry arches and tiled roofs. Oil street lamps hung on iron hooks, and each night a cannon boomed a curfew for sailors, soldiers and Negroes to get off the streets. Business was brisk in New Orleans. Boosters claimed that the port would soon be the most important in the United States. The aristocratic Creoles were inclined to disdain Northern merchants, but the prosperity brought by the latter opened many wrought-iron gates. Yankee businessmen were reluctant to bring their families to Louisiana for the ever-recurring fevers took a frightful toll of newcomers. Soldiers at the Seventh's New Orleans camp suffered greatly; some quarreled with Col. Arbuckle's treatment of those who were laid low by the prevailing sicknesses and/or "frolicking."

America surged westward. The United States Army, already operating in the anonymity which would almost delete it from the history books, was expected to move ahead of an expanding population, to clear the terrain of Indians and foreign traders on a frontier over a thousand miles from north to south, and of phantom and fluid depth from east to west. This meant building and fortifying posts as footholds of settlement and surveying and constructing roads.

After years of bloody revolution, the neighbor on the south had won independence from the mother country, Spain. Mexico was a proud young nation, princely in size, for it included besides Mexico, territory that would one day comprise California, Nevada, Utah, Colorado, Arizona, New Mexico and Texas. The War Department appeared wary of the new nation, for the majority of the Seventh Infantry—six companies—was assigned to the Texas border with the no-nonsense commander Lt. Col. Zachary Taylor.

Steamboat Travel on the Mississippi River

Lt. Bonneville drew duty with the commander of the regiment, Colonel Arbuckle, who, with four companies, was directed to take post on the Indian frontier at Fort Smith on the Arkansas River. Virginia-born Arbuckle had served in the Army for many years with a usual quota of disputes. His military reports and letters show him as earnest, persevering, testy and undistinguished—a typical officer of the regular Army, for the heroes were vastly outnumbered by the workhorses of the officers corps. Col. Arbuckle's Seventh Infantry did, however, have something to be excited about. They would go up the Mississippi by steamboat.

More than a score of steamboats now chugged on the Mississippi, for Henry Shreve had succeeded in breaking Fulton's government-granted monopoly. Steamboating was dangerous: boilers blew up, shipboard fires broke out, and snags and sandbars lurked at every turn. Twice a day the boats stopped to take on wood, for the fires gobbled tons of it to keep up steam. The paddle-wheelers could travel six miles an hour against the Mississippi's mighty current and a breathtaking twelve miles an hour downstream!

The "Tennessee," with Col. Arbuckle and his infantrymen, left New Orleans November 6, 1821, gliding miraculously up the great river without the aid of pole or sail. Cold rains peppered the "Tennessee," which was dangerously overloaded, but during the first week in December, the ship negotiated passage through the swampy lowlands at the mouth of the Arkansas River and docked at Arkansas Post. The Seventh camped in tents while officers tried to find keelboats for the journey up the Arkansas to Fort Smith.

The muster rolls of the Seventh Infantry for November and December, 1821, prepared at Arkansas Post on December 31, show that Lt. Bonneville was present commanding C Company. Half a century later, a news item would state that Bonneville was first married on November 30, 1821. Since he was on board the "Tennessee" with his regiment on that day, this was obviously not true. Another fiction concerning the same period went through early printings of G. W. Cullum's "Biographical Register of the Officers and Graduates of the United States Military Academy:" it asserts that Bonneville was "on march from Ft. Smith Ark. to San Antonio, Texas, 1821-1822." There was no such march. Texas still belonged to Mexico.

To New Orleans and Back to Arkansas on Horseback

Before the Seventh could move on to Fort Smith, Lt. Bonneville was summoned to a court martial at Fort St. Philip at the mouth of the Mississippi. Records show that he was there in January and February, 1822. One company manned Fort St. Philip; across the river stood Fort Jackson, equally remote in the loneliness of the land's end. Whoever the culprit and whatever his transgression, the court-martial provided a respite from routine, a season of fellowship and conversation, at least for the board of judges.

"From New Orleans, all the way on horseback . . ." Bonneville wrote of his springtime trip to Fort Smith, Arkansas, in 1822, tracing his route with references to Baton Rouge, Natchez, Ouachita and Little Rock.[3] The road from New Orleans led past well-kept plantations and into cypress and maple forests. On rising bluffs, Baton Rouge village clustered around a century-old military post and lookout point. Upriver, rolling hills thick-grown with oak, hickory and magnolia alternated with grassy meadows, and farther north there were locust trees and blue poplar.

There were legends about almost-abandoned Fort Adams, a few miles inside the state of Mississippi. Once important, it had been commanded by General James Wilkinson who, it was said, considered setting up a kingdom in the Mississippi Valley with Aaron Burr. From Fort Adams to Natchez the moist and shady path worn deep between clay banks bore the name "Lower Natchez Trace." This trail had known Spanish explorers looking for treasure and the shadowy golden cities, and French wanderers who discovered and claimed and touted for settlement and then moved on until, as happened many times, the wild country claimed their bones. For Americans in this springtime of the 19th century the great river path opened to a potential bounty of food and fiber and enterprise waiting to be taken.

Natchez, overlooking the Mississippi from the bluffs, had been French and British and Spanish before it belonged to the United States. In 1822, with new enterprise spawned of the late war and Eli Whitney's invention, Natchez laid claim to being the capitol of cottonland, a mixture of aristocratic vanity and newly-rich impudence, with ornate buildings, busy wharfs and a tawdry Gomorra, "Natchez Under the Hill."

The road to Arkansas crossed the river, cleared bottomlands and led westward over pine-covered hills to the Ouachita River. Monroe village had formerly been Post Ouachita, built and garrisoned by the Spanish. Before that, there had been other sojourners, DeSoto, LaSalle and Bienville. A few place-names survived, such as Ouachita, sometimes anglicized to Washita. Bonneville turned north, where trails led through pine and oak forests. This had been Quapaw land; the tribe had ceded it in 1818.

Little Rock, a robust town on the Arkansas River, basked in the importance of being the capitol of Arkansas Territory. Little Rock boasted a weekly newspaper, the "Arkansas Gazette;" the editor was W. E. Woodruff, one of Bonneville's boyhood friends in New York City. Woodruff had worked his way west as an apprentice printer and managed to buy a small printing press which he rafted to Arkansas to launch a long career.

Bonneville rode upriver past the mossy sandstone Big Rock, sometimes called French Rock for Bienville's Benard de LeHarpe, who had ridden there one hundred years before to see if it was actually a mountain of pure emeralds, as reported by the Indians. In his letter describing his journey, Bonneville also mentioned Petit Jean, the name given high bluffs on the south valley wall near Cadron settlement. The settlers said that an aristocrat with his family had fled the French Revolution into this wild country. The wife and son died, and Petit Jean, alone and insane, played his flute on the mountain top. He could still be heard, it would be said for years to come, especially when the wind blew.

The river veered west; the blue Boston Mountains on the north and the Ouachitas on the south narrowed the valley. At last the timber stockade of Fort Smith came into view, rising from Belle Pointe, a sandstone bluff at the confluence of the Poteau and Arkansas rivers. Built in 1817 and named for a general, the fort was laid out with the main gate of the hewn-timber stockade facing a parade ground. Blockhouses at the corners overlooked the wooded bottoms of the two rivers. Inside the work were log huts for officers' quarters, a storehouse, the beginnings of a barracks for soldiers, a cannon for sunrise salute, and a towering flagstaff from which the thirteen stripes and twenty-four stars of the flag proclaimed the Americans had come to stay.

Keeping Peace Among Indians at Arkansas' Fort Smith

The Secretary of War had commanded the Governor of Arkansas Territory to take immediate measures to terminate the war between the Osage and the Cherokees. The governor's task seemed simple to the military. He had only to pass out gifts after the Army had consulted and cajoled and bullied the Indians into bargaining moods and monitored councils to see that nothing got out of hand. Fort Smith, on the fringes of settlement, was established for the express purpose of keeping the peace while eastern tribes were hustled into territory already claimed by other Indians. Thomas Jefferson had suggested that Indians who rebelled against being absorbed into white men's patterns could be transferred to the vast reaches west of the Mississippi. Some tribes voluntarily moved—portions of the Cherokees from Georgia, Choctaws from Alabama and Mississippi; many Delaware, Shawnee and others also capitulated. Tribes already claiming the area protested sharing with the newcomers. On the heels of the Indians and sometimes intruding among them, white settlers clamored for their rights too.

Seldom had a conquering people concerned themselves about the dispossessed. The Indians had waged war among themselves for centuries, with stronger nations wiping out the weaker at will. Americans tried to do better. Efforts by the United States to trade fairly for or to purchase Indian lands were sometimes lopsided and bungling, but the notion was too newborn to be very robust. Like other facets of the American dream, the idea would have to be labored for and sought after for countless generations.

Shortly after Bonneville arrived to join the Seventh, the Osage staged an attention-getter. In full regalia and war paint, they swooped down to the river bank opposite the fort. Their whoops and yells brought a quick alert. Col. Arbuckle ordered the cannon loaded and pointed down at the assembled braves. Leaving instructions that if an attack began for the garrison to fire away, the Colonel crossed the river alone in a small boat. A fine gesture, it impressed both Indians and soldiers. Arbuckle promised a parley soon, and the Osage went "on an excursion against the Cherokees" according to the "Arkansas Gazette."

Close-quarter camping and wind-driven rains brought sickness; ten soldiers died, including the bugler. Col. Arbuckle suggested to headquarters that the Army claim a reserve of land for troop subsistence and to keep at a distance people not to be desired near the military post. The most pressing need was more and better quarters to house the garrison, and he requested iron and nails for his building projects. Lt. Bonneville is listed on post returns as directing construction work throughout the following year.

By grace of high water during April, 1822, the "Robert Thompson," the first steamboat ever, arrived at Fort Smith, and later made other trips, towing keelboats with supplies. The "Arkansas Gazette" greeted the first voyages with delight, but shortly began to wonder why Army supplies were imported from Ohio instead of being procured locally. The "Gazette" carried notices from the Army offering a $30 reward for three deserters. One was a new recruit from Lt. Bonneville's company; he was "stout, healthy" and was "learning to play the fife." He was sixteen years old. The "Gazette" described also the loss of the steamboat "Tennessee" when it struck a log near Natchez, drowning most of the passengers and crew.

Encampments of Indians gathered at Fort Smith in July 1822, the culmination of months of effort by the Army and civilian officials to settle the differences between the Osage and the Cherokees. Grievances were legion: the Cherokees held many Osage captive, but the Osage had killed a number of Cherokees. Discussions, promises and flattery smoothed away most of the grumbling, at least temporarily, and a treaty was signed.

Less tension in Indian country produced more turmoil inside the palisade of Fort Smith—more soldier drunkenness, fighting, desertion and theft. One soldier killed another with an axe. Lt. Richard Wash "thrashed" Surgeon

Lawson. Col. Arbuckle tried to remain aloof, even in the face of a letter to the War Department from Lt. Col. Zachary Taylor in faraway Fort Jesup complaining of Arbuckle's lack of talent for command of a regiment. Sickness continued. Calomel, castor oil, mustard plasters and bloodletting comprised the available remedies. The Colonel, in desperation, sent to Union Mission, over one hundred miles away, for "Jesuite Bark" to treat the afflicted.

Cooler weather brought relief from the fevers, but not from Indian troubles. The Osage reported the slaughter of several dozen of their tribe by Delaware and "Camanchy" Indians. Other complaints were brought to the post with monotonous frequency. Detachments tramped out to consult with or to bring in wrong-doers, who protested worse crimes against themselves, or vanished in the distance. Still, the patrols preserved a semblance of peace, though gloryless to the Army.

In the spring, Col. Arbuckle assigned Lt. Bonneville an agricultural detail to expand the garrison farm. "His careful management of the crops and livestock produced a bountiful and varied table for the troops . . . rations issued regularly with no complaints . . ." according to the Quartermaster General's report in 1823. In November, Lt. Bonneville rode to the Territorial Land Office at Batesville, directed to cash an Army draft, presumably for the post payroll, since considerable currency would be received there in an advertised land sale. But he was also on an errand of surveillance, judging from his report to Col. Arbuckle, who considered it important enough to send to headquarters in Washington. Batesville settlers were apprehensive about the large numbers of Indians assembled nearby, Bonneville reported. As he returned through Cherokee country, he was informed of activities against the whites and complaints about the boundaries being run and the quality of land the Cherokees were receiving.

Col. Arbuckle had other gloomy news for Washington; food supplies were running low. The officers were able to add small comforts from the post store, which was outside the stockade and near the river. Sutler John Nicks' establishment may have been new, for the previous sutler had been so unpopular with the garrison that the cannon for the sunrise salute was somehow, one morning, pointed in the direction of the log store, blasting the sutler out of bed. Captain John Rogers, a quartermaster with the Seventh during the war of 1812, remained as a civilian employee listed as "military storekeeper." He was associated with Nicks in business for many years. Both Nicks and Rogers became Bonneville's good friends.

In Yale University's Coe collection is an account book for the post store at Fort Smith. Officers bought large amounts of sugar, coffee and tobacco. For some, liquor was the chief entry; Bonneville was not one of these. In October, 1823, he bought a pair of spurs, a shotgun, two pounds of shot, one curry comb, and two hundred cigars. The same autumn he bought shoes, wool hose, a quart of Jamaica Rum for seventy-five cents and a quart of molasses. At Christmas time, he bought paper, ink, shoe brushes, one quart of cordial, four ruffled shirts, and one hundred cigars for fifty cents. On March 24, 1824 he bought two yards of blue cloth at ten dollars a yard, a pair of silver epaulettes, and a beaver hat.

Building a New Fort in Osage Country

The Governor of Arkansas had not succeeded, as ordered by the Secretary of War, in bringing peace between the Osage and Cherokees. Washington sent orders for the Seventh Infantry to push deeper into Indian country. Moving supplies by flatboat, the soldiers trudged along the shore some eighty miles up the Arkansas. As assistant commissary, Lt. Bonneville remained a few weeks at Fort Smith to tidy up. On June 1, with doors, windows and lumber loaded on flatboats, he and a small crew set off upriver into the sienna prairies and wooded hills which would become Oklahoma.

Near the junction of the Grande, the Verdigris and the Arkansas—the crossroads known as Three Forks—Col. Arbuckle had chosen a landing on a wide ledge three miles up the Grande. The Seventh cleared brush, cut logs, and laid out a new post. Lt. Bonneville resumed his duties in subsistence, apportioning food, clothing, bedding and tools. A typical "Arkansas Gazette" advertisement for bids specifies "200 barrels of pork, feet, legs, ears and snout inadmissable; 470 barrels flour; 210 bushels beans; 3,300 pounds soap; 1,100 tallow candles; 800 gallons vinegar; 2,650 gallons good proof whiskey."

The new post was indeed closer to the trouble. Soldiers sent to hot spots found villages burning and bodies hacked to pieces in appalling eye-for-eye savagery. A Cherokee complained that his son had been beheaded; he believed by Osage. Mad Buffalo, Osage Chief Clermont's son, faced a death sentence for killing a white man. Col. Arbuckle intervened for his life, since old Clermont was a stabilizing force. The Army had two alternatives—endless negotiations for compromise, or show of military force. The latter was more show than force, and officers pleaded for mounts so the troops might be as mobile in the field as the red men. A few horses were kept for dispatch riders, but the infantry trudged on foot to police most of the frontier quarrels.

If the Indians were impressed by the five hundred man army thrust in their midst, there was no indication of it in their continuing vendettas. Their proximity, though, afforded perspectives of their differences and understanding of their travail. One printed account described Osage males as tall, arrogant and naked. The latter was not totally true, for among purchases at the agency store were many yards of blue strouding, a coarse fabric used for breechcloths. A. P. Chouteau presided over the Osage agency on the Verdigris, and lived with his Indian family in baronial style. Another trader, Nathaniel Pryor, had traveled with Lewis and Clark across the continent; he also lived with his Osage wife on the Verdigris. The Osage had been pushed out of the Ohio and Wabash valleys by the Iroquois, and after living for many years in the area which became Missouri, yielded to pressure and drifted down their traditional buffalo-hunting trails to Three Forks. Still depending on bows and arrows and mobility to survive, the Osage claimed that the Cherokees had been thrust into their turf by treaty fraud. The Cherokees, many with English and Scottish surnames, brought with them guns, plows, livestock and looms; some had acquired Negro slaves in imitation of their southern white neighbors. To the Osage, the industrious Cherokees were as dangerous to their free style of life as were the whites.

Work continued on the new post; storehouses and quarters described as snug were completed. By spring three sides of a hewn log palisade were finished, with barracks lining the inside of "Cantonment Gibson." The men enjoyed some diversions: among Lt. Bonneville's purchases at the post store were fiddle strings for a musician. And in spite of the dreary business as usual in Indian country, officers were given leaves, now and then, to enjoy a holiday.

Travel to France with the Marquis de Lafayette

"Major Phillips and Lts. Dawson and Bonneville of the Seventh Infantry passed in a keelboat on Friday from Cantonment Gibson," the "Arkansas Gazette" reported on June 7, 1825. "Lt. Bonneville has obtained a furlough for a considerable length of time and intends to visit his native country, France."

Bonneville was to travel with the most celebrated visitor ever to come to the United States, the Marquis de Lafayette. The newspapers had been full of Lafayette's visit. The celebrations had lasted more than a year, as the colorful old Frenchman was whisked from city to hamlet to battlefield in celebration of his service to the colonies half a century before. Lafayette limped, his shoulders had begun to sag, but his enthusiasm and warm wit charmed the throngs who greeted him at every stop; he spoke of himself as an American just returned from a long visit to Europe.

Lafayette wrote to Margaret Bonneville of his efforts to help her son secure an extended leave of absence so that he might visit his family. He invited Benjamin to travel with him and wrote "I am very sorry to hear from you that M. de Bonneville is in a bad condition and I would be ever so happy if I could contribute to procure him as well as yourself, the pleasure to see a son . . ." This letter, and perhaps others from Lafayette are in private hands. One note from Lafayette to Bonneville is said to begin "My Son" and would appear to be the basis of gossip that Lafayette was Bonneville's father. Lafayette's imprisonment, from 1792 to 1797, precludes the notion.[4]

Lafayette laid the cornerstone for a library in New York City on July 4, 1825; Bonneville may have joined the party there, and attended to other business as well. In a deposition executed in Arkansas he had signed power of attorney to Charles D'Espinville, consul of France, stationed in New York City. D'Espinville sold eight and one-half acres of Bonneville's Thomas Paine land in April, 1825, to Leonard Seacord; he had previously sold fourteen acres.[5]

After leaving New York, the Lafayette party spent a week in Philadelphia and toured the battlefields of Germantown and Brandywine. In Washington, Lafayette paid his respects to Thomas Jefferson, James Monroe, James Madison, and President John Quincy Adams. Bonneville's only extant comment: "In 1825, Genl. Lafayette an old friend of my father procured me a leave for one year . . . went with him to France in the Frigate Brandywine where I remained ten months."[6]

On this maiden voyage of the 44-gun "Brandywine" the hold sloshed with water, and ballast had to be jettisoned. After twenty-four days the vessel moored at LeHavre, the tide-water harbor at the mouth of the Seine. Chalky cliffs marked with lighthouses sloped down a long seawall and a massive tower, said to have been built by Julius Caesar, stood guard. The carriage road followed the Seine past pinnacled Rouen, then wound up the slopes of St. Catherine's Hill. From this vantage point could be seen cities with many-shaped towers, and remains of city walls of by-gone centuries. A tree-lined road led through the Champs Elysee into the boulevards of Paris. Lafayette's destination was his country estate, LaGrange, thirty miles beyond Paris. Lt. Bonneville was bound for a second-hand bookstore on Rue de Pres St. Jacques and a reunion with his parents.

Nicolas de Bonneville's bookstore was his last link to the literary world. The popular young writer Victor Hugo was one of his friends, but "some who had admired his writing of a former day found they could not talk to him, and some who had been his friends went unrecognized when they came to visit."[7] There were other relatives to visit; attorney Jean Pierre de Bonneville was probably still living in Evreux, for—much later—Bonneville said that his grandfather had lived to the age of 106 and fell dead on the steps of the church there.

Writing home to American newspapers, a correspondent noted visitors in Paris "from all our states, including doctors studying, merchants, diplomats and travelers, one from the wilderness of Arkansas," and later described a journey to LaGrange in response to an invitation from Lafayette.

"In the carriage a gentleman presumed from his complexion a Portuguese or a Spaniard turned out to be a Lieutenant in the United States Army who was going to LaGrange." Editor Woodruff footnoted in the "Arkansas Gazette," "Probably Lt. Bonneville of Cantonment Gibson, a Frenchman by birth, who is now in France on furlough."

The great home at LaGrange was of hewn grey stone, with ivy-planted towers. According to visitors, the endless house-party there included dinners of meat, game, fruits and all the wines of the world; family and guests sometimes totalled forty-five at the table. Georges Washington Lafayette, now a middle-aged man and his father's alter ego, toured the grounds with the gentlemen guests or took them shooting. According to one writer, Bonneville and Georges Washington Lafayette attended the "Polytechnical Institute" together at this time. The account lacks credibility for the two are called "boys," and Adrienne Lafayette, called "motherly," had been dead for many years.

In the 1820s, citizens of Paris appeared to have forgotten their desperate struggles for freedom. Aristocracy was again in style, along with a strutting soldiery wearing towering crests and glittering medals, as visitors described them. Lt. Bonneville, watching the pageantry, may have pondered that he was more Yankee than French. In his world, working people predominated. He may have observed, too, the differences between the conquest-oriented Napoleonic soldiery and the road-building, boundary-surveying, treaty-arranging American military establishment. He was mindful of his status as an American citizen, for as a task of honor he served on the committee which sponsored a Paris fete on July 4, 1826 to celebrate the fiftieth anniversary of the signing of the Declaration of Independence.[8]

Promotion to Captain and Return from France

> Boston, Sept. 24, 1826: Sir, I have the honor to report myself thus far on my way towards my regiment which I will lose no time in joining. I am, sir, Most Respectfully, Your Most Obedient Servant, B. L. E. Bonneville, Captain, U. S. Army.

Bonneville's letter to the Adjutant General, written as soon as he landed, conveys an eagerness to be back at his post. Perhaps it was the captaincy; the promotion came in October, after he had sailed to France. And he was some weeks overdue, though all the officers stretched their leaves. In New York, new buildings reached in every direction, for New York City's population had climbed to 200,000. The prosperity was due in part to commerce on the Erie Canal, the grand project connecting the Great Lakes with the Hudson River. Captain Bonneville traveled the new waterway enroute to his post. The scientific wonder of age, the Erie Canal had come to fruit in spite of scoffing, political infighting and stubborn resistance of hills and boulders, plus the awkward fact that water only runs downhill. There were eighty-three locks along the way, where boats were raised from six to twelve feet. Besides transporting boatloads of produce, the Erie Canal was a scenic excursion for travelers. Narrow, bright-colored passenger boats glided to the rhythm of trotting hoof beats of tandem-hitched horses on the towpath. The panorama of neat farms, marshy wastes and forested ridges slid by at the speed of three or four miles an hour. It took almost a week to travel from Albany to Buffalo.

At Gibson little had changed. The Cherokees still complained of the Osage and of white settlers claiming farms. Col. Arbuckle complained to headquarters of the excessive fatigue—work duty demanded of his troops. Nevertheless, orders came to open a military road from Cantonment Gibson to Fort Smith. Arbuckle protested the want of money, tents and tools, and epidemic sickness to no avail. Shortly Lt. Dawson and Captain Bonneville were ordered to survey the road. A civilian commission had already been paid for laying out a route, but Bonneville and Dawson were able to cut off twelve miles by taking short cuts over low hills.

Reconnoitering in Red River Country

In response to urgent War Department messages of "great disturbances" on the Texas border, Col. Arbuckle ordered Captain Bonneville and his company to reconnoitre a portion of Red River country. Bonneville and his men followed an Indian trail over the prairies to the Canadian River and on to Sulphur Fork of Red River where Indians of many tribes traditionally hunted. Now white stockmen were moving in, and the Indians threatened to unite against the common enemy. Caddo Indian Agent George Gray, pleading for a military post, told Bonneville of the restless and dissatisfied of all Indian nations and languages settling on Caddo lands. Captain Bonneville patrolled, as ordered, conducting the talks that were part of the Army's probes whenever the Indians could be induced to take part. The airing of their grievances to listening soldiers with assurances that the government intended to deal with them fairly sometimes quieted the discontent. These battles-not-fought added no luster to the military, and both Indians and Army were betrayed, on occasion, by those of other ethics.

From the Caddo agency, Bonneville traveled seventy miles down Red River, listening along the way to complaints from settlers about the Indians stealing their livestock. Raiders had simply to cross the river to be in Mexican Texas and thus out of reach. But settlers on the Mexican side of the river also wanted the Army's protection; presumably all the bad Indians belonged to the United States. At Fort Towson, Major Alfred Cummings added his own complaints—he had not enough men to patrol hot spots, and in addition he had been ordered to work on a road to Fort Smith. Cummings had learned, however, that the reported trouble which had alarmed the War Department was far south of the border, where Americans on Mexican land grants were rallying Indian support to set up a republic "Fredonia." Bonneville and his company turned back to Cantonment Gibson.

North of Fort Towson, the Kiamichi River winds through Ouachita forest, thickgrown with pine, holly and sycamore. Through the mountains the Poteau begins as brooklets and tumbles toward the Arkansas. This game-stocked land belonged, at least for the time, to the Choctaws.

Life at Cantonment Gibson

There was news at Fort Smith: Forty-seven-year-old John Rogers had made a trip to New Orleans and brought back a pretty young bride, Mary. At Cantonment Gibson, Col. Arbuckle was smarting over criticism from Washington for lack of progress on the road to Fort Smith. He had asked for an increase in pay for his road workers; this was denied. Surgeon Baylor had asked permission to claim nearby land to support his large family; his answer too was "No" which seemed unfair, since other Army men managed similar deals. Zachary Taylor, while stationed at Baton Rouge ran a plantation nearby. Some said Col. Taylor was a better commander than farmer, for his crops failed, but others said he farmed better than he commanded.

The Seventh completed the fifty-six mile road to Fort Smith in the autumn; they were ordered to build another twenty-six miles toward Little Rock. Making his rounds at this time, Inspector General George Croghan deplored the Seventh's roadbuilding burden, writing that the Army should not be "looked upon as the pack horses of the public." The crisp-spoken inspector urged—as did every officer who had a chance—that frontier troops be mounted. "An infantryman might as well be sent to chase the elk or deer as the Osage or Pawnee."[9] The soldiers agreed. Too often after long marches on foot, plodding patrols saw only mocking silhouettes on the skyline or heard the clatter of hoof beats in the woods.

Between Indian patrols and road-building assignments, soldiers were hustled through inspections, drills and instruction, cleanup, and constant repair of the log buildings and puncheon floors. The garrison highlighted holidays with festive dinners marked with toasts and oratory, and with sociables and dances enjoyed by settlers, Cherokee families and traders' retinues as well as the military men. A goodly number of soldiers courted the young women of the region and stayed in the area to make homes on their bounty land. The government's offer of 320 acres of good earth for service completed kept recruits in plentiful supply. The Seventh, though foot soldiers, loved horses; soldiers, officers, traders and Indians enjoyed betting and racing at the improvised track near the post. Fishing was good, and prairie chickens were plentiful. There were also the pleasures of conversation, some of it gossip, some serious discussion of events and ideas. Officers' quarters were small, with rough-hewn furniture, but each was furnished with a stone fireplace where bright wood fires warmed both body and soul and friends might talk of many things.

Steamboat arrivals were gala events, especially the first ones in the spring. Officers returning from leave debarked, some bringing new brides or families, with visiting female kin to spice the leisure of the unattached. Resident traders arrived and so did itinerant merchants with tools and finery. Mail bags bulged with letters and newspapers. Accompanied by a bevy of territorial officials and a full staff, Department Commander Winfield Scott docked in March, 1827, for a week's inspection of Cantonment Gibson's facilities, practices and personnel. Scott was said to have high hopes of being named Commander in Chief of the Army. General Edmund P. Gaines also plumped for the position, and the two campaigned so avidly that President Adams bypassed them both and named General Alexander Macomb to the office.

Guaranteeing the Safety of Incoming Creek Indians

The Seventh Infantry was instructed during the spring of 1828 to guarantee the safety of an incoming party of Creeks. Shortly, eight hundred Indians arrived by keelboat, carrying a meager amount of worldly goods from their homes in Alabama and Georgia. Their bright calico tunics and kerchiefs belied their somber prospects, for at this point in their history, these people were not welcome anywhere. They were outcasts from Creek tribes who still clung to their southern homes; some of their leaders had paid with their lives for signing away their peoples' birthrights. The once great Creek nation had made the mistake of siding with the British, and later resisted white pushiness into their domain. Now, under pressure, many agreed to move west. The Osage bristled at this new invasion into the groves and grass of the Verdigris.

To protest white incursions on their reserve, the Cherokees sent a delegation to Washington. There, a treaty divided up the disputed area; both sides insisted they had been robbed. Almost unnoticed in the settlement was a grant for $1,000 to the Cherokees to buy a printing press. One delegate, a crippled silversmith, had devised an alphabet by which the Cherokee tongue could become a written language. In territorial papers he was listed as George Guess, and years later the magnificent redwood trees in the far west were given his Cherokee name, Sequoyah.

George Gray, the earnest Indian agent near Red River, died in November. His pleas for military support had been rejected but he had stayed on in the dangerous area, serving his Caddo and Quapaw charges. Osage Chief Clermont died, and his people mourned their "Builder of Towns." The village where he lived later became Claremore, Oklahoma.

The Death of Bonneville's Father

Captain Bonneville, too, suffered a loss. Nicolas de Bonneville died November 9, 1828. His friends Victor Hugo, Alfred de Vigny and others "donated to give him a suitable burial." One said of Nicolas, "He never ceased to be the most helpful and kind man I have ever known in my life, though stripped of his talent, a fire extinguished by misery and malady."[10]

On Military Business in St. Louis

Bonneville's enduring fancy for St. Louis may have dated from the first time he saw the lusty frontier city at the mouth of the Missouri. With Colonel Arbuckle, he was summoned there to a court martial in January, 1829. St. Louis spread up gentle slopes from the west side of the Mississippi, and its inhabitants were a pot-pourri of the American scene. Besides old-family French, there was a new aristocracy of bankers and slave-owning landed gentry, and voluble lawyers who regarded office-holding as vital to their profession. Shopkeepers sold the staples of everyday living plus frills like jewelry and locally brewed beer; other merchants did volume business in pack-saddles and hunting rifles and Indian trade goods. Frontiersmen loafed about the waterfront and grog shops, waiting for springtime and a summons to join ventures into the wilds. These men were French and Spanish and Indian and Yankee or mixtures of all. They were a floating population of heroes, for they had bested man and beast and rampages of nature against fantastic odds, according to their stories—some of them true. Among them were veterans of fur expeditions into the mountains of the west.

The streets of St. Louis were paved with cobblestones. The houses were steep-roofed in French sections and adorned with balconies in Spanish nooks, while solid new-England type buildings dotted the town like sturdy pilasters. But St. Louis was not in truth built of stone or Yankee brick but of furs. Furs had been used instead of money in earlier days. Dreams, plans and pursuits of livelihood had been based on furs for so many years the newer lead-mining and river commerce seemed of small importance.

The last of the original founders of St. Louis died while Bonneville was there in 1829. Rene August Chouteau had helped pole flatboats one thousand miles up the Mississippi from New Orleans. With his step-father and brother, he launched fur and related enterprises which dominated midwest industry for decades. He married Marie Therese Cerre: the Chouteaus, Cerres, Pauls, Valles and other French families were all related by birth or marriage. Bonneville's association with these families may have begun in 1829, possibly through Rene Paul, who had recently completed a Cherokee surveying assignment from Cantonment Gibson.

The business at hand for Arbuckle and Bonneville was nine miles downriver at Jefferson Barracks, a large brick and stone Army post which General Henry Atkinson had built three years previously. In 1829, his command included three regiments of infantry; among his lieutenants there were Albert Sidney Johnston, Philip St. George Cooke and Jefferson Davis. These recent West

Point graduates enjoyed recounting their escapades in out-maneuvering their dour instructor, "Old Hitch," Bonneville's classmate Ethan Allen Hitchcock. The mission of Col. Arbuckle and Captain Bonneville to Jefferson Barracks was less light-hearted. Though some courts martial appeared to be footwork for advancement or diversions during idle time in the barracks, this charge was serious, for the Major accused of cruelty to his men was found guilty and sentenced to be dismissed from service.

Andrew Jackson Becomes President

Andrew Jackson took office as President while Bonneville was in Missouri. The new executive enjoyed solid backing of frontier America. He had been touted as a champion of the common man, which was quite true, when the common man's views mirrored those of Jackson or unless the common man happened to be an Indian. In St. Louis, one of Jackson's most vociferous backers was Senator Thomas Hart Benton. With Congressman Lewis F. Linn, Benton plumped for expeditions and roads and Army posts to the Rocky Mountains and beyond.

Attending a Cherokee Council; More Trouble

The ladies of Cantonment Gibson were a-twitter with excitement in May, 1829, peeking from their windows for a glimpse of handsome Sam Houston: this according to a Houston biographer.[11] The ladies of Cantonment Gibson were scant in number—a few officers' wives, Sutler John Nicks' Sally, the washerwomen and the family of Dr. Baylor who had recently been relieved of part of his burden when his daughter Sophie married Lt. James L. Dawson.

Picturing himself as a champion of the Indians, Houston fired off advisory notes to Washington. There, President Jackson heard alarming rumors that his friend from Tennessee was trying to use Indians to seize Mexican Texas and set himself up as emperor. The President advised Arkansas officials to watch him.[12] In response to the alert, Col. Arbuckle sent Captain Bonneville to attend a Cherokee council.

Tribal leader John Jolly's plantation was the scene of the meeting. Middle-aged Jolly's Indian name was translated "He Who Put the Drum Away," but his followers were not amenable to the regulations the military was directed to enforce. Sam Houston claimed to be John Jolly's foster son. But Sam Houston was not present at the council; this was another tempest, a "council" arranged by a Cherokee agent who faced removal because the Army had seized from him thousands of dollars worth of merchandise containing liquor. Though Bonneville had told the Indians he had come only to confer as a friend, he was bombarded with numerous petty grievances, listed in writing.

"As the agent was present, I accused him of using measures to undermine confidence and good feelings toward the military, and I told him I did not believe the chiefs had ever seen that talk." Continuing, Bonneville chided the Cherokees for pettiness and delivered charges of his own, "Some of your bad people keep grog shops where our soldiers go and get drunk, where they are kept so 2 or 3 days; finding the soldiers have no more clothing to sell, your people bring them to the cantonment as deserters and claim thirty dollars as the reward." The air thus cleared, Bonneville concluded the council on a happier note, "May we always meet as brothers, may you rest in quiet, and may your people prosper and be happy."[13]

Unrest continued. The Creeks wanted their agent fired. The Osage protested being crowded by the Cherokees. Sam Houston said the Indians wanted Cantonment Gibson removed, and also claimed that he was trying to dissuade the Cherokees from a planned foray against prairie Indians. The warriors were spoiling for a fight, and if the United States Army was determined to keep the peace at Three Forks, they would go elsewhere. They did, with considerable loss. Such expeditions were part of their pattern of life and Sam Houston, or the Seventh Infantry, or He Who Put the Drum Away could not abolish a custom overnight. Sam Houston's importance to the red people was not what later legend-makers reported. He ran for a position on the Cherokee council and was defeated.

The Seventh Infantry had other trouble. A great log jam piled deeper each year on Red River, blocking boat traffic and leaving Fort Towson remote from communication and support in an international area bristling with unrest. Only weeks after Bonneville's patrol was there, two soldiers were killed near Fort Towson and farther west Comanches killed five traders. Col. Arbuckle decided to withdraw the infantry; settlers protested that they were deserted. Perhaps these were not the same residents who had berated the Army in Towson's early days and even clubbed an officer in a courtroom. Someone, however, set fire to the post as soon as the soldiers left.

"No soldiers in the world are as well-fed, well-clothed and well-paid as those of the United States," the "Arkansas Gazette" asserted, possibly bringing wry shrugs from the garrison at Cantonment Gibson. Better reading were "Gazette" accounts of fur-trade caravans to the Rocky Mountains. The far west intrigued all America. The "Arkansas Gazette" printed official pronouncements from Washington and many articles about the upper Missouri and Oregon country, mostly warnings that the British were taking unfair advantage of the treaty which stipulated joint occupancy. Returning fur-hunters reported attacks by Indians armed with British weapons and of British impertinence to Americans. Fur trade partners Jedediah Smith, David Jackson and William Sublette aired their opinions in a letter to the Secretary of War reenforcing other reports.

Bonneville's friend John Rogers of Fort Smith advertised in the "Arkansas Gazette" for "one hundred young men of enterprise" to join him in a two-year expedition to the Rocky Mountains. His plans did not materialize. Sam Houston, too, talked of going to Oregon. Houston biographer Marquis James pictures Bonneville's "shelf of Latin and Greek, the plays of Racine and poems of Villon" in his "cabin on Officers Row . . . Between the classics, the Rocky Mountain scheme and a bottle on the table, Houston and the vibrant bald headed little Frenchman would talk all night."[14]

It was business as usual at Cantonment Gibson. "Department of War, March 25, 1830, to Col. M. Arbuckle: Sir, An order issued to you yesterday to take immediate steps to secure peace on the frontiers."[15] For eight years the testy commander and his Seventh Infantry had struggled to do just that. Now, the Osage were beating war drums against the Cherokees because of a new rash of murders. White squatters on the Choctaw reserve refused to move. The Creeks had not received their promised money; the last several hundred Creek families had suffered disease and starvation on the long journey to Three Forks, and arriving, found their promised land had also been granted to the Cherokees. Yet here was a faraway politician demanding instant— and ungrammatical—tranquility.

The Jackson Indian policy was now fully defined. The Indians must move west. Gold had been found in Georgia, and this sealed the fate of the Indians remaining there. In other areas too, where Indians still clung to their homes, white settlers insisted that the "savages" be hustled away. Congress approved, passing the "Indian Removal Bill" in June, 1830. Since so many Indians had already been sent to the region which would become Oklahoma, it seemed logical to send more. If, as the Army protested, Indian settlements were already too crowded for peace, then push westward further; the prairies were limitless, were they not? They were not. Besides the human barriers of fierce Pawnees and Comanches, an almost impenetrable belt of black-jack, oak, hickory and briars called Cross Timbers formed a twenty-mile-wide no-mans-land from Cimarron River on the north to Red River on the south. But new reserves must be found.

Assessing the Upper Canadian River for Indian Settlement Locations

Captain Bonneville drew an assignment in late September to assess the upper Canadian River for possible Indian settlement. Along the way, he named the north fork of the Canadian "Atkinson River" and gave the name "Macomb River" to the later-designated Gaines Creek, either for the Commanding General, or for his nephew Jasper Macomb, who was the Company's first lieutenant. Bonneville and his men "waded the Canadian upwards of 300 times" to the mouth of Little River, "a beautiful stream; from its current and clearness mostly fed by springs." Here they turned northward, and after exploring twenty-five miles farther upstream turned back to Cantonment Gibson. Bonneville reported few possibilities of pleasant homes for Indian families. "Sand hills frequently make to the River on both banks. The bottoms are small, being generally sand beds . . . little timber. The Prairies are . . . destitute of water . . . little game," and added "My men were much disabled by sickness." He asked for compensation for the private who acted as doctor and "contended with violent fever, dysenteries and spasms."[16]

An Ambitious Plan

On November 3, Bonneville submitted a request for an eight-month leave, to begin the following March. He did not tell his commanding officer what he had in mind. The West, with its unknown resources and magnificent Rocky Mountains intrigued Bonneville to the point of obsession. The British were threatening to preempt these 'vacant backlands' Jefferson had bought; should the nation—the Army—sit idly by and lose a choice portion of the continent? Weary of fruitless Indian patrols, Bonneville had of necessity to balance his desires for action with his duty to the Army. Out of months of thought had come a wonderful plan.

Chapter Three
1832-1839
Exploring the Rocky Mountains

Requesting Permission for an Expedition to the Rocky Mountains

Furlough in hand, Captain Bonneville set out in April, 1831, to put into motion an ambitious project he had conceived and maneuvered for—a mapping and information-gathering expedition to the Rocky Mountains. In Washington, he submitted his proposal to Commander-in-Chief Alexander Macomb.

> Sir: Observing that our countrymen are daily becoming more desirous of understanding the true situation and resources of that portion of our territories lying to the north of Mexico and west of the Rocky Mountains, has determined me to offer my services for the advancement of that object. I ask for no outfit, no presents for the Indians, no command, want no protection, save passports from Our and Mexican authorities at this place and leave of absence for that purpose . . . I would there, by observations, establish prominent points of that country, ascertain the general courses etc. of the principal rivers, the location of the Indian tribes and their habits, visit the American and British establishments, make myself acquainted with their manner of trade and intercourse with the Indians, finally endeavor to develop every advantage the country affords and by what means they may most readily be opened to the enterprise of our citizens. These, sir, are the objects I propose accomplishing. Early next spring, I would leave the United States, with some of the companies there, and on my arrival, immediately begin my labours . . . I have, for a long time had this object in contemplation . . . I can conceive of no time more propitious than the present, while the attention of the country is directed toward an enterprise likely to prove of so much importance . . .[1]

The government needed just such data as Bonneville proposed to obtain, for many citizens believed that America should simply move into Oregon and solve the joint occupancy dispute by sheer force of numbers. President Andrew Jackson distrusted the British and frequently used undercover agents to supply him with information. Besides, Bonneville had requested "passports from Our and Mexican authorities," and Oregon was not the only far west prize being eyed in the 1830s. Expansionist Jackson was known to covet San Francisco harbor "whose value had been reported by American naval vessels."[2]

Approval, perhaps direction, came in short order, it is apparent, since Bonneville spent the next two months collecting instruments and making arrangements. He enrolled in Hall J. Kelley's proposed migration plan, but quickly dropped out. His proposal to travel with a fur company likewise went by the board. Whether by means of strings pulled or by lucky chance, John Jacob Astor furnished money for Bonneville to head a large, independent probe to the far west. Bonneville's first license to trade with the Indians bore only his name, the second, "Astor, Bonneville and Company."[3]

At this time Astor's American Fur Company partisans were battling competitors for dominance in the well-gleaned trapping grounds. Why put another company in the field? In introducing the later- published *Adventures of Captain Bonneville,* Washington Irving touched the truth obliquely, writing that a boyhood friend who had grieved at seeing the British haul down the American flag at Astoria in 1814 was of great help in securing Bonneville's finance. Without a doubt the "schoolfellow" was Alfred Seton, who was on the scene at Astoria, and continued to be a business associate of Astor.[4]

Another Bonneville family friend, Albert Gallatin, may have had a hand in the arrangements. A promoter of western expansion, Gallatin had in the past strongly defended Astor's endeavors. He and Astor had established the National Bank of New York in the spring of 1831 with, as the financier put it, Astor money and Gallatin's good name. Elderly John Jacob Astor was relinquishing his business world to his son, but failure of the Astoria project still rankled. If, with his assistance, a clear American title to the Pacific northwest might become a reality, his long ago efforts would not have been in vain.

High-ranking army officers put in a good word for Bonneville's expedition. "That I started as a trader and acted as such, is what I never attempted to conceal. Generals Scott, Eustis and even General Macomb assisted me to become one, as letters now in my possession will show," Bonneville would write when he was later criticized for the commercial aspects of the expedition. "It was deemed more proper for me to go as such, and without expense to the government, furnish them with such information as they believed useful and interesting to the Country, than for the Government to be at the expense of hiring men for that purpose, and of making presents to every Indian nation they should meet."

Of those who have taken the time and effort to study the contemporary documents of Bonneville's expedition, historian Wm. H. Goetzmann sums up the conclusion: "There appears to be strong evidence for believing, as Bernard DeVoto and others believe, that Bonneville was a 'spy' in the same sense as Lewis and Clark, Zebulon Pike, and others."[5]

In July, Captain Bonneville wrote to General Macomb that he had assembled "sextant and horizon, microscope, pocket-compass of instruments and patent-lever time pieces" among other items, and that he had "examined every work that was likely to yield me any information respecting the country."

> "Headquarters of the Army, Washington, 29 July 1831. Sir, the leave of absence which you have asked . . . has been duly considered and submitted to the War Department for approval, and has been sanctioned. You are therefore authorized to be absent from the Army until October, 1833 . . ."

Approval included the government's disavowal of expense and possible blame if something went awry, "It having originated with yourself," but charged him to furnish information on every conceivable dimension of the country and people he would see. Historian Edward S. Meany has observed "The letter was one of the most remarkable ever received by an American soldier . . . He was to do all that has since been attempted by such costly agencies of government as the Bureau of Ethnology, Census Bureau, Agriculture Department and Geological Survey. He was to do all that at his own expense."[6] Nevertheless, the stocky balding black-eyed officer was jubilant as he turned westward with his packet of instruments and the joint blessing of the Army and of John Jacob Astor. "Curious and intelligent, he had felt at first hand so strong a pull from the western lands that . . . he simply had to walk toward Oregon," David Lavender has written.[7]

Benjamin's Mother Returns from France

Margaret Bonneville arrived from France to make her home in the United States at this time. Bonneville and his mother traveled to St. Louis by the Erie Canal to Erie, south by stage to Pittsburgh, then by steamboat down the Ohio, around the muddy delta at Cairo and upstream on the Mississippi to St. Louis. Margaret Bonneville went to live at the home of widow Marie Therese Chouteau in a "splendid mansion" where with "French manners, cookery and habits, she seemed to enjoy life."[8] The Chouteau house on Main Street, built when that thoroughfare was called La Rue Royale, was now in the middle of town among mercantile establishments: Wilson Price Hunt's Fur Emporium, Durkee's Bank, and "Mr. Dongan's Silversmith Shop—He has on Hand a Heap of Whiskey, Plenty of Peach Brandy, Linsey, Shoes, Cut and Hammered Nails which he will sell low for Cash or Beef Hides," the "Missouri Gazette" advertised.

Preparations for Departure from St. Louis

Captain Bonneville hurried on up the Missouri River, stopping at Liberty and other frontier settlements. At Fort Osage he commissioned Joseph Walker to supervise arrangements there. A sturdy Tennessean, Walker had been with a trading caravan to Santa Fe, had been sheriff at Independence, Missouri, and more recently on wild horse roundups southward toward Texas. He had passed through Three Forks the preceding February, and Bonneville may have talked business with him there. Walker's correct name was Joseph Rutherford Walker, according to his biographer, Bil Gilbert. The middle name "Reddeford" appeared erroneously in his 1876 obituary and has persisted.[9]

From Franklin, on December 5, Bonneville reported to Washington, "I have the pleasure to say that all my preparations for the Rocky Mountains progress much to my satisfaction." He stated that he would be in St. Louis for some time "where any communications will reach me." This short note was the last the Army would hear of him for three and one-half years, or so officials would claim. But Bonneville kept a journal, and chance events brought the publication later of *The Rocky Mountains, or Scenes, Incidents and Adventures in the Far West, digested from the Journal of Captain B. L. E. Bonneville of the Army of the United States, and Illustrated from Various Other Sources*, by best-selling author Washington Irving. Later editions bore only the name *The Adventures of Captain Bonneville*. Working from notes and a manuscript which Bonneville had been preparing for possible publication, Irving incorporated into the book information from other sources as well. The original journal disappeared, either from files of the War Department, or from among Bonneville's possessions. That Bonneville had no opportunity to proofread is evident in errors such as "I. R." Walker for Joseph Walker, and location and directional misstatements which he would have corrected. Though he saw flaws, omissions and embellishments in the published work, Bonneville referred to it as his "Journal." Except where otherwise noted, quotations in this chapter are from Irving's *Adventures of Captain Bonneville*—the "Journal." A long "Report" to the War Department datelined "Crow Country, Wind River, July 29, 1833," supplies additional information and clarification. Cited in this work as the "Report," it lay in official files for almost one hundred years before being found and publicized.[10]

In St. Louis Bonneville recruited men and bought supplies. Quartermastering he knew well, though this project called for items the Army had not needed: traps, knives, tomahawks, bright blankets, cloth, beads and bells. The usual guns, lead, powder, liquor, food and tobacco must be augmented for this journey with harnesses, axes, shovels and blacksmithing tools, for Bonneville planned to take wagons, at least as far as he could. During the winter, he received by mail from the State Department the passport he had requested, viseed by J. Maria Montoya, the Mexican charge d'affaires in Washington. Dated January 23, 1832, the passport was issued to Joseph R. Walker at the request of Bonneville.[11]

Bonneville chose fur-trade veteran Michel Silvestre Cerre to be his chief clerk. Surveyor Rene Paul acted as Bonneville's agent in St. Louis. In Paul's "counting room," David Adams signed an 18-month contract. In return for a total of three hundred dollars, generous for the times, he promised to be honest and faithful and to keep his employer's secrets.[12] Other "young men of enterprise," as fur-trade adventurers were called, joined the ranks also.

April saw a mighty push at Fort Osage. Joseph Walker had recruited frontiersmen from the area, who with those from St. Louis made up a crew of one hundred and twenty. Among them were a number of Delaware Indians. Of the original expedition employees, only a few names are known: Clerk William D. Hodgkiss, brigade leader A. Matthieu, Benjamin Hardister, who was killed, as were three whose first names do not appear—Jennings, Ross, and LeRoy. Of the following, some were of the original roster and some joined in the constant realignment of loyalties in fur-trade circles: Antonio Montero, B. Bourdalone, Enos Burdno, J. D. Green, Stephen Meek, Joseph Meek, Nathan Daily, John Enos, William Craig, Wm. S. Williams, Joseph Gale, Zenas Leonard, Mark Head, Alexis Godey, Robert Mitchell, Antoine Janisse, George Nidever, Robert Newell, Mr. Bergen, Mr. Laront, Mr. Stanfield and cook Tom Cain.

Departure: May 1, 1832

At last twenty wagons stood ready with great loads of provisions and trade goods. Extra mules, oxen, horses and a cow would be driven along. Bonneville's license listed his capital at $17,254.77, making him the largest and best-equipped of the many entrepreneurs of that year. His rowdy employees whooped and yelled their goodbys to civilization as the wagon train creaked into action on May 1, 1832. Out on the prairie, the shouting died away in a drizzle of cold rain and the wagon wheels creaked in the soggy earth. Bonneville's "Journal", as edited by Irving, depicts people and terrain in a lighthearted vein with little intimation of serious purpose, but Bonneville's transition from army officer to brigade leader was never total. He deployed front and rear guards, with two columns of supply wagons in the middle. At night, wagons were drawn into a square with the hobbled livestock herded into the enclosure.

Sunshine warmed the gentle hills. Grass grew thick along pleasant little creeks, then ridges and hills gave way to sandstone boulders standing like tombstones along the Vermilion River. William Sublette's large pack train of supplies for his Rocky Mountain Fur Company overtook and passed the slow-moving wagons. Traveling with Sublette was Boston ice-merchant Nathaniel Wyeth, who planned to establish a three-cornered business of furs, fish, and China silks from a base at the mouth of the Columbia. He had many odds against him, among them a crew of complaining greenhorns.

At the Platte River and the Sweetwater

A month's travel brought the wagon train to the south fork of the Platte River. Cottonwood thickets grew on islands of the meandering river, though the trail was bare of wood or game. The men ferried the wagons across the South Platte in buffalo hide boats and traveled over rolling prairie to reach the north branch. Past Chimney Rock, a landmark spire, flocks of big-horn sheep kept vigil on cliffs of clay and sandstone known as Scott's Bluffs. The Journal's was the first published account of Hyrum Scott's tragic desertion by his companions.

The expedition's first encounter with Crow Indians presaged their later dealings with these handsome, aggressive high-country Siouans. Yelling warriors thundered over the prairie toward the caravan. Captain Bonneville gave battle orders to his men, and then rode out towards the approaching chief and "extended to him the hand of friendship." At once all was peaceful, the Crows explaining that they were pursuing enemy Cheyennes. They affected a comradery that flattered the travelers—until they found their pockets had been picked.

Leaving the meadows of Laramie's Fork, Bonneville's wagon train headed northwest into the "Black Hills" (Laramie Mountains). Here the wagons had to be let down over abrupt bluffs with ropes and guyed with stout cables to keep them from tipping. The horses limped, their hooves broken by sharp stones. The Crows visited again, this time flaunting Cheyenne scalps. Bonneville's men learned something from the Crows—besides the lesson of watching their valuables—buffalo hides made admirable horse shoes.

Beds of sandstone, craggy rocks and two sienna hills called "The Red Buttes" marked the point where the overland trail veered southwest to the Sweetwater. In the dry heat of mid-July, the men suffered cracked lips and high-altitude abdominal cramps. At one point the Sweetwater squeezed through a deep canyon: "Devil's Gate," later travelers would name it. From a rocky ridge, the "Eutaw" mountains could be seen far to the southwest, and dominating the landscape to the west and north, the Wind River Mountains shimmered in white and jagged splendor. Bonneville pointed out that this great backbone of ice and granite fed both the Atlantic and the Pacific oceans and the Gulf of California as well.

Crossing the Continental Divide—South Pass

The midday sun was blazing hot, but waterbuckets froze overnight. The wagons were falling apart. Leaving the Sweetwater, Bonneville led his company up the stony slopes of the "great steppes" and over a 7,750-foot saddle of the continental divide, the South Pass. He camped on a small south-lowing stream, exulting that he had succeeded in taking wagons to the waters of the Pacific. Bonneville and his men set off across a dry plain and in three days reached the Colorado of the West.

Green River had many names: Colorado of the West, possibly because it was a fork of the Colorado; Spanish River, because the dons and the priests knew its lower reaches; Siskadee Agie, spelled various ways and said to mean Prairie Chicken River in Crow language.

"Having ascended this river on the right bank forty miles, we built a picket work," Bonneville wrote in his Report. Green River valley is emerald and blue in summertime. Cradled between Gray's River range and the Wind River mountains, the meadows are marshy around the area later called Daniel, Wyoming, where evidence of Bonneville's camp has been found. Cottonwood

Creek and the combined branches of Horse Creek feed the Green here; the lowlands between the converging streams grow thick grass; willows and cottonwood shade the water's edges.

A Fort Built in the Green River Valley

While his animals rested—recruited, in Army jargon—Bonneville set his men to building a "breastworks."

> "It is situated in a fine open plain on a rising spot of ground, about three hundred yards from Green River on the west side, commanding a view of the plains for several miles up and down that stream. On the opposite side of the fort about two miles distant, there is a fine willowed creek called Horse Creek, flowing parallel with Green River and emptying into it about five miles below the fortification. The fort presents a square enclosure, surrounded by posts or pickets firmly set in the ground, of a foot or more in diameter, planted close to each other, and about fifteen feet in length. At two of the corners diagonally opposite to each other, block houses of unhewn logs are so constructed and situated as to defend the square outside the pickets and hinder the approach of an enemy from any quarter. The prairie in the vicinity of the fort is covered with fine grass, and the whole together seems well calculated for the security of both men and horses," according to Warren Angus Ferris, who saw it the following year.[13]

In the twentieth century, Wyoming historians including Dr. Grace Hebard and Mr. Perry W. Jenkins located the site of the fort, described as in the northeast quarter of section 30 township 34 north of range 111 west, or about six miles west of where Horse Creek runs into Green River, Sublette County, Wyoming.[14]

The finished work looked exactly like a United States Army frontier fort. A cavalcade of Indians rode into the area, eyed the picket work, and moved on.

"Fell in with the Gros Ventre of the Prairies, Blackfeet, about 900 warriors, had no difficulty with them," Bonneville summarized.[15] Known as the fiercest of all the tribes, the Blackfeet and their relatives, the Piegans and Gros Ventres, were said to be ever avenging the murder of one of their number by the Lewis and Clark party. Their hostility extended equally to members of their own race. The Blackfeet claimed the Canadian plains, plus most of the later Montana, and when they sallied southward, the native Indians usually scurried out of their way.

During the four weeks he spent at his picket work, Bonneville learned facts of geography, climate and allegiances of the Indians. He also learned about the uncertainties of the fur trade. Lucien Fontanelle and his partner Etienne Provost of American Fur camped near Bonneville and waited for their trappers to bring in their furs and be restocked for the coming year. French-Canadian Provost—(pronounced Provo)—was a veteran of twenty years in the fur trade. New Orleans-born Fontanelle was cordial to Bonneville, but hired away the Delaware Indians. In return, Bonneville dispatched scouts to intercept Fontanelle's free trappers and entice them with a "free allowance of grog" to transfer their allegiance, fleeting as it might be, to Bonneville.

In late July, William Sublette and Robert Campbell arrived with news of a battle with Indians near a rendezvous of fur companies in Pierre's Hole. Sublette had been wounded. Bonneville listened to a number of reports; his account in the "Journal" of the "Battle of Pierre's Hole" has been called the most comprehensive of printed versions. Sublette and Campbell were on their way to St. Louis with their Rocky Mountain Fur Company harvest of furs. With them were deserters from Nathaniel Wyeth's party, including Wyeth's disgruntled nephew hurrying home to publish his journal. William Vanderburgh and Andrew Dripps also arrived from Pierre's Hole. These field partners of American Fur collected their supplies from the still-waiting Provost and Fontanelle, and set off with their men to the trapping streams.

Trapping Parties Sent Out

Bonneville, too, began to deploy trapping parties. With "Meldrum's map, forty animals with their equipment and Sundry merchandise and twenty-one men," David Adams was commissioned in writing to recross the South Pass and trap along the eastern base of Wind River mountains. He was to go up Shoshone River and the Yellowstone, "cross over to the Salmon River and descend to the forks." It was a large order, entailing hundreds of miles travel through Crow and Blackfoot country. Bonneville cautioned Adams: "Nightly parks and close Staking, you are aware, are the only true methods of keeping your Animals in Security." The men were expected to know how to take care of themselves. As it turned out, they did not, though some writers have suggested that Adams chose, or was assigned, the ne'er-do-wells hired in St. Louis waterfront bars, for David Adams was a sometimes barkeeper.[16]

To recruit the thinner horses, Bonneville sent a party to Bear River under A. Matthieu, who as a former employee of Etienne Provost knew that country. This group was to trap, to trade with the Shoshoni and when the horses were fit, to join the others on the Salmon River. Other ventures not mentioned in the "Journal" were tried as well. One party was "sent south and wintered on the shores of Salt Lake" either at this time or subsequently. Another was "sent through Crow country and came around by the north and wintered with me on Salmon River."[17] David Adams failed in this, though some of his men may have done so. Or some of the free trappers Bonneville hired away from American Fur may have traveled as they had planned through Crow country. The "Journal"'s detailed account of the rival companies' movements there support this idea. It must be presumed as well that other projects took place which were not recorded.

Northwest through Jackson's Hole

Bonneville and a few trusted men dug pits at night and hid the surplus goods, including the wagons, or such parts of them as remained, carefully obliterating traces of the caches. On August 22, with mules and pack horses carrying 200-pound loads, the expedition "went a north west course" according to the "Report." In the "Journal," the direction is printed "east north east" which leads into the Wind River mountains, and must be regarded as an error. The "crystal cascades and bright little lakes" noted in the "Journal" could only belong to another foray. Wispy evidence points to other probes. W. O. Owen, a government surveyor in the 1890s, wrote that he found a large cave with "B. L. E. Bonneville" carved on a rock inside the cavern. Owen wrote of reading a Bonneville report to the War Department describing the cave and locating it "on the west slope of Wind River chain, in Latitude 42-46' 09 N. Long. 109-20' 00 West." No such entry has been found in the Bonneville file in the National Archives, but it is a fact that other known communications have been lost or misplaced. Owen was a capable, though sometimes controversial mountain climber.[18]

The route west from Green River Valley led over the western rim to the Hoback, where the trail was "passed upon the river, and upon a cornice of the Mountain from which horses fell from every party, descent perpendicular 270 feet high."[19] From Jackson's Hole, Bonneville mounted thc range on the west and "arrived at the summit of a mountain which commanded a full view of the eventful valley of Pierre's Hole; whence he could trace the winding of the stream through green meadows and forests of cottonwood and have a prospect, between distant mountains, of the lava plains of Snake River, dimly spread forth like a sleeping ocean below."[20]

Bonneville made camp at the scene of the recent battle between the trappers and Gros Ventres, then followed Pierre's (Teton) river west, crossing Henry's Fork of the Snake River and sixty miles of sagebrush desert to reach Cota's Defile and the stream later named Birch Creek. The defile led upward in gradual ascent between ranges of mountains, and from a high plateau down to marshy meadows marking the headwaters of the Lemhi River, known to the trappers as the East Fork of the Salmon. A Nez Perce hunting party rode into camp and offered to share their food. When they left to continue their hunt, Michel Cerre and a number of men went with them.

Preparations for Winter on the Salmon

Curving northwestward, the Lemhi washes coral bluffs until it joins the main Salmon coming in from the south. At this sheltered spot, Bonneville halted and set his men to building corrals and log shelters. Told that this was to be a "permanent post for trading with the Indians," one trapper was disappointed when he saw it "situated on the west bank of the river in a grove of cottonwood trees . . . its total want of pickets proved that it was only intended for a temporary shelter for the company during the winter."[21]

Joseph Walker led a band of men eastward across the continental divide to Horse Prairie; other brigades departed as well. Hunters sent out to replenish the food supply came back with game, but with Indian friends; the camp overflowed with Flatheads, Nez Perces, and several Iroquois, remnants of a group imported by Hudson's Bay Company to teach Western Indians how to trap beaver. Bonneville observed, listened and asked questions, and on occasion told the receptive Nez Perces about Christianity. In early November, Michel Cerre and his Nez Perce companions arrived from Horse Prairie (Big Hole Valley, Montana). They brought in meat from a successful buffalo hunt. Walker, too, had found fair hunting in the same area, though he had lost a number of horses. Bonneville sent Walker and forty men to trap on Snake River and its tributaries, with arrangements to come to the picket work on Green River for a rendezvous the following July.

Rival Trapping Parties

The rival trapping parties of Rocky Mountain Fur and American Fur arrived. These brigades had traveled north from Green River to the headwaters of the Missouri. Jim Bridger and Thomas Fitzpatrick of Rocky Mountain Fur had lost two men and gained few furs. Most of their time had been spent dodging the Blackfeet and annoying their competitors, Dripps and Vanderburgh's American Fur trappers. The latter had fared even worse; Vanderburgh had been killed in an ambush. Employee Warren Ferris was wounded, and he believed that the Bridger party had deliberately led them into disaster.

Grass and game were soon gone from the wooded banks of the Salmon at the forks. For the Indians it was time to seek new fields. Caching goods at the encampment, Bonneville joined the Nez Perces "in a secluded part of the country at the head of a small stream," one day's journey from the forks. Two weeks' balmy weather fattened the horses but brought sickness to the Indians. Some died, in spite of ministrations of medicine men and also in spite of Bonneville's prescriptions of sweating and bleeding.

Scarcity of game dictated another move to a spot the "Journal" describes as "at no great distance . . . on the right branch or head stream of the river, locked up among cliffs and precipices . . . so narrow rugged and difficult as to prevent secret approach," an apt description of the Upper Salmon River gorge, where high crags force the river into a narrow passageway. From this gateway for a dozen miles, the Salmon twists through grassy dells interspersed with slide rock barriers and towering palisades. One "Journal" mention of the "north" fork of Salmon River does not refer to the creek-sized later-designated North Fork, which drains a gentle valley. The "right branch, or head stream" as the "Journal" also states is correct, and "up" is south.

Bonneville stayed at the new camp less than a week, though during that time one of the free trappers married a Nez Perce woman. Typical Irving verbiage describes the Indian bride, and explains the trapper-squaw relationship. Bachelor Irving viewed marriage with tongue in cheek; perhaps this encouraged later writers to assert that this wedding was Bonneville's own. This must be said: in all the thousands of words of contemporary accounts studied for this work, there is no mention of Bonneville having Indian wives or mistresses. H. H. Bancroft, writing in the 1880's after Bonneville's death appears to be the first, but not the last, to print this fiction.

On the day after Christmas, Bonneville set out to see what had happened to Matthieu, long overdue from Bear River. Leaving the gorge with eleven men, he passed widening meadows, then left the main branch of the river to follow the "Little Salmon (Pahsimeroi) south toward a pass called John Day's Defile" and down the stream later called Little Lost River. Bitter wind, deep snows and a Blackfeet alarm plagued the men. They killed a buffalo on an icy swamp, but the horses suffered from lack of forage. From the sinks where the mountains end and the Snake River plain begins, the party traveled south to Big Butte, crossing Godin's (Big Lost) River on the way. The Snake River desert from this point was a frosty etching. In the "Journal," Irving credited Bonneville with the delightful description of the scene, and added, "Winter has its beauties and glories as well as summer, and Captain Bonneville had the soul to appreciate them."

The "Three Buttes" rise from the high-desert plain. The Big Butte, the remnant of a volcano, is sculptured and eroded with ravines which support vegetation. On the north side is a spring, an oasis for travelers. Bonneville and his men camped there on January 9, 1833. One of the mules froze to death. The next day, Bonneville found a southeasterly trail between two lava fields and followed it to the belt of wooded lowlands along Snake River in the later Fort Hall Indian Reservation. Sheltered by cottonwoods and willows, this was the traditional wintering place for Shoshoni and Bannocks. Elk, deer and buffalo were usually to be found, and most advantageous, the marauding Blackfeet were reluctant to attack in open country, preferring to trap their prey in the bends of small streams like the area river named for them.

Bonneville found Walker and his brigade camped near the mouth of the Blackfoot River. Matthieu came in from Bear River on February 3. His luck had been all bad; early snows stalled him. Indians had killed three of his men at Sheep Rock (near Soda Springs). He had lost many horses; he had found no friendly Shoshoni to trade with, and had set no traps. Robert Newell, a Rocky Mountain Fur employee, left Milton Sublette's nearby camp to join Captain Bonneville. His new loyalty proved only fair, but he was a good man to have, a saddler, and with such talent for administering remedies and minor surgery to man and beast that he was known as "Doc Newell." Shoshoni and Bannock Indians, related tribes, were wintering near the mouth of the Portneuf. Bonneville called this encampment "Bannocks" and observed that they were cunning warriors. Fulfilling his assignment he described their habits, attitudes and armament in his Report.

Plans for the Spring Beaver Hunt

As the willow clumps turned carmine along the sheltered river bottoms, Bonneville planned his spring beaver hunt. Leaving Walker with most of the trappers, he took sixteen men and set off across the "Plain of the Three Buttes." The snow was deep; at night they dug holes for shelter from the winds. They reached the caches at the forks of the Salmon on March 12.

Bonneville sent out detachments to trap; he planned to make his own spring hunt on "Malade River" (Wood River). With twenty-three trappers and a dozen Nez Perces, he moved slowly southward up Salmon River, pausing in the greening meadows to graze the horses. At a broad riverside bowl with warm springs and rust-colored bluffs, (Challis, Idaho) the Salmon turns westward, and Bonneville left it to travel southeast over a high plateau. At a marshy basin (Thousand Springs Valley) Godin's River (Big Lost) comes in at a right-angle bend from the west. Up that stream and over the mountains was the Malade, but snow blocked the trail. Alerted by tracks of a rival trapping brigade, Bonneville moved south, down the valley, planning to reach the beaver streams as soon as melting snow permitted passage of trails. It was May before the fur brigades reached the Malade, and there the trapping was poor; Hudson's Bay Company's John Work had stripped the streams bare during the past several years.

Westward to the Boise River

Bonneville pushed on westward "towards the Comanche Prairies, laying on the route of the lower Columbia."[22] He reached Boise River, written "Boisee" in the "Journal" and "Boisey" in the "Report." It is an Idaho tradition that Bonneville's men exclaimed "Les bois! Les bois!" at a spot later designated Bonneville Point, confirming the name Boise for the river, valley and in due time, Idaho's capitol city. Earlier, Peter Skene Ogden had written "Boissie" in his journal, and the stream had other names as well. Bonneville wrote "The country . . . is the most enchanting in the Far West: presenting the mingled grandeur and beauty of mountain and plain; of bright running streams and vast grassy meadows . . ." From the "Boisey and LaPayette rivers," he "tried to cross the mountains . . . the great depth of snow forced me to seek another pass."[23]

Hudson's Bay Company—A British Monopoly

Back in Snake River country Bonneville found his Hodgkiss brigade camped near Indians who had assembled to do business with Hudson's Bay Company's "resident trader." That gentleman was present, and though his packtrain of supplies had not yet arrived, "he held such control" over the Indians Bonneville was unable to buy furs from them, though he "displayed the most tempting wares: bright cloths, and scarlet blankets and glittering ornaments." The "resident trader" was Francois Benjamin Payette, described as genial and courteous and also as fat and merry. As a boy he had been one of the boatload of singing Canadian voyagers who paddled down the Hudson in 1810 and sailed to Astoria. He had been errand boy for Alfred Seton, transferring his allegiance to the British when the Americans withdrew.

The encounter with Payette was Bonneville's personal introduction to Hudson's Bay Company, the British monopoly which American fur interests claimed was intruding and inciting the Indians to fight. Bonneville believed this to be true. "Americans have to steal their own fur making secret rendezvous and trading by stealth."[24]

The Hudson's Bay Company supply train arrived, commanded by Francis Ermatinger, and with it Nathaniel Wyeth, the Bostonian who had brought his ambitions to the mountains the previous year. With the help of trapping parties, Wyeth had made his way to Hudson's Bay's Fort Vancouver on the Columbia River, only to find that his supply ship had wrecked coming around the Horn. Nevertheless, he scouted for a site for a salmon-curing plant he planned to build. Most of his crew had deserted, but he proposed that Hudson's Bay furnish him with men and outfit him for a trapping venture. Chief Factor John McLoughlin refused, and nudged him to return to the States, offering safe passage to the Snake River plain with the company's caravan of supplies. Wyeth accepted, but enroute, wrote to McLoughlin's superior making the same proposal. Now he made another attempt to avoid going home empty-handed, offering to lead a hunt "south of the Columbia" for Bonneville. He wrote, "a meeting with Mr. Bonneville gives me the power to make jointly with him a party for a hunt this season . . . I shall go southward in the vicinity of San Francisco in New California."

Perhaps, thinking it over, Wyeth had doubts about the project, or he may have been ill. He wrote on July 4, "I am shivering with cold . . . nothing but a few skins to cover my nakedness . . . the enterprise I am upon is a dangerous one." Wyeth locates this large encampment of British, Americans and Indians as on Camas Creek (Clark county, Idaho) sixteen miles downstream from "a luxuriant clover meadow nurtured by numerous cold springs."

The deal collapsed. Bonneville may have decided that Wyeth, trying to play on everybody's team, was not to be trusted with the mission he had in mind. It is also possible that none of the men would agree to take orders from the unlucky Wyeth, or to follow him into unknown country. Though the partnership failed, the two remained friends, and Wyeth made it a point to defend Bonneville to Ermatinger.[25] And Bonneville learned much from Wyeth about Hudson's Bay Company's posts and their strength, or lack of it.

Fear of the Blackfeet hung thicker than the smoke from the sagebrush campfires along Camas Creek. The Blackfeet were everywhere and thirsting for blood, according to the rumors. As Bonneville prepared to move to Green River and the rendezvous, some of his free trappers elected to hunt the headwaters of the Salmon rather than risk going through Pierre's Hole. Obliged to accede to their wishes—Ermatinger was on hand to hire them away if he did not—Bonneville fitted them out and sent them on their way. Ermatinger's packtrain of furs headed north—seldom did the British meet with Indian trouble. Bonneville with the twenty-three men remaining to him plus Wyeth and his small retinue "traveled East 18 miles to Henrys Fork here wooded with narrow leafed cottonwood . . . our route over a very dry plain passing some low hills of pure sand," according to Wyeth. Crossing Henry's Fork at a "belly-deep ford," they covered the rolling hills to Pierre's Hole, passed the battlefield and climbed the mountains in an "east south east" direction to reach Jackson's Hole. Wary of Blackfeet, Bonneville demanded scrupulous attention to night watches and staking of horses.

Near the southern end of Jackson's Hole, the trapper trail left Snake River at Game Creek, and crossed over foothills in a shortcut to join the Hoback at Camp Creek. This was the scene of a fatal attack on two of Wyeth's men the previous year, as Wyeth noted in his diary. Bonneville's men had found the bones bleaching in the rocks by a small stream and buried them. Bonneville lost one horse from the Hoback trail between Jackson's Big and Little Holes at a spot the "Journal" called "The Cornice." (Red Ledges) The trail ascended Granite Creek some distance to pass northeast of the hump later called Battle Mountain, then rejoined the Hoback. Bonneville led his party across Jackson's Little Hole to the Hoback Rim and down into the valley of Green River.[26]

Rendezvous at the Green River—1833

The rendezvous was already underway at Bonneville's picket work and the rival fur company camps nearby. Shoshoni—most of the tribe, it appeared, as well as the scores of trappers had a good start on the feasting, brawling and bragging. The taut armor of wariness which mountain men carried in order to survive dissolved in a fog of raw liquor flowing from the kegs. Past enmities slumbered. Pack trains from the States spread open their goods. From Bonneville's caches, Joe Walker set up a store in one of the blockhouses, exchanging munitions, knives and ornaments for skins.

Faces were missing from every company, a total of twenty-seven men killed, by one count, including four with Matthieu and another Bonneville man,

Benjamin Hardister, who died of illness. Bonneville's greatest loss was the party he had sent into Crow country. None returned except the leader, David Adams—not named in the "Journal," but called "the unlucky partisan." Some of Adams' men had been killed; others deserted, taking with them all the horses and gear they could carry off. On Powder River (Wyoming) for a spring hunt, Adams' remaining men lost their horses to Arickaras, whereupon the trappers carried out their threat to burn their Arickara prisoners to death, then fled down the Yellowstone. The "unlucky partisan" mustered his courage and returned to report the sorry tale.

Joe Walker's men had long stories to relate of battles with rival trapping parties. One brigade had moved from the Blackfoot River east to Salt River, north to Pierre's Hole and thence to Green River. Walker's main brigade trapped on Bear and Snake Rivers and reached the rendezvous in early June. None of the fur companies had found riches. What the Americans knew but did not like to admit was that the golden age of trapping was past; the British had seen to that. In their own bailiwick in Canada, the policy of Hudson's Bay Company was to harvest judiciously, but of areas open to both Great Britain and the United States, company officials wrote "The country is a rich preserve of Beaver, which for political reasons we should endeavor to destroy as fast as possible."[27] Peter Skene Ogden and John Work with their Snake River brigades had obeyed orders, and by 1833 the results were painfully evident.

The New Alliances at Bonneville's Fort

Into the middle of July the emerald bowl around Bonneville's fort echoed with the sounds of the biggest and rowdiest rendezvous of them all. Trappers traded in their year's work for new supplies and monumental sprees. Gossip flew, and braggart tales, while allegiances shuffled freely. Doc Newell left Bonneville to join American Fur. William Sublette sold his interests in Rocky Mountain Fur, and he and Robert Campbell formed their own supply partnership which they called the St. Louis Company.

Convoyed safely through the hostile country, Nathaniel Wyeth busied himself at the rendezvous writing letters, making new plans. In a polite thank-you note to Ermatinger, he itemized the numbers, locations, successes and failures of the American brigades, with remarks about the collective group's being a majority of scoundrels. Amenities taken care of, he looked about the camps at Green River for an escort back to the States. Robert Campbell and William Sublette agreed to provide for him. Before his departure Wyeth contracted with Thomas Fitzpatrick and William's brother Milton Sublette to bring a sizeable supply of goods the following year—an order which the St. Louis Company thought was theirs. It was a sharp deal, and Wyeth would find it had more than one cutting edge.

Bonneville Sends Joe Walker on an Expedition to California

A new project intrigued the mountain men. Captain Bonneville planned to send forty men under Joe Walker to spend a year in Mexican territory. Announced in the "Journal" as an exploration of the Great Salt Lake, the destination, as all knew, was California. "I was anxious to go to the coast of the Pacific," wrote Zenas Leonard, clerk of the expedition.[28] George Nidever, formerly of Fort Smith, and Texas and other frontiers, brought a dozen free trappers to volunteer. William Craig and the Meek brothers, Joe and Stephen, signed on later as did others. Captain Bonneville instructed Walker to keep a journal and to record "minutely the events of the journey and everything curious or interesting, making maps or charts" of the route and surrounding country. It was a large order for a man who apparently left not a single written word to posterity. Accustomed as he was to reports and map-sketching, Bonneville may not have realized the capable mountain man Walker was not a scribe. Lavishly fitted out, Walker and his brigade set off.

Bonneville's Responsibilities to the U. S. Government

At this point, Bonneville was solvent. There was ample time to travel back to the States before his leave expired in October. The love of adventure which Irving stressed had surely been fulfilled. Did he hope to make a fortune, as critics would later cry? If he ever had any illusions on that score, the past year had furnished him with an unvarnished picture of that possibility. In his whole lifetime Bonneville was never more than casually acquisitive, nor was he a gambler. Why did he risk his career by planning to overstay his leave? Why did he send a company into Mexican territory? Everyone knew that Jedediah Smith had found cold treatment and few furs in California. Jim Bridger and others had seen the sterile Salt Lake basin, and Joe Meek had only lately been hungry enough to eat grasshoppers in the barren country west of the salty lake. Why did Bonneville send Joe Walker and a brigade to California? The reason "may have been that the Secretary of War ordered him to," according to Bernard DeVoto. Why did he not go himself? The government needed information of California, but soft steps were indicated for any walk into Mexican territory. Mexican roughing-up and imprisonment of civilians, as had happened, was one thing; detention of an officer of the United States Army was another. Army officer Bonneville probably never set foot south of the forty-second parallel, and probably because of strict orders not to.

Critics have scoffed at Bonneville's lack of commercial success, though no other company made money either during those years. Showing no great dismay at his monetary losses, he spent his time listening to the Indians, moving about the area. He was interested in Hudson's Bay Company posts and by what routes they might be reached. He built a shelter like an Army fort and then didn't stay in it, so some trappers called it "Fort Nonsense." It was poised to cover the South Pass, which led to Salt Lake, Oregon and California. Historian Bernard DeVoto has written, ". . . the letters of Western traders, the reports of Indian agents, half the press of the United States and the speeches of all the Western senators and representatives were clamoring about the British threat to Oregon. So here was an army officer trapping furs in the international area, but not many furs. There was nothing nonsensical in the location of Fort Bonneville . . . it made sense to the War Department . . . and on its site a year after it was built, Captain Benjamin Bonneville of the Seventh Infantry, U. S. A. entertained Captain William Drummond Stewart of the King's Hussars."[29]

Stewart was a Scot, semi-retired from the British Army. He had paid Robert Campbell five hundred dollars to bring him to the rendezvous, professing to be interested only in hunting and the comradery of mountain men. His hunting trip lasted six years and took him to every sizeable American gathering in the mountains as well as to the Hudson's Bay Company posts and visits to the British consul in New Orleans. If, as appears likely, Stewart's mission, like Bonneville's, was to observe and report to his government he filled his assignment with theatrical flair. His equipment was excellent; he carried plentiful supplies of the niceties of civilization which he shared freely. He was a good trooper, an excellent shot; he relieved the life-and-death grimness that could settle over the mountains.

In 1833, most of the furs went east by a long packtrain-and-water journey around the Wind River range by way of the South Pass, then north to the point where the Big Horn became navigable, down that stream to the Yellowstone and into the Missouri. Bonneville elected to send his furs by this route; Michel Cerre would deliver them to St. Louis. Men who wanted to go home would make the journey with him. Bonneville planned to escort the homebound to the point where they would embark, then push on to the

Columbia by a northern route to "winter near the Sea," and return "upon its southern branches," a round trip which would furnish a wide view of the whole Pacific Northwest.[30]

The camp-town came down. The fur brigades went their way, while the suppliers prepared to go east with the harvest of furs. Robert Campbell left on July 24 with guests Nathaniel Wyeth and William Drummond Stewart. A day later, Bonneville and his men set off on the same trail to round the Wind River mountains at South Pass. Northeast across a sagebrush upland, they reached a branch of the Popo Agie, which winds along the eastern base of the mountains. Wind River comes in from the northwest and makes a right-angle bend; the combined streams are called the Big Horn.

Bonneville's Report to General Macomb

It rained all day in Wind River country on July 29, 1833. Hunters went out looking for fresh meat; men and horses rested. Captain Bonneville assembled a many-paged report to the Commanding General in Washington D. C. In it he had recorded his own observations plus information he had gleaned from other travelers and from the Indians. Military possibilities appear first. Though some writers profess to be puzzled by "curiously belligerent phrases," the last paragraph clearly reveals that a military expedition had been discussed in officer circles.

> "Crow Country, Wind River, July 29, 1833. General: This country I find is much more extensive than I could have expected . . . I have visited only the headwaters of the Yellowstone, Platte, the Colorado of the West and the Columbia. I have therefore remained . . . to explore the North of the Columbia in Cottonais Country and New Caledonia, to winter on the lower Columbia, and going to the South West toward California on my return, which will certainly be in the course of next fall. I would not have presumed this much were I not aware how desirous you are of collecting certain information respecting the country . . ."
>
> "I have constantly kept a journal . . . The information I have already obtained authorized me to say this much; that if our Government ever intends taking possession of Oregon, the sooner it shall be done the better, and at present I deem a subaltern's command equal to enforce all the views of our Government . . ." As to trade, since Hudson's Bay Company receive all their supplies by ship "at trifling expense . . . they have every advantage over

the Americans," pushing their brigades far inland "even on the Colorado, the headwaters of the Arkansas, the Platte, and the Missouri; they even speak of making a fort on the Big Horn . . . the Americans have, as it were, to steal their own fur, making secret rendezvous, trading by stealth."

The "Report" summarizes the origins of the British trade and American bids to compete. Pages are devoted to numbers, locations, strength, habits and loyalties of Indian tribes. The outward journey and first year's travels are summarized, clearing up some points of confusion in the "Journal." The last pages of the "Report" are filled with observations about geology, geography, climate, flora, fauna and soils of the area.

"This much, General, I have been able to collect in compliance with my promise, and I hope will be satisfactory when you consider how extensive this country is . . . if you shall have any instructions for me, I shall be glad to receive them; either to join any party that might be sent, to comply with any other commands in the Country, or to return to the States. I have the honor to be, General, with every consideration, Your Most Obedient Servant, B. L. E. Bonneville. To Major General Alexander Macomb, General in Chief, U. S. Army."[31]

Across the Big Horn Basin

After Wind River joins the Popo Agie and becomes the Big Horn, it plunges through an enchanted canyon, where, it is said, a feather wafted into the air will float, airborne, the entire twisting length of the gorge. North of this "gap," as Bonneville called it, his party and Robert Campbell's traveled together for safety across Big Horn basin. This was the country of the Crows, who also called themselves "Absaroka" or bird people. They bragged of not killing whites, but stealing was another matter. Stalking a camp and swooping off with horses and gear was a sport to compare with hunting the bounties of nature, and excellence in both modes of subsistence proved that the Absaroka were indeed a superior breed. From information gleaned along the way about the mood of the Blackfeet, Bonneville decided that his planned circuit to the north could only lead to disaster, and he must reach the Columbia by a safer route through Shoshoni country. Knowing that he would soon retrace his steps, he sent out trappers "to the west of Horn River on its tributary streams" with instructions to meet him "at the next full moon . . . at a place called Medicine Lodge."

The packtrains continued northward down the Big Horn, passing the mouths of Greybull and Shoshone rivers, the latter called "Stinking Water." John Colter had discovered the hot springs, but "Colter's Hell" was still a laughing matter in the east, though many trappers had seem them, and some had seen the more spectacular thermal wonders one hundred miles westward. At "Bad Pass" the trapper trail mounted the west side of Big Horn canyon, with the magnificent chasm visible at most points. Steep cliffs of vermilion and amethyst rise from the turbulent river, and eagles wheel overhead in this third deepest gorge in the United States. Past Dryhead Canyon the river cuts deep, swirls over boulders and dashes over miles of rapids to smooth out calmly past the mouth of Black Canyon. Here the mountain men assembled bullboats of rawhide over green sapling frames. Bonneville's men put together three boats, Campbell three, Wyeth one. Wyeth transferred to a pirogue at the mouth of the Big Horn, and Campbell to a keelboat at the mouth of the Yellowstone. Whether Cerre, with Bonneville's report and "letters to other gentlemen," his furs and departing men were able to upgrade their awkward flotilla is not a matter of record. The Big Horn empties into the Yellowstone, which joins the Missouri near the Canadian border. The "mighty Mo" meanders through North and South Dakota, divides Nebraska and Iowa, and Kansas and Missouri, and finally twists and turns the entire breadth of Missouri to St. Louis.

After the boats had floated away, the brigade which had accompanied Campbell set off eastward for a fall hunt. Bonneville was uneasy; he had kept but four men, and he had forty-six horses, a tempting target for the Crows. With three days hard riding, he reached the "Medicine Lodge" where he built a horse corral and a log breastwork. Bonneville's "Medicine Lodge" was at or near the great warm springs later called Thermopolis. Two early travelers, Osborne Russell and the Abbe Domenich, label "Medicine Lodge Forks" the tributaries which join the Big Horn near the springs. Bonneville's trapping parties arrived as promised. They had been attacked by Blackfeet and lost horses and traps. Two men had been wounded. Bonneville led his men over the "Little Horn Mountains," (Owl Creek Mountains) and moved up verdant, narrow Wind River valley, directing the trappers to continue working upstream toward the towering peaks. He had another errand, announced in the "Journal" as a trip back to his picket work for more traps. Union Pass—which the Astorians had used—branches off from the upper reaches of Wind River; this was the shortest and quickest route to the fort, but Bonneville did not take it. Instead, he probed the entire eastern flanks of the range, as if looking for another passage across the continental divide.

Climbing Gannett Peak

With three men, he moved south from Wind River and up the Popo Agie. The headwaters of the tributaries all appeared to end in snowy cliffs, impossible of passage. Retreating, he tried other approaches. Several days' riding up mounting slopes and scrambling over rocky precipices brought him to a small valley holding two small lakes. Leaving two of the men with the horses, Bonneville and an unnamed companion climbed higher. Choosing the highest peak, they began to scale it, sometimes clambering on hands and knees and lying exhausted now and then in the snow. At last they reached the summit. The September day was cloudless.

In the "Journal" description of the view from the summit, Bonneville conveyed the wonder of the panorama, the "snowy mountains chain beyond chain and peak beyond peak till they melted like clouds into the horizon." He accurately located the faraway Sweetwater, the headwaters of the Wind River, the Yellowstone and the Snake, the Teton peaks, and the fascinating origins of Green River.

"Captain Benjamin L. E. Bonneville made the first ascent of a major Wyoming peak—Gannett—in September, 1833, starting from the Hot Springs which are now an attraction at Ft. Washakie," writes Orrin H. Bonney. Historian and mountain-climber Bonney, who has climbed and mapped all the major Wind River peaks, points out that Gannett is the only peak to which can be tied the beginnings of Green River as described in the "Journal." Green River flows north from the western slopes of Gannett and over cascades on Wells Creek Fork to Big Bend where it turns south.

"No one had previous knowledge of this trick geography of the Green River. Bonneville was the first to discover it. Only from a northern peak of the range would he view 'snowy peaks to the south' as he describes them; only from the highest would he see those towering landmarks, the Three Tetons. There is an unobscured view of them from Gannett."[32]

Return to the Green River Fort—Winter Quarters

Bonneville and his companions descended the slopes and made their way to South Pass and northward to the Green River fort. He secured the needed supplies, resealed the hiding places and hurried northward up the valley to

Union Pass. Indians stalked the small party, but they managed a safe journey through the mountains. By September 25, they were reunited with the men on Wind River. Bonneville had completely encircled the Wind River range, probed for its non-existent passes and climbed its highest peak.

The autumn hunt was the old story; the trappers spent more time dodging Indians than in trapping. Giving up Crow country, Bonneville and his men rounded the range at South Pass, picked up supplies from the picket work and withdrew to Ham's Fork, a lower tributary of Green River. Thomas Fitzpatrick's men camped nearby; they too had left Crow country. Bonneville moved over sagebrush ridges to the outlet of Bear Lake and on to Soda Springs—"Beer Springs," the trappers called them. Leaving the main group there, Bonneville and three men made a trip to "the bosom of a mountain valley" where they found the free trappers who had hunted the headwaters of the Salmon. Their take had been only fair, but Bonneville bought furs and hides from the Sheepeater Indians, Tukudeka, Shoshoni-speaking small tribes who lived in primitive areas.

Bonneville's winter quarters were "near the Portneuf at the edge of flatlands near fine springs." Historian Miles Cannon believed this to be about ten miles northwest of the later Bancroft, Idaho. Others have speculated that Batisse Springs, farther west, fits the description. Bonneville himself did not winter there. He picked three men and left on a trip which he held so important that he started on Christmas Day.

Captain Bonneville intended "to penetrate the Hudson's Bay establishments on the banks of the Columbia, and to make himself acquainted with the country and Indian tribes; it being one part of his scheme to retrieve for his country some of the lost trade of Astoria." The joint occupancy treaty had served only the British, and until the United States could establish firm footholds, would continue to do so. Astoria sat almost deserted in the mists at land's end, while John McLoughlin ruled Hudson's Bay's Columbia River empire from Fort Vancouver, ninety miles inland. In financing Bonneville, John Jacob Astor perhaps thought to help his adopted country put the legal boundary of the Louisiana Purchase at the Pacific Ocean, where most citizens thought it belonged. Merchant Astor supposed that commercial dominance meant sovereignty; it did, for the British. The Army wanted to be prepared if the dispute must be settled by force.

Bonneville went to the Rocky Mountains because it was his ambition to see and report on this little-known portion of the continent, to serve his profession and his country, and since Astor's money was making it possible, to serve him too. Bonneville probed and observed and jotted down information. He gloried in the streams and the mountains, the good earth of the prairies and valleys, and he counted all living things worthy. To the Indians he extended a hand of fellowship, and succeeded more fully than any other early traveler.

Down the Snake River to the Columbia

Deep snow muffled Snake River country as Bonneville and his three men rode downriver. The "Journal" describes American Falls, Snake River in its varied moods, and bleak lava-strewn plains in the first two hundred miles of the journey. Bonneville traveled some distance from the deep gorges of the river, and missed towering Shoshone Falls and Twin Falls, but noted the enchanting cascades of Thousand Springs. He feasted with Indians at Lower Salmon Falls, "Fishing Falls," where spawning ocean salmon could ascend no farther. A few descriptions in the "Journal" are not from Bonneville's notes but from Wyeth's of the previous year, as Irving acknowledged and may account for some errors in labels on "Map of the Territory West of the Rocky Mountains" as it was reproduced by Irving. "Powder River" is the name given on the map for what should have been the Bruneau, though the spectacular canyon of the latter is described. The map places the Owyhee, "Wyer," correctly, but labels "Little Wyer" the Malheur, opposite Payette River. The Weiser, upstream from the Payette, is omitted, perhaps because Bonneville was some distance from the Snake and on the opposite side.

Bonneville had intended ascending "Gun Creek" (Burnt River), but on advice of an Indian kept to the main river. The Journal's word pictures of the "Shoshoke" Indians are sympathetic, as are Bonneville's observations of all the Indian people he encountered. With a Shoshoke guide he and his men traveled down the Snake until purple and ochre hills crowded close in a tumble of bed-rock boulders. The guide deserted. Sharp granite peaks, called in the "Journal" "Immahahs" (Imnahas), towered in the north and west. The river thrashed "through deep chasms, between rocks and precipices until lost in a distant wilderness of mountains, which closed the savage landscape." The description is apt; this gorge of Snake River would be named Hell's Canyon, and is the deepest gash on the North American Continent. A night's camp was made in a sheltered basin, called Grand Rond in the "Journal," which also names the small stream there "Fourche de Glace," or Ice River. But Bonneville was far from the Grande Ronde valley in what would become Union County, Oregon. Outdoorsmen-historians have traced Bonneville's probable route with only slight variations.[33]

Following Snake River again, Bonneville and his men passed green-hued slopes (Homestead, Oregon) and small boulder-choked canyons (Herman Creek, Nelson Creek and others). Past a wider spot, (Big Bar) slide rock narrowed the gorge. Crossing and recrossing the river, the men crept over icy trails with "a shouldering wall of rock on one side, a yawning precipice on the other," until the turbulent currents funnelled into a narrow passage. (Red Ledges at 32 Point Creek, site of Hell's Canyon Dam.) An attempt to climb out of the canyon failed. Retreating up the river, the discouraged travelers tried again, zigzagging among crags to mount high ridges. Though broken by sharp ravines, the benchlands led higher into the mountains. Downed timber and deep drifts slowed progress. When food ran out, the men butchered a mule and struggled on through the Wallowas, a wild expanse of towering jagged peaks rising from granite ridges. Bonneville reached the windswept summit near Himmelwright Springs and struggled on through the snow to a point where "the valley of the Immahah stretched out in smiling verdure" near Section 25, T3 S Range 48. February grass greened the banks of the Imnaha, and trails led downstream. A lone Indian stretched out his hands in welcome. With food and security in sight, Bonneville lay down and slept. "Wawish," the Nez Perce called this monumental fatigue.

At a Nez Perce camp (Imnaha, Oregon), Bonneville enjoyed royal treatment. He won good will by fashioning turbans for the women from his own plaid jacket; the Indians eyed his shiny pate and titled him "The Bald Chief." In a dos-a-dos of gift giving Bonneville received a fine horse in exchange for a rifle, hatchet and ear-bobs. Chief Yo-mus-re-cut butchered a colt in welcome to his village. Passing Buckhorn Spring and the heads of Cherry and Cook Creeks Bonneville and his men reached the "Way-lee-way, a considerable tributary of Snake River." The Wallowa is a tributary of the Grande Ronde, and the combined streams bear the name Grande Ronde. Bonneville's map labels the whole, Way-lee-way. There were feasts and parades at another village near the mouth of Joseph Creek, winter home of Tuekakas, Old Chief Joseph.

No nation of rootless nomads, the Nez Perces have lived in the mountains of the Wallowa, Snake, Salmon and Clearwater rivers for longer than their memories can reach, one of few Indian peoples who have no folklore of having migrated from elsewhere. Bonneville's "Journal" describes a lodge of mats and poles, and a main building or council house. The Nez Perces welcomed information of the United States, and Captain Bonneville was at his best in the role of ambassador. His skill at doctoring had preceded him from Salmon

River and he administered such treatment as he could. No missionary or government servant ever established a better relationship with a native people.

Yo-mus-ro-e-cut continued with the travelers down Way-lee-way's pleasant canyon of high bluffs and gentle meadows to Snake River; Bonneville turned north to follow it downstream. Here terraces of sienna and vermillion rise from sandbars, and pictographs record an ancient culture. Yo-mus-ro-e-cut introduced the Bald Chief to all the Indians they met, including those within shouting distance across the river. Among the latter was a warrior whom Bonneville had met at the forks of the Salmon. The Nez Perces did not trudge the long circuit of Snake River in their east-west commerce, but traveled the Nez Perce Trail, a primitive passage across one hundred and fifty miles of evanescent blue, blue ridges.

On sheltered flatlands (Asotin, Washington) Bonneville and his men enjoyed a celebration presided over by Chief O-push-ye-cut. (Apash Wyakaikt, or Flint Necklace according to Alvin Josephy.) Because Snake River makes a long circuit to the north, the Nez Perces guided Bonneville over rolling upland prairies in a shortcut to the Columbia. En route, Chief Red Wolf welcomed the travelers, as did Chief Timothy at the mouth of Alpowa Creek. A clipping from an 1894 "Asotin County Sentinel" tells of four aged Indians who were youths in the 1830s and remembered shaking hands with the bald chief, and the gala reception prepared for him.[34] Astor's Donald Mackenzie had reported the Nez Perces inhospitable, but there was another side. The Nez Perces resented the intrusion of martinet Mackenzie who humiliated them in an angry search for missing goods. Alfred Seton reported this; it was he who searched Nez Perce belongings on orders from Mackenzie.

Hudson's Bay's Fort Walla Walla

Hudson's Bay's Fort Walla Walla was exactly as Nathaniel Wyeth had reported to Captain Bonneville: "Of no strength, merely sufficient to frighten Indians." The magnificent Columbia River meandering from Canada, receives the Snake some miles upstream, and the Walla Walla joins it here for the headlong rush to the Pacific. (Wallula, Washington) Dwarfed by a backdrop of bluffs, Fort Walla Walla had been built in 1818 on orders from Astorian-turned-British-entrepreneur Donald Mackenzie. The famous Snake River fur brigades had been launched here with Peter Skene Ogden and others sweeping up every creek and river of the intermountain country. Like other Hudson's Bay posts, Fort Walla Walla flew the Union Jack together with the red HBC pennant; wags said HBC meant "Here Before Christ" but Americans who saw it regarded it as impudence. On March 4, 1834, Captain Bonneville knocked at the door.

Fort Walla Walla's factor, Pierre Pambrun was not surprised. Chief Factor John McLoughlin had sent orders to sell no food to anyone . . . and have no dealings at all with Captain Bonneville of the U. S. Army. Dr. McLoughlin subscribed to American newspapers to learn of events in the United States, and both he and Pambrun had entertained the talkative Nathaniel Wyeth. Pambrun gave Bonneville "great courtesy and hospitality" but quoted company rules when asked to sell supplies. He did bend the rules slightly. Bonneville did not tattle, but someone did, and Dr. Mcloughlin was asked to explain. He wrote "As to Bonneville, Mr. Pambrun sold him a roll of tobacco and some Dry Goods . . . this was injudicious . . ."[35]

Bonneville declined Pambrun's offer that he travel with Payette's supply caravan by way of Flathead House (Clarks Fork, Montana). Instead, he retraced his route, visiting villages and collecting camp followers, some of doubtful value to his progress. Bonneville was one of few diarists who saw individuality among Indians, portraying them as possessing all the virtues and failings of the human family. The worried father, the free-loader, the witty vagabond are a far cry from the stereotyped "savage."

Guided over the Wallowas by Nez Perces, the Bonneville party clambered down the steep sides of Snake River canyon, losing a horse before reaching the sheltered bottoms. Grass was high, and "prismoids of basaltes" rose "to a height of fifty to sixty feet." Canyon meadows were a glory of wildflowers and shining new leaves as Bonneville made his way up Snake River. He looked in vain for the men instructed to meet him; an Indian told him that white men had come, earlier, and left again. On May 12, two months overdue, he arrived at the Portneuf. The winter camp was deserted, but he found the main camp on the Blackfoot River. It was a joyful reunion. The men who had searched in vain for Bonneville on lower Snake River had concluded he had been killed "and so reported."[36] At the Portneuf camp, the men had "been pinched by famine and forced to repair to the caches at Salmon River." Blackfeet had hounded trappers everywhere and the beaver take was scanty for all mountain men that winter.

Bonneville moved his men upstream to the headwaters of the river named for the Blackfeet—not because they lived there, but because of their deadly raids in the area. When a large war party began to stalk his men, Bonneville ordered night-watches and careful staking of horses, with ruses of numerous campfires and noisy movement to give the illusion of strength. He was not attacked. Leaving the timbered hills and grassy basins of Blackfoot River headwaters, the brigade moved south to Soda Springs and up Bear River to Bear Lake, hunting buffalo along the way. In an improvised canoe, Bonneville explored "Little Snake Lake" as he called the blue jewel, Bear Lake. Farther up Bear River, in the vicinity of Smith's Fork, he found Joseph Walker and the trappers he had sent to California.

Reunion with Walker's California Expedition and Their Report

Braggart tales of slaughtering Indians and of wild frolicking rang through the reunion camp and made Walker's adventurers heroic in the eyes of their friends. The reports did not delight the Army officer trying to line up Indian tribes on the American side, and to impress neighboring countries with potential American strength. What of Salt Lake? They had skirted the edge of it at a distance. What of the trade goods? Long since traded off. Then where were the peltries? Traded for provisions for the return journey. But they had brought back Spanish horses—they had started with ten-fold more, but lost them in the icy passes and on the sun-baked desert. Two Mexicans traveled home with them, lassoing Indians along the way and killing them as if they were prairie dogs. Bonneville was "so indignant at the atrocities related that he turned, with disgust and horror, from the narrators," according to the "Journal."

Though Bonneville abhorred the men's excesses and could not have been pleased with Walker's performance, his personal censure of Walker is not mentioned by on-the-spot witnesses who wrote of the trip, and Walker continued to lead brigades for Bonneville. Most disappointing was the absence of the charts and journals. If Walker kept any record of his momentous journey, it has not been found.

But Joseph Walker opened the way for American settlement by blazing five hundred miles of trail which would become a well-used road to California. He discovered the wonders which would become Yosemite National Park, and on his return found the not-too-difficult Indian path through the southern part of the Sierras which would bear his name—Walker Pass. All this historians would conclude from the vantage point of later decades. Walker has been portrayed as so crushed by criticism of him in the "Journal" that he drifted into oblivion. There is no evidence that the brusque mountain man ever indulged in self-pity. He enjoyed good standing as a capable brigade leader and pathfinder. Active and tough, his explorer instincts kept him moving over endless hills as a hunter, and later as a guide. He was his own man.

Besides the account of the California expedition in the "Journal," a few of Walker's men wrote of their adventure. Clerk Zenas Leonard lost some of his notes, but aside from date discrepancies, his book supports the "Journal" and adds specifics and detail. George Nidever reminisced in his later years. Joe Meek, much later, relived the journey to Francis Fuller Victor. Stephen Meek wrote a letter to his home-town newspaper. William Craig in his old age talked briefly of his adventures.[37]

Walker's brigade had left Green River in July, 1833, well-supplied and in high spirits, with instructions to steer through an unknown country towards the Pacific, according to Leonard. August heat baked the north shores of the great salty lake; as far as the eye could reach, there was no stream running into it and no Buenaventure River running out of it, as some had said. There was no evidence on the lake of a hidden whirlpool marking an underground water passage through the mountains to the ocean: that, too, had been one of the trapper tales. According to another legend, a race of giant white men lived on the islands of the inland sea; they rode elephants and harvested fruits and corn for food, and though no one had ever seen them, logs bearing gigantic axe marks were sometimes washed ashore. In night-camp coolness, silhouettes appeared to float on the mirror of water, shadowy and changing; perhaps the eery tales were true!

Leaving the shore of the lake, Walker veered northwest through a sahara of "parched wastes of sand" (Bonneville Salt Flats area). From a snowtopped peak, (Pilot Peak) small watercourses gathered into a considerable stream, later named the Humboldt. When Indians stole traps, trappers shot several of them. Grassy meadows gave way to swamps and to open spaces of water (Humboldt Marshes and Sink). Leonard called the area Battle Lakes; there are several versions of the massacre of almost weaponless Indians there. Outnumbered, the trappers saw fires on all sides, and believed they were surrounded. Joe Meek reported that the Indians had no guns, but carried clubs and some bows and arrows. Fear mounted. When Joe Walker gave the order to chastise a band of warriors, trappers surrounded them and shot thirty-five, according to Leonard; seventy-five: according to Joe Meek. The Indians fled into the marshes. Trapper William Small was killed, others wounded. A week later, according to Stephen Meek, thirty mountain men fired on Indians who sat smoking peace pipes, killing eighteen. Zenas Leonard wrote, not proudly, "The severity with which we dealt with these Indians" was necessary "since we were far removed from the hope of succor." The Indians, he noted, wore almost no clothing, lived in brush huts and ate grass seed, frogs and fish painstakingly speared with crane leg-bones.[38] The "Journal" called them Shoshokos. They were Paiutes, Shoshonean.

Passing other land-locked lakes, Walker probed the Sierra Nevada mountains for a pass. At length, a scout found a promising trail, and Walker and his men set out on a three-week nightmare of floundering through snow-filled ravines and skirting icy peaks. The summit, it was apparent, was many miles across. They ate horse meat, and crept along a few miles a day, emerging finally on a ridge with steep precipices on each side. Cascading streams plunged from crags, and rose in mists deep in the valleys. An Indian trail led downward to a paradise of plentiful game and incredibly giant redwood trees.[39]

Walker and his men traveled toward the Pacific, crossing the coastal range and reaching the sea near Ano Anevo Point. The captain of the American merchant ship Lagoda, anchored off shore, welcomed the trappers, supplying them with food and with information that the Bay of San Francisco was forty miles north, and the provincial capitol, Monterey, sixty miles south. Enroute to Monterey, the party visited Scottish-born John Gilroy and gleaned more information. (Santa Clara Valley) Some of the men remained at Gilroy's, and Walker left most of the others at a mission while he went on to present himself to the governor. Granted permission to spend the winter, but not to trap or to trade with the Indians, the Americans could trade with the Spaniards. The scope of that trade was variously reported. Zenas Leonard wrote the relationships were "most friendly." Joe Meek told his biographer that "one hundred soldiers . . . a wild jaunty looking set" conducted the trappers into Monterey where they were "treated with all hospitality" for a month. The senoritas, Joe remembered, wore gaudy calico or silk, "were wellformed with laughing eyes and soft voices and associated freely" with the trappers at fandangos, bull-fights or bearbaitings.[40] Stephen Meek wrote of a whirl of balls, parties and Spanish ladies.

Joseph Walker and Zenas Leonard toured the countryside, where Leonard learned of the extent of the settlement, crops produced and other assets of the fair land—information which was of interest to Bonneville, if he was able to hear Leonard's voice above the braggart mouthings of the others. Some men decided to remain in California. In the latter part of January, Walker traded off company assets for supplies and moved his men forty miles eastward. The new encampment was a veritable Eden, with shade, grass, and game.

To prepare for the homeward journey, Walker bought cattle to eat along the way, and three hundred horses; they would be as valuable at the rendezvous as the elusive packs of furs.

The journey went well. San Joaquin valley spread out a bounty of grass. Walker traveled southward along the base of the mountains searching for a pass. He was in luck. Spanish-speaking Indians, Concoas, guided the brigade over the mountains by the pass which would be known by Walker's name. Fearful of the desert, Walker kept close to the mountains on a trail of sparse grass and loose sand. Streams coming down from the Sierras emptied into scattered sink-hole lakes. On the men plodded, scanning the horizon for landmarks of their outward trail, wandering through badlands and sandstorms until at last the horses bolted. Following them, Walker and his men came to a stream of water. They had lost many of the animals. Continuing northward, they found their previous trail, and also hordes of Indians.

"Being thus compelled to fight, as we thought in a good cause and in self-defense, we drew up in battle array and fell on the Indians in the wildest and most ferocious manner . . . killing fourteen besides wounding a great many more as we rode right over them," Leonard wrote.[41] The stunned redmen dispersed, and the journey continued up the treeless course of Barren river, as Walker named it. To avoid the great salt desert, Walker traveled by way of Bishop Creek through Thousand Springs valley and into the Goose Creek mountains. Past the later named City of Rocks and across Raft River valley he reached Snake River at the mouth of Calder Creek. The men found game in the timbered hills, celebrated with the last of their brandy and in a few days reached Bear River and their reckoning with their sponsor.

Bonneville's disappointment with his Walker expedition did not dampen the rendezvous on Bear River. This was one of the good times in the mountains, a reunion of friends who had brushed close to death in lonely places. Buffalo meat was plentiful, and heroic tales unfolded around the campfires. Stephen Meek said that "all the cattle, thirty horses and nine mules" perished in six-foot snow drifts on the return trip. Joe Meek claimed that with Bill Mitchell and others, he went from Monterey to "Lulare" lake, then to the Colorado River at the Mohave villages and down to the mouth of the Gila. There Joe's party found some Rocky Mountain Fur trappers and moved with them to the headwaters of the Rio Grande, pausing long enough at a "Moquis" (Hopi) village to kill a dozen Indians. With Kit Carson and others, Joe said, he fought a battle with "Camanches," killing forty-two of them, and escaped in the dark on foot to run seventy-five miles before finding a drink of water.[42]

There are clues that parts of Joe's story were true. Bonneville wrote, many years later, "One of my parties journeyed into the Utes country, farther south, until it met the traders and trappers from New Mexico."[42] Kit Carson is said to have confirmed the Comanche battle, though with fewer Indian casualties.

Kit Carson's fur brigade of that winter included Lieutenant Richard Bland Lee of the United States Army, who was traveling with mountain men along the eastern flank of the Rocky Mountains from Santa Fe northward. By the time he and fellow-officer Bonneville returned to duty in the States they had probed the entire length of the continental barriers. Army officers Lee and Bonneville both traveled as "trappers."

Decision to Stay Longer in the Mountains

"I fell in with Mr. Cerre 28th June, 1834, the gentlemen to whom I had eleven months before entrusted my communications to the General in Chief, which he informed me he had delivered, and that the General appeared perfectly satisfied with my report and also with my determination to persevere in the course I had adopted and pursued; that owing to his remaining longer in New York than he had originally contemplated, he was prevented returning to Washington, and consequently left the former city without bringing an extension of my furlough, or any communication whatever from the Department of War. Highly gratified at the verbal report of Mr. Cerre of the flattering expressions made by the General in Chief, I was inspired with renovated ardor for the enterprise I had undertaken, being now determined to accomplish it at all hazards," Bonneville wrote later.[44] Word of mouth approval was less than satisfactory, but so bright was the dream "to fully execute the order of the General in Chief to furnish the Department of War with every information desired" that Bonneville made plans to stay another year.

Joseph Walker, with fifty-five men, would trap and trade with the Crows, Leonard wrote. A "leader named Montero was to proceed to Crow country and trap upon its various streams among the Black Hills" according to the "Journal."[45] Bonneville prepared new reports and other letters which he entrusted to Cerre who would return to the States with the year's catch of furs, totalled at forty packs. Nathaniel Wyeth wrote that "10,000$" was due Bonneville's men. Wyeth, on his way west, met Cerre's eastbound caravan and because Walker was at that time traveling with Cerre, wrote in his journal that Walker was also returning to the States. Wyeth's saga fills twenty pages of the "Journal" at this point, and appears to be the source of Irving's belief that Walker no longer worked for Bonneville.

Return to the Lower Columbia

Still determined to reach the lower Columbia and break the British stranglehold on Oregon country commerce, Bonneville planned to take more men, and to winter and trade on the Willamette. The Honorable Company was very much in evidence; several Hudson's Bay Company traders "employed to follow up Indians and buy up their peltries" visited Bonneville's camp on Bear River. In return for past "civilities" Bonneville invited them to a feast, providing Irving with grist for merry paragraphs about the effects of whiskey and honey, improvised for the occasion. Later, Wyeth visited Bonneville and unburdened himself of his pique with his fellow Americans. From St. Louis he had brought supplies for Rocky Mountain Fur, as agreed, only to find them rejected. He was angry, and announced his intention to build a trading post at the mouth of the Portneuf in order to dispose of the surplus supplies. Traveling with Wyeth were botanist Thomas Nuttall, ornithologist John K. Townsend and Methodist missionaries Daniel and Jason Lee, with several lay companions. Lately joined was William Drummond Stewart, who had spent the past months shadowing the path of Lieutenant Richard Bland Lee, trapping with Kit Carson along the eastern base of the Rockies north of Taos. Stewart and Hudson's Bay's Thomas McKay paid a visit to Bonneville, who again played host with his keg of alcohol and honey. Tall, lithe and darkly handsome, Thomas McKay was one-eighth Indian. His father, Alexander McKay, had taken young Tom with him on the memorable canoe ride down the Hudson in 1810 to board the "Tonquin." Alexander McKay was killed, and Tom's mother married John McLoughlin, now chief factor at Fort Vancouver. Tom led numerous brigades; he was to be found at all the American rendezvous. This did not net him many pelts, but he gained an accurate picture of rival activities.

Fledgling wild geese supplemented the mess as Bonneville and twenty-three men made their way down Snake River toward the Columbia. They reached the salmon-stocked portion of the Snake in time for the first salmon-run of the season, and a fish-feast with the Shoshoni. Farther on, the country was oven-hot and dusty. Unencumbered this time by a mistaken guide, Bonneville left Snake river to follow a trail up a winding stream he called Gun Creek. French-Canadian trappers had called it "Brule." Translated "Burnt," this name has survived.

West winds brought the scent of burning sagebrush; Indians had set fires to dry summer grasses so green forage could sprout in autumn rains. The smoke thickened, and Bonneville "found all the plains and valleys wrapped in one vast conflagration . . ." He kept his packtrain close to the mountains, groping along Indian trails until he reached "the head of the Way-lee-way River." This was the Grande Ronde; the Wallowa joins the Grande Ronde. Bonneville halted and sent out hunters. He dispatched scouts westward to search "for a convenient pass through the mountains," a route to the coast which would by-pass British posts on the Columbia. Friendly Cayuse and Nez Perce joined the camp, and in a couple of days William Drummond Stewart, traveling with Thomas McKay's men. In the party, too, were missionaries Jason and Daniel Lee. They brought the news that on August 5, Nathaniel Wyeth had raised the American flag over his newly-built trading post at the mouth of the Portneuf, and with fitting noise and toasts, christened it "Fort Hall" for one of his backers. Jason Lee had preached a sermon there.

Stewart and McKay's men moved on, and on August 31, Wyeth himself nooned at the Grande Ronde. With him were scientists Thomas Nuttall and John K. Townsend. Townsend wrote of Bonneville, "His manners were affable and pleasing . . ." He described the Cayuse as "neat and cleanly" and wrote "I observed one young and pretty looking woman, dressed in a great superabundance of finery, glittering with rings and beads . . . She was mounted astride, Indian fashion, on a fine bay horse . . . decorated with scarlet and blue ribbons, the saddle ornamented all over with beads and little hawk's bells . . . her whole deportment proved to us that she was no common beauty, but the favored companion of one high in office who was jealous of her slightest movement." Fifty years later—after Bonneville's death—H. H. Bancroft interpreted Townsend's paragraph to mean that the Cayuse queen belonged to Bonneville, and threw in the opinion there were other liaisons as well. Succeeding careless hacks pounced on the idea, embroidering details to clothe the effigy. It may be pointed out that no contemporary account mentions a Bonneville Indian wife or paramour, though the alliances of many other trappers are described. As for Townsend's ambiguous paragraph, it is white conceit to suppose that the decorated beauty did not belong to one of the "fine looking, robust" Cayuse men described by Townsend.[46]

Townsend called the Cayouse "Kayouse;" Wyeth wrote "Skiuses." In the Daniel Lee diary, the name appears "Kinse" and in the "Journal," "Skynses." Obviously, the handwritten "u" in the latter accounts has been misread "n" in transcribing the manuscripts. In Bonneville's handwriting the "u" and "n" are almost identical. Like the Nez Perces, the Cayuse were rich in horses. The Cayuse spoke the Nez Perce language, and like them, lived well on camas and other roots, salmon and game. Bonneville believed the Cayuse and Nez Perce could be encouraged to cultivate grain and observed that their country was "admirably suited for the raising of cattle." He suggested that "a Christian missionary or two would promote a considerable degree of civilization."

He told the departing Wyeth that the area Indians would welcome an American supplier. Wyeth promised to enlarge his Fort Hall supply caravan and agreed to meet the Indians at a rendezvous Bonneville arranged, though he "would be pleased to make a joint affair of it much better than to proceed alone. Your beaver traded from the Skiuses is so much seized from the common enemy in trade . . ." But Wyeth's plans went astray.[47]

Fortune was not exactly smiling on Captain Bonneville either. His scouts came back to report they could find no westward trail to the Willamette. Prairie fires had spread up the ravines, and smoke obscured possible passes. Time was running out. Bonneville set out on the Indian pathway over the Blue mountains. From the bare heights at the top, a grassy prairie spread northward. This was the home of the Walla Wallas, Cayuse and other tribes, who after years of dispute would become good citizens of this choice land and go by the name Umatilla Indians. Bonneville descended the mountain, and called the little stream where he camped the Ottolais; others wrote Ualla or various spellings of Umatilla.

Refused Trade by Hudson's Bay

From a camp near the future site of the proudly-Western cow-town Pendleton, Bonneville sent men to Fort Walla Walla to buy "a little corn for the subsistence of his party." To no one's surprise, they could buy nothing; in addition, Pierre Pambrun tried to hire away the messengers. Stewart, Wyeth, the missionaries and the scientists had preceded Bonneville; all would report the warm welcome they received at Fort Walla Walla.

As Bonneville and his men pushed down the willowed Umatilla to the Columbia, Indians scurried away and hid. Hudson's Bay Company had forbidden them to trade, and Bonneville's men could not get within shouting distance of the forewarned natives. Westward, down the Columbia, brown hills rise into cliffs of layered lava, with lichens clinging on shady ledges. Snowy Mount Hood shimmers in the west. To Bonneville, land's end beckoned, and yet it was out of reach.

"The broad and beautiful Columbia lay before them but the resources of the country were locked against them, by the influence of a jealous and powerful monopoly," the "Journal" put it. To winter on the Willamette, as Bonneville had planned, appeared of doubtful wisdom; the missionaries and Nathaniel Wyeth were already there to beg the strained hospitality of the British residents. Captain Stewart, too, was headed for Vancouver; Bonneville would have been obtuse not to be chary of the influence of this sightseer. To spend a hungry winter on the lower Columbia would be a waste of time. Bonneville decided to withdraw to the mountains.

It would have been easiest to retrace his steps, but Bonneville turned his course up John Day River. This large tributary of the Columbia rises in the heartland of Oregon; various forks have their beginnings in the Blue Mountains, and might be expected to lead to passes to the Snake River drainage. Bonneville was looking for such a trail when he sent his scouts westward from the Grande Ronde. Now, with depleted supplies and limited time, he tried again to find an alternate route. John Day country is a wonderland of sharp twisting canyons and painted badlands, of thick-growing forests and summit plateaus. Prehistoric fossil beds reveal traces of palms and ferns; basalt walls show ancient writings. The "defile was rugged and difficult;" the travelers "mistook their route and wandered for ten days among high and bald hills of clay," according to the "Journal."

Familiar ground appeared at last, and on October 20, Bonneville and his men reached the Snake River, probably upstream from the mouth of the Boise River, for the newly-built trading post in the area is not mentioned in the "Journal." Thomas McKay, after watching Wyeth begin to construct Fort Hall on the Portneuf, had hurried to the mouth of the Boise River and built a competing post for Hudson's Bay. Grass fires are thought to have destroyed the original cottonwood Fort Boise, or perhaps the Indians did; they burned John Reed's earlier post in the area.

Osborne Russell, one of the men Wyeth had left at Fort Hall wrote on November 16 of news that Captain Bonneville had returned from the lower country, and passed within 30 miles of the Fort on his way to Green River.[48] Fort Hall is not mentioned in the "Journal"; Bonneville may have taken a short cut eastward over the low Bannock range and up the Portneuf. This route would take him past the 9,200-foot later-named Bonneville Peak in Caribou National Forest.

Winter on the Bear River

Brigade leader Montero, still in Crow country, sent messengers for additional supplies, and to fill the needs, Bonneville moved from the headwaters of the Portneuf to caches he had made on Bear River, and then into winter quarters. Game was plentiful, for "the people on Snake River"—Bridger and his Rocky Mountain Fur men—were so noisy and careless in their fall hunts that immense herds of buffalo "of unbelievable bulk and spirit, all rushing forward as if swept by a whirlwind . . . came trooping over the mountains." Deep snow fell, and "the vast herds which had poured down into the Bear River Valley were now snow-bound, and remained in the neighborhood of the camp throughout the winter."

This winter encampment was "on the upper part of Bear River" but not too far, for the herds had stampeded over the mountains from Snake River. Joe Meek considered Thomas Fork the headwaters of Bear River. Traveler Frederick A. Wislizenus in 1839 described a spot on Smith's Fork where "the Blackfeet several years ago had shot into Bonneville's camp."[49] Both Smith's Fork and Thomas Fork join the Bear through grassy meadowlands. The main Bear River comes from higher meadows, (Randolph, Utah and Evanston, Wyoming) locations which appear too far removed from Snake River and too high of altitude to have been the likely wintering spot. Like many of Bonneville's camps, this 1834-35 bivouac could have been in any of the numerous remote vales, sheltered with cottonwoods and fragrant with sage.

A band of Shoshoni sold Bonneville "lodges, furs and other articles of winter comfort" and camped nearby for security. Utes were also camped in the little valley. Reporting to the War Department, Bonneville wrote that they "Came upon a village of Eutah Indians that had been caught there by the snow—as the two tribes were at war, I used all my influence, and a treaty of peace was made and all united for greater safety from the Blackfeet tribes continually prowling for plunder and delighting in bloodshed."

In the spring, the Utes and the Shoshoni went their separate ways, friends for a season. Bonneville retrieved his goods from his Bear River caches and set off eastward. He spent several weeks on Green River, making a last visit to his picket work. By June he was on the eastern slopes of the Wind River Mountains.

Rendezous at the Forks of Wind River

Bonneville's final rendezvous took place at the forks of Wind River where he built storage sheds. Near the later Hudson, Wyoming, a marker locates "The Bonneville cabins, built by Captain B. L. E. Bonneville in 1835 to store his trade goods. Three cabins were constructed, and later two more. They were long known as the Five Cabins, the first mercantile establishment in central Wyoming." A Hudson native, Harold H. Rogers, saw the remains of the cabins when he was a child.

Walker and Montero, with their trapping brigades, came in to Bonneville's camp in late June. Once again there was feasting and tale-telling and noisy celebration of being alive. Some were not, including "Mr. Bergan and Mr. Laront," according to Zenas Leonard. In his journal, Leonard wrote of Walker's considerable journeys of the past year. He had built a "temporary trading house;" letters from there designated it "Wind River Fort" (near Crowheart Butte). Business with the Crows was brisk, and in the spring Walker's men trapped the headwaters of the Missouri.[50] Antonio Montero, assigned to trap on Powder River, built stout cabins—later called "Portuguese Houses"—of hewn logs surrounded by a log stockade, near the forks of Powder River (near Kaycee, Wyoming) but Indians managed to steal many horses, and rival trappers harassed Montero's men.

When the stories had all been told and the explanations offered, Zenas Leonard wrote, "We set about packing and sorting our fur, etc. and making arrangements." He added that Walker was to continue trapping for Bonneville. Walker, however, was already busy with his sideline of horse-trading, and he trapped for American Fur during the ensuing season. Montero was left "with a brigade of trappers to open another campaign," according to the "Journal." Leonard wrote that the season had been a good one; he decided to join those who were eagerly heading for the States.[51] Captain Bonneville may have been more anxious than eager, for he was two years overdue from the Army.

Return to Civilization and Dismissed from the Army

The Wind River mountains receded into an ice-blue backdrop, and midsummer sunshine baked the high plateau as Bonneville and his men trudged eastward. On August 22, they reached the outermost settlements. In sheer joy at finding themselves among the living after years of danger, the trappers "saluted civilization scattering their silver like sailors just from a cruise." A homecoming of a different nature awaited their commander. The news was devastating. He had been dropped from the Army.

> "Order No. 42. Adj. Genls. Office May 31, 1834. Cap Bonneville of the 7th Regt of Infantry having been absent without leave since October 1833 and Lieut Lee of the 3 Regt of Artillery having also been absent since 15 Feby, 1834, are this day by order of the President of the United States, dropped from the rolls of the Army. By order of Alex. Macomb, Majr. Genl."

Bonneville was out, dismissed, in his own eyes, disgraced. What had gone wrong? What of Michel Cerre's assurances that the General appeared satisfied with the 1833 report? What had become of the 1834 reports Cerre had promised to forward from Council Bluffs? Final as the dismissal sounded, there was a glimmer of hope. General Macomb had waited eight full months after Bonneville's leave expired before he moved to drop him. Lt. Richard Bland Lee was accorded only three months' grace. Perhaps, when the maps and journals were presented, the decision could be reversed.

Report to John Jacob Astor in New York City

In New York City, Bonneville reported in person to John Jacob Astor. The aging millionaire was spending the summer in his Hellgate country home facing East River. Reported at this time to be sickly and feeble, the immigrant Midas was in his early seventies. In the years Bonneville was in the West, time had not dealt kindly with John Jacob Astor. His daughter Eliza died in Switzerland—of a broken heart, the gossips said, because her father insisted she marry a count instead of the dentist with whom she was in love. Astor's wife Sarah, who had worked by his side in musty fur warehouses in long-ago lean years, died in 1834. He held deeds to an important share of New York City, but his attention now focused on the image he would leave behind in his adopted country.

What did Bonneville report to Astor? The fur fields were well-gleaned? There were too many trappers? Astor's company knew this; their instructions were to operate at a loss, if need be, to erase the opposition. They had done just that while Bonneville was in the mountains. The price of beaver was falling? "It appears they are making hats of silk in place of beaver," Astor himself had written months ago. The British did, in fact, control the Columbia River? This was what many Americans had been telling the government for years. Bonneville confirmed it from frustrating first-hand experience.

He may have told Astor that he had written the War Department in 1833 suggesting that the Army could seize the whole territory quite easily, and that "the sooner it shall be done, the better." He had received no answer from that proposal, however much the Army high command might have favored such decisive action. Bonneville may have added ruefully that he had no written answer, either, to his request for an extension of leave, and for that reason was no longer an officer in the Army.

Meeting with Washington Irving

Another guest at Hellgate in early September, 1835, was Washington Irving, the popular essayist who had returned to America after many years abroad. Irving had visited Cantonment Gibson and Indian country soon after Bonneville left for the mountains, and had written of his adventures in *A Tour of the Prairies*. Now he had accepted John Jacob Astor's offer of access to reports of the Astorian expedition in order to memorialize that ill-fated venture. There was irony in the situation: Astor's son William had wanted to be a writer but his energies had been channeled into the world of finance.

Irving listened to Bonneville tell of his sojourn in the West "at the table of John Jacob Astor," explaining that since Astor was patriarch of the fur trade, he liked to entertain adventurers both within and without his own realm of business.

"Among these personages," Irving continued, "one who peculiarly took my fancy was Captain Bonneville of the United States Army, who, in a rambling kind of enterprise, had strangely ingrafted the trapper and hunter upon the soldier . . . he was too much of the frank, freehearted soldier . . . to make a scheming trapper, or a thrifty bargainer." Bonneville had traveled many of the trails of the Astorians, and Irving was delighted to examine maps of the very terrain he would portray in writing of the Astorian expedition. Irving plied "the mild, quiet-looking personage" with questions, and "drew from him a number of extremely striking details, . . ."

"There was something in the whole appearance of the captain that prepossessed me in his favor. He was in middle size, well made and well set . . . His countenance was frank, open, and engaging, well browned by the sun . . . He had a pleasant black eye, a high forehead . . . a bald crown gained him credit for a few more years than he was really entitled to."[52]

Lengthy Efforts to Win Military Reinstatement

At Army headquarters, Bonneville found only disappointment. His long report from Crow Country, July 29, 1833 could not be found. Bonneville's classmate Samuel Cooper, now aide to General Macomb, remembered that in the fall of 1833 Michel Cerre had delivered a document, but it was not in the file. The 1834 reports, sent with Cerre to be mailed from Council Bluffs apparently had never been received (and have never been found, though the 1833 report resurfaced many years later). What went wrong? Had someone taken the reports from the files for consultation and failed to return them? Or had they been lost through simple mischance? There was no comfort in any of the possibilities.

The missing report—and perhaps the original blessing of the expedition—were an embarrassment to General Macomb, but whether or not he was sympathetic to Bonneville, the matter was out of his hands. The Secretary of War must be consulted. Secretary Eaton had departed; the new man was Lewis Cass. Bonneville wrote him on September 30 announcing his return with information, maps and charts and pointing out that he went with consent of the War Department and charged by Secretary of War Eaton "with instructions to guide me in collecting information with which he considered it advantageous for the Government to be possessed. During my absence, and at a time when a report of my death by the Indians received general credence my name was stricken from the rolls of the Army."

Samuel Cooper submitted a two-page supportive "Report in the Case of Captain Bonneville" to Secretary Cass. In it he stated that "Captain Bonneville received special instructions from the General in Chief, a copy of which accompanies this report." Concerning the dropping of Bonneville's name from the rolls "It may be proper to state that at the time the General in Chief made his report to the War Department a report was in circulation and was generally accredited, that Cap. Bonneville had been killed by the Indians." This letter went to President Andrew Jackson who returned it asking for verification "whether the commanding General approved of his continuing his exploring expedition and gave the messenger to understand that his furlough would be extended."[53]

While Bonneville waited, gossip of new problems and new alignments met his ears. The Jackson administration, said by one writer to be not a government, but a battle, had disputes flourishing in many directions. Cotton-growing states complained that high tariffs on imported goods subsidized manufacturing New England while the South, which must export, was penalized overseas.

There was a financial muddle too, when the President withdrew government deposits from a long-patronized bank. Public interest had shifted. In 1831, many talked of the Rocky Mountains. Now there was little enthusiasm for that far-away real estate; other crises and projects filled the news columns. Andrew Jackson's determination to remove all eastern Indians to the prairies had not gone smoothly. Cherokees still fought through legal channels to hold their lands. Some of the not-yet-removed Creeks had filtered into Florida to join the Seminoles, and there trouble mounted. There had already been a "First Seminole War," a brutal curtain-call from the War of 1812. Now, several Indian treaties later, the Seminole balked at being deported to Arkansas. Loosely federated bands rallied around a fiercely dedicated leader Osceola. White settlers in Florida bombarded the War Department for help. Secretary Cass had more pressing problems than the case of a chagrined captain who had overspent his leave far away from 1835 trouble spots. The stocky, bald Secretary, however, may have felt a measure of rapport with Bonneville, for he too had known the pull of the far borders of the country. As territorial Governor of Michigan in 1819 he had asked for and received sponsorship of a large expedition to the northern reaches of his domain. "I think it very important to carry the flag of the United States to these remote regions," he had written. His expedition was expanded to include soldiers for protection, presents for the Indians and an official historian, Henry Schoolcraft. Treasury watch-dogs grumbled, and future explorations met with resistance. Cass was assistant to Secretary Eaton in 1831, and may have had a hand in the directives handed Bonneville at the time, for the language bears definite resemblance to Cass's own prospectus for his exploration of Michigan.

General Macomb, perusing the maps and journals which Bonneville submitted, appeared to concede that the tardy captain had accomplished his commission. He indicated this to Secretary Cass and wrote, "The Captain, after he reached the Indian country was heard from through a Mr. Cerre, who brought a letter from him dated some time in June, 1833. After this nothing was heard of him except a vague report that he had been killed by the Indians . . . If the report of Captain Bonneville's death were not well founded, it was thought, that as he was engaged in mercantile concerns, and as the officers of his Regiment, the Colonel in particular, were complaining . . . he ought no longer to be continued on the Roll of the Army. Captain Bonneville has now returned to Washington after an absence of four years, reported the causes of his detention in the Indian country and brought with him interesting and important accounts of what he has seen, and fulfilled satisfactorily the instructions given him on his departure."

General Macomb's statement that "the officers of his Regiment, the Colonel in particular, were complaining" revealed at whose insistence Bonneville had been dropped. Uneasy, Bonneville wrote Secretary Cass on November 25, explaining more fully about Cerre and the reports. Cass talked to Macomb. Bonneville was advised to be patient.

Now there was a flank attack. Col. Arbuckle and some of the officers at Fort Gibson sent a petition protesting Bonneville's reinstatement on the grounds that the expedition was strictly a commercial venture. To officers with new commissions Bonneville was merely a name on the muster roll: "Absent for the purpose of exploring the Rocky Mountains," adventuring in faraway places while others drew the Indian-minding patrols. He was not present, but received his salary and retained his place in the line of promotions, a line that was all too stagnant. As Macomb wrote, previous complaints from Fort Gibson had precipitated the decision to drop him. Bonneville was shown the petition and quickly penned his reply.

"Referring to the memorial of a portion of the officers of the 7 Infantry—I cannot but express my regret at this ungenerous act. I scarcely could have believed had I not seen it." He reiterated his account of his efforts to accomplish the directives and to report to headquarters. "That I started as a trader and acted as such, is what I never attempted to conceal. Genl Scott, Eustes and even Genl Macomb assisted me to become one, as letters now in my possession will show. The whole Army knew it. It was deemed more proper for me to go as such, and without expense to the Government, furnish them with such information as they believed useful . . . than for the Government to be at the expense of hiring men for that purpose, and of making presents to every Indian Nation that they should meet. His Excellency, the President, who has yet seen merely the first part of my labours, I am induced to believe and hope, approves of what he has read . . . General Macomb communicated to me through his aide de camp, as a result of his conversation between himself and the Secretary of War, that I would be nominated to the Senate . . ."

General Macomb bristled a little at this letter. In a message to Cass dated December 12, he pointed out that the leave of absence "was for an unusual period" and that he was under the impression Bonneville intended to resign at the end of it. Further, he added, "I do not remember to have given any assurance to Capt. Bonneville through Mr. Cerre that his leave would be prolonged" and he insisted the directives were not "obligatory" but only to be performed "at his leisure." Plainly he preferred to forget the whole affair. Disappointing, too, was Michel Cerre's reply in answer to Bonneville's frantic appeal for corroboration. Indeed, he had delivered thc report to General Macomb and "he then told me that your letter had given him great satisfaction . . . It may be that Genl Macomb told me that your furlough should be continued . . . but I cannot say positively that he did. However . . . it was my impression . . . the Government was satisfied that you should remain some time in the mountains for the sake of acquiring information . . ." This letter went into the file, though it was not as positive as Bonneville had hoped. Had he heard only what he desired to hear? Regardless, he was not about to retreat. He had not lost sight of his dream, and though the prize seemed to flutter out of reach and had suffered loss of value in the eyes of his military peers, he still pursued his goal: to regain his reputation in the Army and to prove that he had contributed something of value to his country. General Macomb could not deny his initial approval nor his November 19 acknowledgement of the value of the reports, though he may never have seen the vision in the same brightness as Bonneville.

Bonneville had no need to be apologetic. Army historian R. Ernest Dupuy has pointed out that Bonneville brought back "the first authentic geographic study of the entire region, including its flora and fauna, as well as the habits and numbers of the Indian tribes." He had explored Green, Snake, and Salmon rivers, "scrambled through the Big Horn and Wind River Mountains," made two trips to the Columbia, and furnished direction and means for Walker's party to skirt the Great Salt Lake, chart the Humbolt River and lakes, cross the Sierras by two different passes, and report the status of Spanish California. In addition his maps were the "first to correctly represent the hydrography of the regions west of the Rocky Mountains, and determine the existence of great interior basins without outlets to the ocean."[54]

Secretary Cass appears to have turned the vane in Bonneville's favor. Cass had no need for the approbation of the officers of the line; he answered only to the crusty old soldier at the top, President Andrew Jackson. On January 4, 1836, two letters came out of the Adjutant General's office to Cass, the first beginning "In conformity with your instructions . . ." detailing how Captain Bonneville could be reinstated without changing the list of promotions, the second "Re-Appointment of Benjamin L. E. Bonneville . . . restored to his former rank and Regiment." Secretary Cass wrote a supporting letter to the President when he submitted the re-appointment papers.

It would be pleasant to report, as some have, that Andrew Jackson looked at Bonneville's maps and reports, pounded the table and exclaimed "By the eternal, sir, you shall be restored!" Historical honesty does not admit this face-to-face encounter. Though records mention verbal conferences, no one, apparently, wanted to admit he had a hand either in Bonneville's expedition or his dismissal. The fact remains that President Jackson did have a lively interest in Oregon. Less than two months after Bonneville returned with reports that he was literally shut out of Columbia River country, the government sent a civilian observer by sea to the British installations which Bonneville had not been able to reach. The Secretary of State instructed William A. Slacum to visit the settlements on the Columbia and "without exciting British suspicions bring back a report." Slacum left in such haste on his journey that he had to use his own money; this would come to light when he billed Congress for his expenses.[55]

President Andrew Jackson sent Bonneville's re-appointment nomination to the Senate on January 8, 1836, but the mills ground exceeding slow. The nomination went to the Senate military committee where it lay for months. Chairman Thomas H. Benton told the anxious Bonneville that he need not haunt the committee room, and he was kept in agonizing ignorance of his chances. The final decision lay with the complete membership of the Senate, and that body had not always been amenable to the President's wishes.

One hopeful note: Rocky Mountain explorer and fur trader Lt. Richard Bland Lee, dropped in the same general order with Bonneville, had been quickly reinstated. But Lee was not so many months overdue. He was also the son of a member of Congress. He did not escape entirely unscathed. Months later he wrote the Adjutant General's office requesting copies of letters concerning his mountain probes "which I deem necessary to my vindication . . . my reputation as an officer having been assailed during my absence."[56]

Bonneville could only wait. Major James Harvey Hook, with whom Bonneville had served, made room in his own quarters, and apparently encouraged him to put his notes and journal into shape for publication. Washington Irving found Bonneville there "writing at a table covered with maps and papers . . . rewriting and extending his travelling notes and making maps of the regions he had visited." Irving had written to General Macomb requesting copies of maps of the Rocky Mountains from Bonneville's journal; now he sought out Bonneville concerning the maps he had requested. His *Astoria* was almost ready for publication, and when it appeared the "Sketch of the routes of Hunt and Stuart" was Bonneville's map, though simplified, presumably by Irving. To express appreciation, Irving labelled the Great Salt Lake "Lake Bonneville." Later critics derided this gesture as "conceit" on the part of Bonneville, though it was Irving's choice. A footnote: in the late 1860s geologist Clarence King of the "Fortieth Parallel Survey" asserted that the Great Basin held the remains of two huge prehistoric lakes. He named the western one Lake Lahontan. His colleague Grove Karl Gilbert studied the Salt Lake basin, and named the great vanished lake there Lake Bonneville. The name became official in an 1890 government publication.

Sale of His Manuscript to Washington Irving

While Bonneville toiled over his manuscript, the newspapers and the military buzzed with excitement about events in Texas, where long-simmering disputes had erupted into Mexican massacres of Yankee Texans at the Alamo and Goliad. Sam Houston, his wasted days behind him, now commanded Texas troops, bent on revenge and determined to set up an independent republic. In Florida, too, trouble mounted. Indians killed over one hundred troops on the Withlacoochee River. Militiamen and regulars swooped in for revenge, but Osceola mocked them from the shelter of trees, and the Seminole killed and wounded more soldiers.

It is doubtful if Bonneville found authorship easy. Whether he worked with materials from his original journal or from other personal notes and diaries is not known. Dr. Edgeley Todd, introducing a 1961 edition of "The Adventures of Captain Bonneville," writes, "What Irving had seen at Hellgate was clearly the original journal that Bonneville immediately turned over to his superiors upon his arrival in Washington from New York. What Irving found Bonneville working on three or four months later . . . was a second manuscript." John Francis McDermott writes that Bonneville may have produced "two or even three manuscripts or sets of documents."[57]

Bonneville reworked his maps into "Map of the Territory West of the Rocky Mountains" and "Map of the Sources of the Colorado and Big Salt Lake." Years later he wrote that he had also made one of "the waters running east to the Missouri state line" as well. That map, plus the sketches from which he worked, as well as the original journal and diary have not been found. They may have been destroyed, or they may yet come to light.[58]

Bonneville had not yet been restored to duty. He had promised new supplies to Montero, and he had left some of his property "in the care of agents." On March 12, he packed up his "mass of manuscript" as Irving called it, and set out for New York to find a publisher. In 1836, as in all the years that followed, publishers were cool to unpolished manuscripts by unknown authors. After two weeks, Bonneville requested an interview with Washington Irving. Irving promptly called on Bonneville, examined the manuscript and "bought it for a price which I conceived to be above what he could procure from any Bookseller," Irving wrote. Irving promised in a letter to Major Hook to deal fairly with Bonneville in the literary work "as he is a gentleman for whom I have already conceived a high regard." He mentioned also that he would use Bonneville's dedication of the work to Hook.[59]

Return to the West

Bonneville left New York the instant he had disposed of his manuscript. It was springtime, and once more he simply had to walk to the West. With fifteen men and a capital of $1,122, he intended trading with the Arapahoes "at a point of timber on the south side of the Grand River Platte, called Laramais Point," according to his license. The small amount of goods indicates that he had no large trapping brigades in the field. He reached American Fur's new Fort William on the Laramie River on June 6, and pushed on to the Portuguese Houses on Powder River, two hundred miles north. Montero's business with Bonneville apparently ended at this time, for a little later a Fort William employee wrote to an associate "Captain Bonnville has settled his affairs in this country and is on his way down with part of his equipment which he expects to sell here . . . I'm told he has eight kegs of liquor to dispose of, that we never have too much of, if he will take a reasonable price for it I may bargain with him; the Sioux are all along Riviere Platte and if he should attempt to take it down he's sure to be robbed."[60] Whether Bonneville allowed himself to be robbed by the Sioux or by the trader at Fort William was not recorded.

Chapter Four
1839-1845

Seminole War Years; Marriage

Reappointment to His Former Rank and Regiment

> Fort Leavenworth, August 7, 1836. Sir, Upon reaching this post this day I find order No. 46—received yesterday—announcing my reappointment to my former rank and Regiment. I have now been absent from the settlements since 8 May last, at which time not being able to hear of any decision being had, I proceeded to the far West to make a final close of every interest there— and now have the pleasure to say I shall proceed immediately to the post Cantonment Gibson where my regiment is stationed.[1]

"Immediately" meant only as quickly as the jubilant captain could hurry on down to St. Louis, dispose of his trappings of the fur trade, and see to his mother's welfare. The mayor of St. Louis, John Darby, visited often at the Chouteau home in the 1830s. "Mme Bonneville was then an old woman and talked entirely in French," Darby wrote.[2]

The local press took note of Bonneville's visit to St. Louis: "Captain B. L. E. Bonneville of the U. S. Army returned to this city on Sunday morning from a tour to the Rocky Mountains, where he has been (with the exception of a few months) for the last five years. We are happy to learn that the captain, in connection with Washington Irving, Esq. contemplates compiling a narrative of his travels, together with an account of the various tribes among which he sojourned, and a geographic account of the country through which he passed. We await with impatience the appearance of this work."[3]

Duty at Fort Gibson on the Arkansas River

When Bonneville reported for duty, Col. Arbuckle demanded to know why he had not arrived until September, though his re-instatement was dated April 22. Possibly the testy colonel still smoldered that he knew nothing of

Bonneville's expedition until it was an accomplished fact. And he had lost the re-instatement skirmish. Bonneville, now that he was back on the rolls, could view the petition against him in perspective. Most who had signed were newly assigned and had never met him; he was merely an obstacle to their personal progress. In the years ahead he would count as good friends signers Theophilous Holmes, Gabriel Raines and Dixon S. Miles, among others. As the story of the past five years unfolded, Bonneville could see why he had been a target of the officers' discontent.

It had been no picnic at Fort Gibson, as the post had been officially named when the fourth side of the stockade was completed. With Andrew Jackson's Indian policy moving into action, additional hundreds of displaced families were thrust into the area for the Army to escort, settle, and keep from being annihilated by each other or by the native tribes. Post facilities bulged, but several companies of Dragoons were also moved to this hub of Indian country. The Dragoons—there was the sore spot. The flashy blue and gold uniforms, the arrogance of mounted men toward those on the ground, the clouds of dust settling on the whitewashed buildings after the squads had clattered away—all these were galling to the footsoldiers and their officers who had pleaded for horses for their Indian patrols. Col. Arbuckle had suffered another indignity when Dragoon General Henry Leavenworth superceded him in command. However, a grand tour of the prairies by the Dragoons brought death to General Leavenworth and one hundred and fifty men—not at the hands of Indians but from fever and dysentery. Colonel Arbuckle resumed command.

Congress had recently appropriated money for the Army to build a military road from Minnesota south to Red River—a picket fence boundary, some had scoffed. Planners decided that Fort Gibson was too far west and a new Arkansas River site must be found. When Col. Stephen Watts Kearny arrived at Fort Gibson to choose a location, Col. Arbuckle complained that he should have been consulted. He declined to accompany the party, but sent Captain Bonneville as escort.

After a pleasant swing about the countryside, Bonneville brought the delegation to Fort Smith. Residents there wanted the new post located at the site of the old one; other towns bid for the plum too. Arkansas was exulting in its new statehood status; the transition from territory to 25th state meant more local office-holders and less political appointees from Washington. "Arkansas Gazette" editor W. E. Woodruff was serving as state treasurer. The current "Gazette" advertised Washington Irving's "Astoria; Two volumes, with maps, $4." Included in the book were an essay on Indian problems by

Albert Gallatin and "Suggestions With Respect to the Indian Tribes, and the Protection of our Trade . . . quoted from a manuscript written by Captain Bonneville."

Albert Gallatin had published in 1835 an article about Indians for the American Antiquities Society. His accompanying "Map of the Indian Tribes of North America" shows dotted lines tracing the travels of the late Jedediah Smith, indicating the information may have come from him. Names, placement of rivers and other features show that Gallatin had not yet seen Bonneville's maps.

In his treatise, Bonneville cautioned that expecting peace among tribes transplanted into the midst of the prairie Indians was unrealistic. He advocated military control and well-distributed trading posts. Of the Indians of the Rocky Mountains, Bonneville wrote, "the residence of the agents of the Hudson's Bay Company among them renders the condition of our people in that quarter less secure."

Captain Bonneville was back at Fort Gibson in time for lively Christmas festivities. There had been weddings and there was gossip too: sutler John Nicks' widow had been courted by many, including, it was said, Colonel Arbuckle, who was willing to give up his bachelorhood for her. She chose another.

Indian alarms were still the order of the day. Not all the prairie Indians had signed treaties; the Kiowas had not. Captain Bonneville wrote the Adjutant General's Office on January 24, 1837, offering to head a mission to settle the issues. Years later, he wrote of the episode "The Indians had assembled in large numbers, and becoming sickly, they dispersed suddenly, thinking there had been some foul play toward them. Thinking my experience might be of some service, I felt it my duty to offer myself to go and bring in any chiefs the government might wish to confer with, asking for the purpose my company and only the remnant of merchandise, presents, etc. the commissioners had not disposed of." The answer was some time in coming, and when it did Washington announced that A. P. Chouteau would be going on the mission Bonneville had proposed. Bonneville remembered the incident with resentment: "An influential trader on this frontier, learning of my proposition, applied for the 'job' as he called it, got it, and afterward said to me 'You do this for honor; I do it for profit.' "[4] Chouteau delayed going to the prairies until autumn, but succeeded in sending Kiowa chiefs to Fort Gibson, where they signed agreements with the government. Bonneville signed as one of the witnesses.

The Army, ponderous and solid, had changed little while Bonneville was absent. Hustle the Indians westward. Keep the peace among them. Build roads into the hinterlands. Guard thousands of miles of frontier—this with a few thousand men. The pulse of America pounded westward and the nation needed the Army more than any civilian would ever acknowledge, yet improvements in the profession were hard to come by. Medical and mess standards had been slightly upgraded, and small pay increases approved. Officers and men were proud of the few new tools of the trade, among these, new brass field artillery pieces, superior to the old iron cannon. A six-man crew could load a twenty-four pounder with bags of lead bullets and powder cartridges encased in oiled flannel, ignite a long fuse which burned into a paper packet of powder and the charge was off—almost always.

Still interested in his mountain men, Bonneville wrote to David Adams asking about his welfare. Adams had confided that he intended to publish his own journal, and Bonneville assured him that his, soon to be published, did not include Adams' "journey" and that he hoped Adams would not fail to publish his own story. "Where is Bourginon, how did he get through—also the others who had sued the company—how has it been fixed with them?" Bonneville asked, referring to Adams' men who had left before their contracts were completed. A search of Civil Court Records at St. Louis has failed to reveal suits against Bonneville but legal hassles were common in the declining fur-trade years. David E. Jackson, who left his name to Jackson's Hole at the foot of the Tetons, had a number of law-suits against him in 1837, according to St. Louis newspapers.

"Although I am far from the Voyagers, yet I take great interest in knowing all about them—let me hear how things go on with the Rocky Mountain companies and their men, and in fine everything about the mountains," Bonneville wrote.[5] If David Adams responded, he may have described Thomas Fitzpatrick's 1836 trek to the rendezvous with a supply train for American Fur. Fitzpatrick escorted Marcus and Narcissa Whitman, Henry and Eliza Spaulding and other missionaries bound for Nez Perce country. William Drummond Stewart required two carts for his personal supplies, which included "an assortment of luxury foods and liquors such as the mountains had never seen."[6] The 1836 rendezvous was held at Bonneville's picket work on Green River. One of the missionaries wrote that nothing was left but a "square log pen covered with poles."[7] Nathaniel Wyeth had sold Fort Hall to the British, it was said; Antonio Montero too would soon be out of the trade. Jim Bridger's brigade had harassed him until he had very little property remaining. This year, 1837, American Fur supply trains were again bound for the rendezvous with more missionaries as well as William Drummond Stewart. The perennial hunter had hired painter Alfred Jacob Miller to go along to paint scenes of the American wilds.

In national news, President Andrew Jackson was reported to be thundering mad at failures in Florida. Generals Winfield Scott and Edmund P. Gaines, at odds in the field of action, were summoned to Washington to account for the absence of victory. Andrew Jackson was quoted as sputtering that with fifty women, he could defeat all of the Indians who had been ravaging Florida. The old soldier hated to leave unfinished business, and he was about to turn over the presidency to his hand-picked successor, Martin Van Buren.

Premature "Arkansas Gazette" headlines proclaimed in March, "Florida War Ended. Osceola Surrendered." General Thomas Sidney Jesup, to whom the Florida command had fallen, summoned Seminole chiefs to a council where "Capitulation of the Seminole Nation of Indians" was signed by some. But Osceola did not come, and a little later visited by night and freed seven hundred Seminole prisoners. The war was far from ended.

"Washington Irving has a new work in the press entitled *The Rocky Mountains: Scenes, Incidents and Adventures in the Far West*, the "Arkansas Gazette" announced in July. True to his promise, the writer had put Bonneville's manuscript into shape for publication. When Bonneville obtained the two-volume work it is a fair guess that he agonized over the inaccuracies and omissions, but appreciated the sprightly tone. Later editions were titled simply *The Adventures of Captain Bonneville* and it was published in England and translated into Dutch, French, and German. One reviewer wrote, "The graces of pen have literally made the solitary wilderness blossom like a garden."[8]

Captain Bonneville spent September and October, 1837, in the russet and gold hills of Choctaw country "on special duty, to muster friendly Indians," according to Fort Gibson records. Other Indian soldiers had proved to be of value in Florida but their terms were expiring and generous terms were offered Choctaws who would enlist. Soon five hundred young warriors converged on Fort Gibson to claim the $272 each Bonneville had been authorized to promise them. But headquarters had erred, and the stipend was much less. The disgruntled Choctaw departed.[9]

However, the Seminole War was really over, according to headlines. Osceola had been captured in October, and without his leadership resistance must surely fade away. Later, details were made public. Osceola and his party were surrounded and made prisoners while they talked beneath white flags at a peace conference. But Osceola's capture did not bring Seminole families to the docks for emigration. Nettled, General Jesup planned to sweep the Indians together with converging columns, where, in battle, the war would be over. General Abram Eustis succeeded in pushing a sizeable number of Seminole into the Kississimee River area. Chafing for action, Col. Zachary Taylor received permission to charge. Army casualties were high, and the Seminole withdrew into their familiar sanctuaries, but reports reaching the newspapers gave the impression that Taylor had won a great victory at Lake Okeechobee.[10]

Transferred to Fort Towson

In February, 1838, Captain Bonneville and F Company were ordered from Fort Gibson to augment the garrison at Fort Towson, where trouble mounted between settlers and Indians. The area was assigned to the Choctaws, but white settlers were scrambling to extend their claims, resulting in raids, counter-raids, and stealthy killing.

New and attractive Fort Towson stood on bluffs overlooking Gates Creek, six miles from Red River. Disgruntled settlers had burned the first Fort Towson after troops were withdrawn in 1827. Major Stephen Watts Kearny was sent in 1831 to build a new one, not to protect the settlers, but the Choctaw. General Gaines had ordered "a small strong fort" and wrote scathingly of the finished "country palace . . . calculated to give our promising young officers the effeminate habits of fashionable idlers . . ." Officers stationed there wrote of the shaded porches fore and aft of their quarters, and of the stone fireplace, large enough to roast a whole beef. Though often at odds with the civilians of Red River country, the Army got along well with the Indians and with the missionaries working among them. One man of the cloth wrote of the "friendly attitude of the officers." He noted that "half the garrison" belonged to the Temperance Society.[11] The other half, perhaps, were among those recorded by the "Arkansas Gazette" as celebrating one occasion by drinking thirteen patriotic toasts, "including a final salute to Col. Vose and the officers: May they never feel want, or want feeling."

New recruits began to arrive at Fort Towson. Rank and file soldiers were easy to get, for the nation had fallen on hard financial times, brought about, some said, by the clumsy juggling of government fiscal policies. When jobs became scarce, young men were eager to join the Army. With Fort Towson strengthened by newcomers, Bonneville and F Company departed.

At Fort Gibson Col. Arbuckle was nervous. The Osage were raiding area farms because their hunting grounds were being overrun. The Cherokees had worse trouble. Years before, some had moved from their southern hills to the prairies. Families continued to trail westward, but the pace was not fast enough for those who clamored for their eastern homes. General John Ellis Wool succeeded in removing several thousand Cherokees before he was replaced in command, some said because his sympathies veered to the Cherokees. To General Winfield Scott fell the ugly task of removing the remainder of the tribes. During the summer of 1838, seven thousand armed regulars and militia herded the Cherokees west. Fever, measles, whooping cough and dysentery stalked the exiles every weary mile of the way. Over four thousand Cherokees, one-third of the total, died along "The Trail Where We Cried." Fully as bitter as their resentment of white men's injustice was the Cherokees' internal strife, the white-hot hatred of the Cherokee East for the Cherokee West leaders whom they blamed for their betrayal. Broken-hearted patriarchs like Sequoyah tried to patch up a peace. They were whispering into the wind. Captain Bonneville submitted a plan of his own for policing and guarding Indian country, as evidenced by a map of the Three Forks area he sent to the Adjutant General's office at this time. Among notations on the 1838 map: "The Fort I plan is only intended as a depot for stores, etc., the Army being always in the field or cantoned near the depot . . . B. L. E. Bonneville."[12]

The garrison at Fort Gibson staged a full military funeral for A. P. Chouteau, who died there in August. A West Point graduate of 1804, he had served only briefly before devoting his life to the fur trade and to the Osage as their agent with the honorary title "Colonel." His Chouteau kin still dominated the fur business in St. Louis, but packtrains from the mountains brought scanty harvests. The fields were too well-plucked to justify a rendezvous, and it was said there would be no more of them. Change was in the air. At the last pow-wow, a supply caravan had brought a new adventurer, Swiss-born John Sutter, along with numerous missionaries. In Washington, Congressman Linn introduced a bill authorizing the United States to occupy Oregon country. Newspapers carried his long speech, in which the Missourian cited Lewis and Clark, William Slacum and others, and outdid himself with eloquence quoting Washington Irving's rendition of Bonneville's view from the top of the Wind River peak.

The New Fort Smith

In the scramble for the proposed new post on the Arkansas River, Fort Smith won. The government already owned a good sized tract at old Fort Smith, but John Rogers would ever be envied for the handsome deal he made with the Army for additional land. A later writer asserted that Bonneville served on the final selection committee, went to Washington and swung the decision in his friend's favor in return for a gift of two lots. This was not true, for Post Returns show that Bonneville was on duty continuously from 1836 to January, 1839 in Indian country. He purchased his Fort Smith holdings in 1837 from the government.[13]

As the new Fort Smith project got under way, Bonneville and his company were ordered to repair the old post buildings for storage. Arriving at Fort Smith, Captain Bonneville found Quartermaster personel occupying the government housing; his men had to make do with tents. Resented too was the importation of civilian laborers at handsome wages, while infantrymen worked for subsistence. Some townspeople criticized the new Fort Smith, pointing out that the Vaubanne-designed establishment sat in the middle of a thriving, settled town. And as workmen turned Belle Point into a quarry, chipping and blasting away that ferncovered landmark, oldtimers and others had second thoughts about the good fortune which had come to Fort Smith.

A Transfer to Fight in the Second Seminole War

In an autumn assignment, Captain Bonneville and Major W. B. Belknap surveyed the Fort Smith to Fort Towson segment of "The Great Frontier Road." Shortly after Bonneville returned to Fort Gibson the Seventh Infantry received orders to serve in the Florida War.

> A company of Seventh Regiment of U. S. Infantry under Captain B. L. E. Bonneville numbering forty arrived by keelboat on their way to Tampa, where the whole regiment has been ordered— "Arkansas Gazette," January 16, 1839.

At Little Rock, F Company transferred to a steamboat for the trip to the Mississippi and the voyage downstream from winter frosts to the gray mists of the deltas and across the Gulf to the bright sunshine of Florida's west coast. Built on an inner nook of Tampa Bay, Fort Brooke bustled under the command of Brigadier General Zachary Taylor. As in 1821 when Bonneville had been a green subaltern on the Jackson Military Road, Taylor was ramrodding his campaign in a manner to delight his superior, Andrew Jackson, not quite retired as President of the United States, for the Van Buren administration was hewing to Jackson's line. In the first months of his command of the Florida War, General Taylor deported over a thousand Indians. Then, as had his predecessors, he suggested letting the remainder of the Seminole remain in the southern "worthless" areas of Florida. Settlers wanted the Indians removed or exterminated. Critics of the war argued that civilians wanted hostilities to continue for the commerce it brought them, and so their militia could make slave raids in Indian country while on the government payroll.

Army patrols had logged hundreds of miles, while the Seminole moved out of reach in the shadows and raided outposts and travelers on lonely trails. Preparing to lead an expedition southward, General Taylor ordered Captain Bonneville to precede the columns with stores of rations. Shortly, F Company headed down a dim wagon-road with supplies to establish a depot on the Caloosahatchee River, a hundred miles south in strictly Indian country.

Bonneville and his men learned new words. Hammocks were groves, sometimes so thickly grown with tall trees as to produce perpetual twilight within, and protected on the perimeters with tangles of bushes. Some hammocks sheltered loamy meadows where the Indians planted corn. Palmettos were squat trees with enormous root systems, their fan-shaped foliage covering dry ridges in thick mats. Savannas—small prairies—supported drifts of cabbage palms. Yellow lotus and water hyacinths floated in ponds and sloughs; there were springs and swamps in every lowland.

Broad and of uncertain shorelines, the Caloosahatchee flooded over spongy banks to nurture miles of green-misted oak and grapevine forests. Beyond the river, southeastward, grew the sedge called saw-grass, bristling in prairies of water mile upon mile to the very end of the land, with fibrous roots reaching to primeval muck shelved on limestone. Here copious rains and lake and river overflows moved through the water grasses in a never-ending surge to the sea. This southern tip of the enchanted peninsula was known as the Everglades.

At a dry spot along the Caloosahatchee, approximately midway between the later villages of Alva and Labelle, Bonneville chose a site in open country for the depot. Berry patches were heavy with fragrance and snowy ibis soared serenely in the sky. The idyllic scene belied the grim Army business at hand—to seek out and capture every Indian family in Florida. Captain Bonneville had escaped much of the onerous duty of uprooting the Choctaw, the Creeks and the Cherokees. In Arkansas and in the West, his Indian dealings had encompassed only attempts at peace and friendship. Now he must call the red men enemy.

Back from the supply depot mission, Bonneville found that the planned expedition had been cancelled. Approval had come from Washington for a divide-and-conquer plan of squares, and General Taylor lost no time in implementing it. He moved his own headquarters to Fort King (Ocala) and directed the quartermaster at Fort Brooke to send all the ponies fit for service to Captain Bonneville by boat to Fort Clinch; F Company would then take the horses overland for use at the several posts. Fort Clinch, near the mouth of the Withlacoochie, bore the name of the first of the war's many commanders, General Duncan Clinch, who met defeat when Osceola caught him with half his army on one side of the river and half on the other side.

Along the Withlacoochie, cypress, oak and gum trees grew in profusion. Captain Bonneville was assigned to build a post in the area, but green scum floating on the sloughs made him wary for the well-being of his men. He chose a spot ten miles north of the river near the edge of Wetumpka Hammock, and established a station known as Fort Number Three. General Taylor sent his approval of Bonneville's efforts to use game for subsistence, and informed him that he would send two companies of the Seventh to join him as soon as they arrived. Taylor was peevish that Col. Wm. Whistler had not yet brought the balance of the regiment. When they came they were pressed into service constructing wagonroads, bridges and posts.

In May the War Department announced that Commander in Chief Alexander Macomb would come to Florida for a peace conference in lieu of the elusive military victory. Traveling by steamboat, stage and horseback, the Macomb entourage reached Fort King to be greeted by most of the military units then in Florida, including the entire Seventh Infantry. Captain Bonneville and his "cavalry" are recorded as escorting Macomb.

In response to enticements by scouting patrols, Seminole delegations began to assemble. Chitto Tustenuggee, Halleck Tustenuggee and Thlocklo Tustenuggee with their followers gathered in a hastily built council house—Tustenuggee meant Chief. As an observer described the Indians, the warriors greased their straight black hair, and some cropped it in two narrow strips at right angles with feathers stuck in the top. They wore little more than breech cloths; a few adorned themselves with silver and brass ear and nose rings. Many of the women wore forage bags. The Seminole liked liquor and frequently asked the soldiers for whiskey. It was said that the men would imbibe one day, and when they had sobered up, the women would have a turn; in that manner, there were always clear heads to watch over the safety of the tribe.

The Army treated the visitors to full dress reviews and the mighty volume of the Seventh Infantry band, with huge night bonfires for the Seminole dances. After negotiations through interpreters, peace pipes were smoked, and General Macomb proclaimed on May 20 that the war was ended. The Indians had agreed to withdraw southward within sixty days where they were to remain until further arrangements were made, as the General smoothly put it. No treaty was signed, but the staff was certain that Macomb had succeeded in winning the Seminole with pomp and presents.

General Macomb returned to Washington, and once more the newspapers carried headlines that the Florida War was over. General Taylor, absent while Macomb visited, resumed command. The shaggy-browed commander had no admiration for General Macomb, and no faith at all in Indian promises. There remained at large many hostile bands who had not come to Fort King to be dazzled by military pageantry. The Army had traveled this road before. The Seventh Infantry, too, had reason to doubt that all would be peaceful. On the very day the Commanding General was declaring the end of the war, a sergeant from K company was killed by Indians near Bonneville's Fort Number 3. His death presaged the fact that before the Seventh was finished with the Seminole, one man in four would lay down his life in this wonderland of foliage and water.

Florida: the legendary Juan Ponce de Leon named it when he landed among the blossoms and claimed it for Spain early in the Sixteenth century. As Spanish, English, French and Americans battled for the smooth beaches and sheltered bays, the original inhabitants, called Calusas, were almost obliterated. They died of civilization, it has been said, meaning, rather, of the cruelties and diseases of invading peoples. Remnants of the Calusas survived, and uniting with Creeks and Muskogee fleeing from Alabama and Georgia became the proud and defiant Seminole. By adoption, the Seminole included the rebellious spirits of many strains, including some Negroes who had escaped their bondage.

The Negro refugees were a source of contention, and the first Seminole uprisings were reprisals for raids in which slave-hunters attempted to round up every black, slave or free, as well as mixed bloods and numbers of pure Indians. In the early 1800s, the Seminole had farmed northern Florida, collecting herds from wild Spanish stock. Whites moved in, building homes and claiming great tracts. Treaties committed the Seminole to moving out of the way, but the Indians claimed each had been exacted by fraud. In other parts of the nation, the Indians could move westward; in Florida they were trapped, with no place to go but the swamps and the sea. Their resistance, 1835 to 1842, is chronicled as the Second Seminole War.

It was an undeclared war. At Andrew Jackson's and Floridians' demands, Congress began to appropriate money to subdue the few thousand Florida Indians. The several tribes—Tallahassees, Creeks, Mikasukis, Yuchis, and Alachuas each with subdivisions—united loosely for their common cause. All were referred to as Seminole. By 1839, when Bonneville reached Florida, the heartland was dotted with destroyed plantations. It would continue to be a no-man's land of stealth and stalking for three years, and the Seventh must call it home for that length of time.

In Florida, rain spatters down, then rainbows arch the skies, and vapor clouds rise like air-born castles. The overhead pageant was enchanting, but on the ground were the same miseries the Seventh had known in Arkansas, plus the added discomfort of oppressive humidity and a wider variety of pests. Salt-water mosquitoes blew in on the west wind; there were fleas and cockroaches and rodents and snakes. Bonneville and his men adapted their clothing, hanging flaps from their caps down over their collars to keep the rain from running down their necks. Their blue uniforms, which made them easy targets, soon blended with the color of the mud.

Commanded to observe an armistice after the May Conference, the troops kept close to their posts. Col. Whistler took a short leave, and Captain Bonneville commanded regimental headquarters at Fort King during his absence. Built to protect the Indian agency near Silver Springs, Fort King was set atop a knoll, with a 20-foot-high cupola. Sentries could scan the surrounding forest and hammocks; they heralded both friend and foe by ringing a large cowbell. Osceola had grown up in this verdant area; the blackened timbers of the Indian village said to have been his home were a few miles northwest of Fort King. Osceola's death in prison had given him immortality, but numerous leaders vied to take his place: "bitter, bold" and handsome Coacoochee, "Wildcat," Thlocklo, "Tigertail," and others.

During the uneasy peace that followed General Macomb's visit, Indians gathered in Mikasuki territory at Silver Springs, east of Fort King. Presumably, they were assembling for their move south, and the Army, as instructed, hovered near. This was the season of the green corn festival, a religious holiday held during the full summer moon, when priests and elders meted out punishment and honors. Rituals, some preserved from ancient times, included fasting and displaying a medicine bundle. Old fires were quenched, old quarrels laid aside. At the climax of the celebration, the warriors shared a drastic emetic of button snakeroot, chanting "Asi-ya-ho-lo" in a long yowl. This was said to be the origin of the name Osceola, adopted by the part-Scottish martyred leader. After the purification of the black drink, the elders stoked the embers into new fires, symbolic of rebirth. According to Marjory Stoneman Douglas, the 1839 green corn festival featured long discussions of what to do about the latest white men's edicts. Plainly the Seminole were not ready to submit as meekly as General Macomb had supposed. In frenzied oratory, Creek Chief Otulke Thlocco, "The Prophet," exhorted the tribes to unite and drive the white men into the sea. Rattles and drums beat wildly as new fires burned bright, and when the night's dancing was over, there were "dawn prayers and the baths and the feasts" and ominous promise.[14]

War exploded on the Caloosahatchee, very near the spot Bonneville had found tranquil in March. Dragoon Colonel William S. Harney had been sent to escort a trader. In a night attack, Indians killed and captured eighteen men. Fourteen escaped, including Col. Harney, clad only in his underwear. All the trade-goods were lost, as well as the newly-developed Colt rifles which Harney had managed to obtain for his men. News came that the captives were tortured to death. Never gentle, Harney from that day forth became an Indian executioner of no mercy.

As if by sparks scattering in the wind from the Caloosahatchee, murder and destruction blazed all over Florida, and destroyed the shaky peace structure. Small bands of Indians moved silently through hammocks and swamps, ambushing unwary whites. Two militiamen were killed and mutilated near Micanopy; six bridge-building regulars were slain on the Suwannee, and there were killings near Fort Lauderdale and Picolata. On the other hand, peaceful Indians bringing their skins to trading posts were hustled into stockades and deported.[15] Several hundred prisoners were sent from Florida during 1839. The Seventh manned Forts Russell, Micanopy, Brooke, Heileman, and 2, 3, 4, and 5 as well as Fort King, with patrols constantly on the move. A dozen soldiers of the Seventh died of yellow fever, cholera, dysentery and "disease unknown." Others suffered chronic fevers.

The Christmas season brought no peace to Florida in 1839; presumably it did bring letters and papers from home. Bonneville's mother, Margaret, completed a business transaction for him in 1839, buying a lot in St. Louis for $1,000 from Major Floyd Smith, a son-in-law of Mme. Chouteau.

Frustrations and New Commanders

The bloodhound episode of the war, variously reported, brought no credit in any version. Bloodhounds were used to track down fugitive slaves in the West Indies, and Florida territorial officials, reasoning that the dogs could ferret out Indians hiding in the hammocks, imported thirty-three from Cuba. General Taylor agreed to try three. Trained to track down black men, the dogs—muzzled on orders from the War Department—could not be induced to trail Indians.

Zachary Taylor's faith was in his regulars. He assembled a force of Infantry and Artillery for a three-columned thrust, hoping to push the Seminole east of the Suwannee, and from there southward. Fugitive Indians struck with new fury in the Fort King district. During the first months of 1840, six privates of the Seventh were shot while on patrol. A scouting party was ambushed only two miles from Fort King. Three men were killed, and Captain Gabriel Raines rallied the remainder in a charge back to the post. Raines was critically wounded. General Taylor ordered reinforcements to Fort King, and directed Col. Whistler to move the Seventh Infantry headquarters to Fort Micanopy. Taylor was frustrated. He had given his best, and for a longer period than any other commander in this endless conflict. Territorial officials disliked him. Unlike his predecessors, he would not allow slave owners to come into the prison encampments and claim Negroes, or part-Negroes, as their property. Taylor asked to be relieved of the command in Florida, and in April, 1840, his request was granted. General Walter Keith Armistead arrived.

Many Indians had slipped through General Taylor's lines. Skirmishes were fought the length and breadth of Florida, with heavy toll from sneak attacks. At Indian Key, thirteen settlers were killed, among them Dr. Henry Perrine, a noted horticulturist. A theatrical troupe traveling near Picolata was ambushed; the Indians carried away loads of costumes which would appear in the future on innocence-protesting Indians who came to posts to bargain or beg. Lt. James S. Sanderson surprised forty warriors in a hammock eight miles from Fort Micanopy. In a savage engagement, six of the patrol were killed, including Lt. Sanderson. A little later, Captain Bonneville and Captain T. H. Holmes with their companies probed Big Swamp, west of Fort King. The Indians fled, leaving behind the plunder they had taken, including Lt. Sanderson's ring.

In the absence of Col. Whistler, Captain Bonneville commanded the Seventh Regiment headquarters post at Micanopy in July and August, 1840. Named for a chief who had been made prisoner while conferring under a white flag, the post was sturdy, with blockhouses on all four corners of the stockade. Quarters were small, but "tidy," and great oak trees growing within the palisade spread welcome shade. The fort itself was a secure haven, but in the midst of woods and brush, even nearby forays were dangerous. Along with the regimental returns for August, 1840, Bonneville sent a report of an attack on a detachment he had sent with the post ambulance to bring in a sick man.

"Upon their return, they were attacked at 1 p.m. The escort fled. The sick man jumped out and so severely wounded an Indian that they had to make a litter to carry him off. Two of the escort were killed and one wounded and one missing . . . The sick man reached the post in safety, and saved the life of one of the escort."[16]

In November, reinforcements arrived, including Col. William Jenkins Worth's Eighth Infantry Regiment. General Armistead now commanded an army of almost five thousand regulars plus fifteen hundred militia. Like the commanders before him, he concluded that a military parade would convince the hold-out chiefs they would be better off to capitulate. Previously emigrated Seminole brought from Arkansas contacted friends and relatives. Runners brought word that Tiger Tail and Halleck would meet with General Armistead at Horse Shoe Hammock.

Captain B. L. E. Bonneville and his dragoons escorted General Armistead and Col Worth to the conference, according to John T. Sprague, formerly General Macomb's aide and now with Col. Worth.[17] At the edge of the hammock, Halleck stepped out of the woods bearing a white flag. He was tall, with an engaging smile which belied the story that he had killed his own sister because she favored surrendering. General Armistead tried bribery, offering each chief $5,000 to surrender and bring in his people. The chiefs replied they would have to think it over. With a show of reluctance, Halleck and Tiger Tail went to Fort King, where they were showered with attention. Followers came to the fort and left with gifts of food and drink. Then in the night both chiefs and their warriors vanished.

During the winter, Captain Bonneville commanded at Fort Wheelock, fronting on Orange Lake. Floating islands dotted the water's blue depths and drifted in the winds. The Indians were said to bury their dead on the islands. Private John Milne died of fever at Fort Wheelock; he was the first man lost from Bonneville's F Company. Not far away, the Seventh's Lt. Walter Sherwood and twelve men escorting the wife of Lt. Alexander Montgomery from Fort Micanopy to Fort Wacahoota—a distance of nine miles—were ambushed from a hammock. Mrs. Montgomery, Lt. Sherwood and three men were killed and mutilated. Swift searches yielded no traces of the culprits; some said the attack was by Halleck of the sweet smile. In reprimand to General Armistead for the ambush, Secretary of War Joel Poinsett scolded that a mounted infantry man would always be thrown from the horse's back or keep himself on by throwing away his musket. The Secretary's views were not shared by the soldiers in Florida. Militiamen flatly refused to serve without their mounts, and regulars preferred riding too. Horse-lover Zachary Taylor had ruled that Infantry regiments could keep horses at the posts for patrols—half as many horses as men, he judged, would be adequate. The fact that the Infantry used horses may explain why Bonneville was called a dragoon in a number of accounts.

Still hopeful he could bring the war to a close, General Armistead asked if Indians might be granted permission to stay in the southern reaches of Florida. The answer was "No." In small actions, some Indians were captured, some bribed. Among the latter was a sub-chief who had taken part in the Sherwood ambush. He received $5,000 for bringing in his band of sixty. Wild Cat came to a post a number of times, secured bounties of food and drink and slipped away again. Once, he and his henchmen appeared in Shakespearean costumes taken from the ambushed theatrical company.

F Company's Owen Cowley died of his wounds in January, eight months after the Sanderson ambush. Three more of Bonneville's F Company privates died of dysentery during the spring. The beleaguered Seventh made their patrols through mud and brush, sun-blistered, rain-chilled, flea-bitten, scratched, weary and discouraged. Fifty soldiers of the Seventh died during the year.

General Armistead left scarcely a ripple in Florida when he was replaced. In his earnest one-year tenure, he had captured, bribed, coaxed and/or browbeaten almost seven hundred Indians into submission. This number did not include those shot by soldiers nor the score or so hanged by Col. Harney. The General's achievements equalled those of his predecessors, but he lacked an aide who possessed a facile and flattering pen. Zachary Taylor was soon to acquire W. W. Bliss to help his snowballing popularity. Armistead's successor enjoyed a special relationship with John T. Sprague, who left the only history of the war as seen by one who was there.

"Haughty Bill" was the nickname of William Jenkins Worth, named to replace Armistead to command in Florida. Though lame from the War of 1812, Worth rode a horse superbly; he was handsome, crisp, aggressive. His military stance demanded decisive and immediate victory. He did not achieve it in Florida, but so convincing was his aura that most observers believed he did. Of the chroniclers who mention the Seminole War, at least one, a Winfield Scott biographer, credits Scott with bringing hostilities to a close. A fair number of writers veer to other subjects after Zachary Taylor's engagement at Okeechobee, awarding the laurels to Old Rough and Ready. Many historians credit Worth with swift and satisfactory end to the conflict, leaving only a minority to conclude that this war, like so many others, was a many-splintered thing.

All the tactics had been tried before—patrols at all seasons, destruction of the Indians' crops and villages, bribery, negotiation. Hundreds of families had been deported, yet there were still ambushes and terror throughout the territory. Somehow, the "Colonel commanding," as Aide Sprague called Worth, managed to project a vision of victory. Col. Worth ordered detachments to scout in all directions: find the enemy, capture or exterminate. Worth's self-confidence was bolstered by the fact that his ideal and mentor, Winfield Scott, had been named Commanding General after the death of Alexander Macomb in June, 1841. General Scott, still smarting from his long-ago thirty-day failure in Florida, wanted a quick victory as keenly as did Worth.

Transferred to Fort Fanning

Captain Bonneville was ordered to Fort Fanning, and with detachments destroyed fields on the Suwannee River and in the Wacassassa hammock. Fort Fanning was new and clean, built on a high bluff on the east side of the Suwannee River. A nearby tepid spring poured forth thousands of gallons of water; Indians had left arrowheads from centuries of camping. Across the Suwannee was Old Town, the Creek stronghold where Andrew Jackson had captured an Englishman in 1818 and hanged him for conniving with the Creeks. The Suwannee here was big enough for ships, and there were tales of pirates' treasures buried along the shores. Captain Bonneville reported that most patrols found no Indians, nor even tracks, for the Seminole were adept at traveling for miles by stepping only on fallen trees.

Detachments combed dozens of small streams and intervening hammocks. Few captives were taken, but there was no longer sanctuary in any part of Florida for the Seminole. Citizens complained that the enemy, like wounded animals, would now be more dangerous, and insisted that additional Florida volunteers were needed. In disagreement, Col. Worth told the settlers to go back to their homes and protect their own acres. To the objection that they had not been able to plant crops and thus were destitute, the Army sent money to help them until they could sustain themselves. Troops assisted in building a blockhouse in each community, and arms and ammunition were furnished civilians brave enough to go back.

Coacoochee, Wild Cat, had been captured in one of his food-and-whiskey forays, and by the time Col. Worth took the reins, was already on his way to Arkansas. The Colonel ordered him brought back to use as hostage in securing the surrender of others. At first belligerent, Coacoochee was kept in chains and threatened with death unless his messengers brought in his followers. One story has it that on the Fourth of July, Coacoochee asked what the celebration was about and was told, not exactly with pride, "Freedom." Bribery money plus a concession permitting him to take off his irons and dress up in his crimson turban convinced Coacoochee he must cooperate. He was true to his word, under the Army's watchful eyes. He contacted Tiger Tail, who insisted he must confer with Alligator, already in Arkansas. That Alachua chieftain too was sent for.

Bonneville Commands Micanopy District

During the summer, Captain Bonneville was transferred to Fort Wacassassa, a hammock-side post on the upper reaches of that river. During the fall, he commanded the Micanopy district in the absence of Col Whistler. In his reports, Bonneville commended his men for scouts made on the Suwannee, and wrote that he inspected the posts in the district. These included some of notable history, and others designated only by number. At the site of Fort Wacahoota (later Gainesville) a Spanish mission had been built in the early 1600s. Later, white invaders burned villages and slaughtered or sold the natives into slavery. Fort Drane, at the edge of Wetumpka hammock, occupied the ruins of a sugar plantation General Duncan Clinch had claimed for himself in the early 1830s. Near Fort Call, several miles north of Newnansville, the Santa Fe River disappeared into a sinkhole and traveled some distance before emerging. At Fort White, near the confluence of the Santa Fe and the Suwannee, abundant springs created a good-sized stream. The entire district was quiet at this time, Bonneville's inspection tour revealed.

Already out of favor with territorial officials, Col. Worth had no qualms about carrying out the often-sent orders to wean off civilian employees. Clerks, teamsters, smiths, wheelwrights, express riders—several hundred, long on the public payroll, were cut off. Because Indian villages were so often found empty after carefully arranged raids, hard looks were taken at interpreters, whose importance and incomes hinged on the continuance of the war.

Wildcat's value as bait ran out. In the middle of October he and over two hundred Alachuas and Mikasukis were hustled aboard ship. When Halpatter, Alligator, arrived from Arkansas, Tiger Tail came to Fort Brooke and set up camp. He appeared to be as tired as the soldiers of the deadly game of hide and seek.

The action shifted northward. According to alarms from the settlements, Creek bands from Georgia had joined the Mikasuki still lurking in the hammocks. Some of the depredations were rumors; some all too true. Across Florida to the east, Indians burned Mandarin village near Jacksonville. Col. Worth sent troops to police the area. Here and there, small Seminole bands were captured or surrendered. They were disillusioned people, tired of the discipline of their zealot leaders, and sick to death of hiding and running. Word from Big Cypress Swamp indicated that the Mikasuki and Alachua there had broken away from the influence of the militant Prophet.

Believing there were only about three hundred Indians left in Florida, Col. Worth wrote to Washington asking that the war be declared at an end. The Third and Sixth Infantry, on the scene since 1836, were transferred out of Florida, and the Second and Seventh were alerted that they too would soon be reassigned. Since the war was all but over, Captain Bonneville requested a furlough.

"I shall be at the North in a few days," he wrote on March 21, 1842, to John Rogers at Fort Smith. Rogers had transacted some business for him, and Bonneville asked to whom he should remit the "424$" owed. "Write me addressed at Washington City. So soon as I shall hear my station assigned I will write you. Will you continue your kind attentions for me—friends must act for each other . . . "[18] The furlough was not granted as quickly as Bonneville had planned.

Halleck, of the Mikasuki, and Tiger Tail and his Tallahassees, were still at large. In addition, there were more Creeks to be dealt with. Nobody expected the Creeks to make a last stand, yet here they were in uncounted numbers, slipping in from Alabama and Georgia to harry the settlements. Andrew Jackson had "wiped out" the Creeks twenty years before, and several thousand had moved to Arkansas in the intervening years. Now, with the Seminole War all but finished, Creek warriors tantalized the Army. It was past time for drawn-out peace talks, Col. Worth tersely informed the Indians, through messengers. Hereafter it was to be capture or death. Quickly, for Worth was ever in a hurry.

The Seventh tackled the tag-end duties of the Florida War in the glory of springtime on the Suwannee and the Wacassassa. Velvety ground-orchids and emerald ferns grew in the shelter of bay and sweet gum trees, and acres of blue iris swayed in the marshes. Woods creatures scurried through the tangled brush, but vultures perched on drowned-out trees, and ducklings squawked in terror before the shadow of hawk wings. It was a bittersweet season for men so near to leaving this mocking paradise.

Patrols probed by night, hoping to intercept the Creeks, who had taken to moving in the dark. Troops destroyed palmetto huts and growing fields, but could not close in on the hunted people who covered their tracks by burning the grass, or by walking in the streams. A band of Creeks swooped down on Newnansville and hacked to pieces a woman and three children, then sped southward where they ambushed and killed two soldiers. Lt. Forbes Britton of Bonneville's F company came face to face with a Creek war party at Clay's Landing on the Suwannee. Two men were wounded, one of whom died. Another private died of consumption, bringing F Company's toll to seven.

Col. Worth led an attack on a wooded island near Palachikaha hammock which yielded little. However, an elderly captive who said he was Halleck's father agreed to try to talk his son into surrendering and in five days Halleck came to the Army encampment at Warm Springs. The game of coy delays began, with the women and children enjoying the Army's bounty. But Worth was wily, too. He inveigled Halleck into going with him to Fort King; Halleck thought he might bargain for powder and lead there. After they left, the Army surrounded the Indian encampment and took all the Mikasuki captive. At Fort King, Halleck was informed that his trail had reached a dead end. The handsome leader for whom the whites had never found a nickname wept and raved by turns. No journalist ever again mentioned Halleck's enigmatic smile

On May 10, President Tyler agreed that hostilities should officially end. Col. Worth was prepared; he had been closing out the war for some time. The Seventh was assigned to garrison posts in Florida, and Captain Bonneville's F Company drew the choice Fort Brooke berth on Tampa Bay. Bonneville arrived at Fort Brooke on June 17, relinquished command to Lt. Britton and set off on his long-awaited holiday—first a stint of recruiting, then a three-month leave.

A Recruiting Assignment to Baltimore

Washington D. C. had taken on big-city glitter. Gas street lights had replaced some of the flickering oilburning lamps around town. Citizens stepped briskly as they attended to the nation's business. Newspapers and coffee houses projected the notion that this, now, was the center of the world. At her home on Lafayette Square, grande-dame Dolly Madison still presided over gracious affairs, but President Tyler's daughter-in-law set the pace of a livelier circle. It included vivacious younger belles and government employees as well as numerous Army personnel and their families. Among the latter, Lt. and Mrs. Philip Kearny enjoyed popularity. Kearny had trained at a French cavalry school and learned in the Nigerian desert to charge with a saber in one hand, his pistol in the other, and the reins in his teeth. General Winfield Scott dominated the military scene; his uniforms were dazzling, displayed as they were on the six-foot-four-inch redheaded general.

Military bands gave daily concerts. Foreign diplomats rode in elegant carriages through the streets. There were flamboyant native personalities as well, including Thomas Hart Benton in his long Spanish cloak. That westward-looking senator had secured authorization for his son-in-law to head a mapping expedition into Oregon country. Unlike Bonneville, Lt. John C. Fremont would have all his expenses paid by the government.

The country had gone mad with railroad building. Earlier, it had been canals, but even before many waterway projects were off the drawing boards there was talk they would soon be made obsolete by the railroads. To get somewhere quickly was an obsession which grew in America as naturally as hickory and maize, only faster. It was a stylish thing to "go by the cars." Engines glistened with bright paint; passenger cars made up a "brigade." There was railroad service in 1842 from the nation's capitol to Baltimore, the port on Chesapeake Bay, and this was Bonneville's recruiting assignment.

Baltimore was a fast-growing city of many-angled streets emanating from a bustling waterfront. Bluffs were constantly being pushed into the marshes to make room for mills, distilleries and warehouses built to process the harvests flowing from prosperous inland farms. Neighborhoods of Italians, Poles, Germans, Irish and Acadian French were promising areas for recruiting. Army troops garrisoned the harbor bastion Fort McHenry, and presumably Bonneville quartered there. Among officers on the roster was Captain John M. Washington, a distant kin of the nation's first president who had entered West Point in 1814 while Bonneville was there. In a challenging new assignment he was to command the "Cavalry School of Practice" in an historic little

Pennsylvania town named Carlisle. Bonneville and Washington may have worked together in signing up new enlistees and in delivering them to Carlisle Barracks, the principal recruit depot in the Army.

Baltimoreans were proud of Fort McHenry, but they had other tales from the War of 1812 as well: a British general bragged that he would eat dinner in Baltimore or in hell, and though the hastily-mustered militia had to load their cannon with scraps of old muskets, they dispatched the enemy officer to keep the appointment in the latter of the two alternatives. Francis Scott Key's triumphant anthem "Defense of Fort McHenry" had premiered at Old Holliday Theatre; more recently, John Howard Payne had introduced a hit song, "Home Sweet Home," in a stage production there.

Baltimore citizens had built Greek revival style houses, a Latrobe-designed cathedral, and a lottery-financed monument to George Washington. Rembrant Peale's Gallery of Fine Arts vied for attention with Barnum's Hotel, seven stories high, with wrought-iron balconies and red velvet hangings reflecting endlessly in gilt-framed mirrors. Here, only weeks before Captain Bonneville arrived, Washington Irving introduced Charles Dickens to the "enchanted julep" and other facets of American hospitality.

Marriage to Ann Callender Lewis

> "Captain B. L. E. Bonneville of the United States Army married at Carlisle, Pa., December 12, 1842, Miss Ann Callender, daughter of the late Charles W. Lewis of Monroe Co., Virginia." *Missouri Republican*, December 29, 1842.

"How many changes since we parted . . . myself married . . ." Bonneville wrote to his friend John Rogers, with the context of the letter indicating joy and a tinge of wonder at this magic turn of events.[19]

When and where did Bonneville meet Ann Callender Lewis? There are slender clues. Many of Ann's relatives followed military careers. In 1831, Commissary General of the Army Callender Irvine, Ann's uncle, resided at Schuykill Arsenal in Philadelphia; if Bonneville secured his "scientific instruments" for his western expedition from that source—and returned them there—he could have met the General and his family, which included Ann at that time. Captain Peter Fayssoux, also an uncle, had served in St. Louis. He lived in Philadelphia with his family for some years before his death in 1833. It is possible that Ann was in Baltimore in 1842, for she had relatives there through her great-aunt Isabella Callender Neill. A family letter reveals also that a close friend of Ann's lived or visited in Baltimore at about that time.

Very likely John M. Washington's wife, Philadelphian Fannie Macrae, at least abetted the autumn romance of Benjamin Bonneville and Ann Lewis. The Washingtons moved from Baltimore to Carlisle for the Cavalry School assignment and were instantly popular. Officers and staff at Carlisle Barracks enjoyed good rapport with the townspeople, and the very name Washington was appealing to citizens whose forebears had drafted their own Declaration of Independence in May, 1776. Carlisle had produced many patriots, including Molly Pitcher. Molly's husband was body-guard for General William Irvine, Carlisle's physician-turned-military-leader. General Irvine was married to Ann Callender, also a heroine in the war. They were the maternal grandparents of Ann Callender Lewis.

Ann's father, Dr. Charles W. Lewis, was a grandson of John Lewis of the Shenandoah Valley, who "Furnished Five Sons to Fight in the Revolution," according to his epitaph (Staunton, Virginia). John's son William studied medicine in Philadelphia, as did William's son Charles. The association with the Irvines, also a family of physicians, resulted in the marriage of Dr. Charles Lewis and Mary Irvine in 1805. They made their home in Sweet Springs, Virginia, and when Dr. Charles died in 1827, Mary Lewis and her seven children returned to her family. They lived in Philadelphia with General Callender Irvine until his death, and then in Carlisle. In 1842, the home in Carlisle sheltered three widows: Mary Lewis, Mary's sister Elizabeth Reynolds, usually called Aunt Betsy, and Patience Irvine, widow of the Commissary General. Patience, paralyzed by a stroke, was cared for by Aunt Betsy, and by Mary Lewis and her daughter Ann.[20]

The Irvines and Lewises loved to gather for weddings, according to extant letters. Ann's brother Thomas and wife and two sons lived in Virginia. Sister Agnes Elizabeth and husband Archibald Campbell and two children made their home in Philadelphia. Ann's youngest sister, Mary B. had married Samuel M. Leiper and lived with their large family at Avendale near Swarthmore. William, the older brother, had lost his life at the Alamo; brother Armstrong also had a fancy for Texas and served a number of years as a Commander in the Navy of the Republic of Texas. The youngest of the Lewis family, Callender, was nineteen years old in 1842. Bonneville appreciated Ann's extended family, as witnessed by his life-long attention to them.

It was an unusual union; he of French descent and Roman Catholic heritage, she a Protestant gentlewoman. He possessed his grandfather's Bourbon-awarded sword, books and medals from his rebel father and a few momentos from the famous Lafayette; Ann inherited fine linen and silver. He was an ardent wanderer; she was the faithful unmarried older daughter who shared her mother's burdens. They were, perhaps, both wondering if fulfillment was passing them by, for she was thirty-one and he was forty-six. Bonneville was short and stocky. Ann's Lewis progenitors are mentioned as tall, and members of the Irvine family were of generous proportions. But by family tradition, Bonneville called Ann "Nina" possibly meaning diminutive, or as a term of endearment. Their marriage proved to be an enduring one, in spite of long separations, of inconveniences of travel and abode, of professional disappointment and serious illness.

The announcement of the marriage in the *Missouri Republican* within two weeks may indicate that the Bonnevilles traveled to the Florida assignment by way of Margaret's home in St. Louis, perhaps spending Christmas with her. Overdue, Bonneville reached Fort Brooke on January 16.

Assignment at Fort Brooke, Florida

Wild orange trees and great live oaks lined the shores of Tampa Bay. Fort Brooke's blockhouses overlooked the countryside, and a six pound battery guarded the sparkling blue harbor. Log barracks stood on stilts; small cottages housed the officers and their families. (The southwest corner of Platt and Franklin streets in modern Tampa has been marked as the site of Fort Brooke.) Civilian stores, repair shops and a boarding house occupied Army property. A boat brought delicacies to the post from a fishery; it was said that the bugler would announce the approach of the fish boat. It was also said that the drinking water was so bad it had to be flavored with molasses, but that the claret was excellent. All the officers liked Tampa.

There was news to catch up on. Col. Worth, promoted to Brigadier General, continued to command in Florida from headquarters in St. Augustine. After exacting a peace agreement, Worth had gone to Washington to enjoy a hero's welcome. The reports of Aide John T. Sprague had contributed to enhance the commander's stature. Sprague, in turn, was rewarded with advancement to Captain. He also became Worth's son-in-law.

In recent action at Fort Brooke, Octiarche and his Creeks had come in, asking for a conference. Instead, they had been surrounded and captured. A little later, troops took custody of Tiger Tail at Cedar Key. Battered and sick, he was promptly dispatched westward. He died aboard ship at New Orleans, it was reported, but years later the legend grew that it was another ailing warrior who had been captured, and that Tiger Tail escaped to live out his days in the Everglades. As Bonneville resumed his duties, more exiles were being put aboard the last boatload sent west of these Indians the Spanish said were too tough to conquer and too stubborn to convert.

On February 26, Bonneville assumed command of the garrison. Throughout Army circles there were recriminations and a flurry of courts martial or inquiry into various misdeeds in the war maneuvers—some of the action requested by the alleged offenders themselves to clear the air and their fiercely-guarded honor. At Fort Brooke, all was tranquil, according to the records. The sunshine was warm, shells of infinite variety lay on the beaches, and the breezes stirred the sweet smell of citrus. It was a time for long-neglected practice of military drills, of band concerts, of reminiscing and recapitulation of past frustrations and hardships, and regrets for those who had died in the campaigns.

Transfer to Baton Rouge, Louisiana

Army orders and transfers traditionally arrived in spring; the Eighth Infantry inherited Fort Brooke, while the Seventh was moved to Baton Rouge. Captain Bonneville embarked with his men on March 24. Whether or not Ann accompanied her Captain to his new station is not recorded. She was in Carlisle during the following August, and she may have returned to her mother's home from Tampa rather than risk the uncertainties of medical care in disease-prone Louisiana. She was "enciente," as it was delicately put. Middle-aged Bonneville and his thirtyish wife were expecting a baby.

Baton Rouge: French explorer d'Iberville saw a "reddened post" placed there by Indians, a diarist with him wrote. But some said the name came from a cypress so high it couldn't be measured because it rose out of sight. Baton Rouge Barracks were fairly new in 1843, built on gentle bluffs beside the Mississippi. Brick buildings formed three sides of a parade ground, and opened to a landing wharf and bath houses on the river. Garrison Bayou mirrored two mounds; a slope of one was used for a military cemetery. In June Col. Whistler arrived from Florida, bringing two more companies and the regimental band.

Army bulletins announced the death of General Abram Eustis, the dignified, unpublicized artillery commander who had spent his lifetime guarding the nation, and who had encouraged Bonneville in his western exploration. Bonneville was by no means the only military man whose efforts at special service went unrewarded. Naval Lt. Charles Wilkes, recently returned from an "Exploration Expedition" of five years, was court-martialed on charges by some of his men that he had been too high-handed. He had mapped the Pacific Ocean and its islands, and discovered a new continent, Antarctica, but his charts and records were treated lightly, some lost. One public servant was luckier. John Charles Fremont returned from his 1842 sojourn to South Pass. His wife wrote his report, she recorded, and his father-in-law, Senator Benton, inserted it into the Congressional Record. The senator ordered extra copies printed, so that one and all might know that Lt. Fremont had "discovered" the Wind River range and climbed its highest peak.

"The British have come down the Columbia, taken possession of it from the head to the mouth, fortified it and colonized it, monopolized the fur trade, driven all our traders across the mountains, killed more than a thousand of them," Senator Benton declared in a burst of oratory. Congress appropriated money for Fremont to make another expedition. He took with him a capable map-maker, Charles Preuss, but there were rumors in Army circles that he also took along a howitzer, against orders, and that his superior officers were furious. There were rumors too that Fremont planned to go into Mexican California.

Ordinary citizens were ahead of official circles. Tales of returning travelers plus books like *The Adventures of Captain Bonneville* were bringing dividends of appreciation of the West, and the value, the downright necessity, of its becoming part of the United States. The missionarics—the Lees, Whitmans, Spauldings, Father DeSmet and others had all taken tools of settlement into the Pacific Northwest—the whole area being called Oregon. In the spring of 1843, many land-hungry families headed west with plows and seed loaded on wagons and herding along cattle and horses. In contrast to the earnest homeseekers, a collection of "doctors, lawyers, botanists, bugg ketchers," as guide Bill Sublette called them, accepted William Drummond Stewart's invitation for a last "hunting frolic" to the West. Stewart, now Sir William, hosted journalist Matthew Field, two German scientists, and a bevy of European and American goodtime Charlies.[21]

Captain Bonneville traveled to Carlisle in October, 1843. He had a sixty day leave and the "joyful prospect of going to seek my wife and little darling pet—a daughter—she has presented me," he wrote to John Rogers. Born during the last week in August at Carlisle, the baby was named Mary, with a second name not certain. "Irving," some have written, presuming she was named for the writer. More likely, the name was "Irvine."

The new father collected his little family and set out for Baton Rouge in November. At Cincinnati "the most violent catarrhal and dysenteric affliction took hold of our pet, and for these past 15 days she has been at the point of death . . . now providence smiles again upon her although her diseases are still disturbing her, yet I am delighted to find her getting fat as a little pig," Bonneville wrote to Rogers, and added, "How many changes since we parted—a large city commenced under your patronage—fortune flowering upon your heels, myself married, and a little daughter to love and to cherish . . . It is now nearly one year since I have been at the head of the list. How anxiously do I hope my promotion may bring me once more among my earliest attachments."[22]

Arriving at Baton Rouge, Bonneville found orders to attend a court martial in New Orleans. This most French of American cities had doubled in size in the past ten years, prospering as world port of the Mississippi Valley. Behind the great doors of the Latrobe-designed bank building on Royal Street, business deals were discussed in English instead of French, and dollars were more popular than "dixies," though the latter name described the whole delightful southern scene. Dixieland meant warmth and music, balcony-shaded streets, noise and color at the French market. Not far out of town a breastwork still remained, where Andrew Jackson's army of regulars, backwoods volunteers and pirate crews outwitted and outshot the glittering victors of Waterloo in 1815. New Orleans Barracks, adjoining the battle site, was the scene of the court-martial.

In Baton Rouge, officers' quarters occupied portions of the barracks buildings, whose white columns supported front and rear galleries, adding grace and shade. (In subsequent years, some of these buildings were surrounded by the campus of Louisiana State University.) Wives of married officers enjoyed this pleasant southern post and the leisurely pace marked by the clock atop the steeple of St. Joseph's cathedral. Business houses clustered along the river. There were two newspapers, one printed in English and the other in French. There were mansions: one featured verandas on three sides, with brick pillars and railings of ironwork; the owners treasured a set of china, hand-painted by Audubon.

Col. Whistler departed for a six-months leave, and Captain Bonneville assumed command of the 220-man garrison. Inspector General George Croghan expressed approval when he visited the post in May: "Discipline, At present good and correct. A great change for the better has been wrought in the habits and temper of this command; but a short time ago there was much intemperance with great insubordination."[23] Later, on orders, Captain Bonneville with men and officers moved to the Gulf Coast, where Major Jacob Brown joined with more companies and the regimental band. Fragmentary records variously datelined "Camp Worth" and "Camp at Pass

Christian" indicate that most of the Seventh Infantry spent the late summer and early autumn by the chameleon sea and white sands of Bay St. Louis. In November, Bonneville was back at Baton Rouge, where he commanded for the next several months.

The year had been unsettling in the nation. Texas had asked for admission to the Union, a move very apt to bring war, for Mexico regarded the upstart Republic her property. For the presidential election, candidates had been in good supply. The Whigs would have no more of John Tyler, but nominated Henry Clay. At the Democratic convention in Baltimore, Lewis Cass was a willing candidate, while one-term Martin Van Buren panted for a come-back. After many indecisive votes, Tennessee unveiled dark-horse James Knox Polk, rumored to be Andrew Jackson's choice. Once kindled, the Jackson spirit crackled like the bulletins being sent to Washington—for the first time—by means of Samuel Morse's device of wires and electrical current. In a flurry of oratory about annexing Texas and occupying Oregon, delegates put together a platform of unbeatable Jacksonian appeal.

One of the harsher events of 1844 concerned an American-born religious movement. Vermont native Joseph Smith had published *The Book of Mormon* and organized "The Church of Jesus Christ of Latter-day Saints." Ridiculed, abused and driven from their homes in Ohio and Missouri, followers reclaimed swampy Commerce, Illinois, and renamed it Nauvoo. But persecution had followed them, and newspapers recounted the June, 1844, "butchery of Joe Smith, the celebrated Mormon prophet," opining that this turn of events would undoubtedly be the end of Mormonism. The year had brought trouble in other parts of Christendom too: in Philadelphia, disputes between Catholics and Protestants triggered riots, and churches and schools went up in flames.

While some citizens turned their ambitions and discontent to quarreling with the neighbors, others looked for new horizons. The road Bonneville had traveled west, the Indian-trapper-trader path along the Platte, Sweetwater, South Pass, Bear River, Snake River and Columbia, was now called the Oregon Trail. California, too, beckoned. Though it was Mexican property, reports of its riches made it a prize too glittering to resist. Adventurers struck south from Snake River on Joseph Walker's trail to reach the eastern side of the Sierras, and with the help of the Indian Truckee, crossed later-named Donner Pass. Farther south, Joe Walker guided a party into California by the crossing he had found, Walker Pass. Home from his second expedition, John Charles Fremont reported he had been to Snake River, the Columbia and Walker's

Barren River, which he renamed the Humboldt. He wintered near the settlement of Swiss adventurer John Sutter, then made his way back by a more southern route.

Winter touches Louisiana lightly, though frosts brown the leaves and signal a change of pace for living things. People came in from the great plantations to attend balls and concerts in Baton Rouge, and to show off the superior horseflesh they owned. Near the end of the February, Bonneville took most of the garrison to New Orleans to spend a week. The traditional mid-winter frolics there had evolved into wild pre-Lenten celebrations known as the Mardi Gras. Whether the troops were sent to lend smartness to the parades or to help keep order is not apparent.

New President James K. Polk inherited trouble. The winning catch-phrase of the campaign had been "fifty-four-forty-or-fight," meaning the United States would go to war to win title to the Oregon country, including British Columbia. The English press snapped about "insults," though some maintained that peace was more important than possessing swampy woods and an untamed river overrun by American border ruffians who had ruined the fur trade. Negotiations continued.

The Texas dispute involved a more peppery people, and many warned that annexation would mean war with Mexico. On the assumption or the hope that money would solve the problem, President Polk sent an emissary to offer five million dollars for New Mexico and twenty-five million for California. Mexico, absorbed with internal trouble, brushed the deal away. The Army was prepared. Poised near the Texas border, Zachary Taylor's large command stood ready to march. On orders, Bonneville sent most of the Baton Rouge ordnance to him.

On the western frontier, the coveted assignments of probing and mapping went to the topographical engineers and the dragoons. Col. Stephen Watts Kearny took his cavalry across the plains to South Pass, then south to Bent's Fort, returning by way of the Arkansas River. Captain John Charles Fremont—he had received a double promotion for his previous jaunts—drew an assignment to scout the southern Rocky Mountains, and to return quickly. Once in the field, Fremont ignored the limitations of his assignment, and with Joseph Walker and Kit Carson among his guides, made a bee-line for California. "This project, like the previous ones, represented a direct violation of official orders . . . Thanks to Benton's powerful backing, he seemed entirely immune from the rigors of military discipline."[24]

Andrew Jackson died in June; his era did not. On July 4, 1845, Texas approved annexation to the United States. General Taylor's "Army of Occupation" marched through the streets of New Orleans and boarded ships for Corpus Christi at the mouth of the Rio Grande.

Promotion to Major

Bonneville continued to command at Baton Rouge during the summer. A twenty-day leave in April presumably had enabled him to take Ann to her mother's home in Carlisle to await the birth of another baby. The annual list of promotions was late, delayed by the bustle of movements to Texas, but at long last, Captain Bonneville won his commission as Major. Among the delights of his new position was a raise in salary from $79 per month to $129. He had served in the Seventh Infantry for twenty-four years; now he was assigned to the Sixth.

Reassigned to Fort Smith, Arkansas

Whether by lucky chance or request, Fort Smith was Bonneville's first post as Major. He took command on August 30, 1845. The garrison—two companies with their officers plus a large quartermaster work detail—still occupied log houses, while the almost-finished new Fort Smith stood nearby. Plans had been revised. The northwest anchor of the fort would be a storehouse; as the "Old Commissary Building" it was destined to outlast all the other structures. The palisades' thirteen-foot walls of cut stone were completed, with portholes for musketry four feet apart. The chiseled stone gateway was massive and striking. The work had been costly. Besides the outlay of money, and the years of labor by the soldiers, the project had required tons of rock, quarried on the spot. Fern-grown Belle Pointe on the Arkansas River was no more.

John Rogers' dream of a town had come true. Several businesses occupied Front Street, while the Rogers' Block at Second and A streets housed the post office and the hotel. Rogers and his Mary had six children, and he served as president of the board of Fort Smith Academy.[25]

During the autumn, Major Bonneville received word of the birth of his son, Nicolas, in Carlisle. A few weeks later, there was another message: the baby boy had died, October 9, 1845, aged one month, nine days, according to his tombstone.

On December 21, Major Bonneville departed on leave according to post returns, and there is evidence that Ann joined him at this time. In a letter to an older grandchild, Ann's mother Mary Irvine Lewis wrote in early 1846, " . . . little Frenchy always gives a P. S. to her mother's letters, but writes in an unknown tongue, and we are little wiser of her thoughts, but conclude from her natural disposition she expresses much love for us . . ." If, as seems likely, Mary Lewis was referring to Mary Bonneville as "Little Frenchy," the two-and-a-half-year-old perhaps resembled her father.[26]

Arkansas newspapers hailed the completion, at long last, of the "new works at Fort Smith." Brick pillars and wide porches graced the three barracks. Other buildings stood ready. On May 15, Major Bonneville with his officers and two companies of Sixth Infantry moved into quarters described by the "Intelligencer" as "substantial, neat and handsome." Not mentioned in the local press was the fact that reasons for the fortress, doubtful from the start, had now become non-existent, but the Van Buren editor noted "The officers want to be off to Texas."

As war talk snowballed, dissent rumbled from eastern states, where editors made snide references to Taylor's "Army of Provocation" and claimed the soldiers spent their time gambling and drinking in the rowdy Corpus Christi camptown. The "Arkansas Gazette" took a solid stand: "It is with regret that we see our contemporaries in the east from both parties withhold support from the government at this time. Our Country Right or Wrong!"

Chapter Five
1846-1847

War With Mexico

Mexican Attacks in Texas

"Mexico has shed American blood upon the American Soil!" President Polk announced on May 11, 1846. A Mexican force had crossed the Rio Grande and surrounded American dragoons, killing eleven and capturing fifty others. Congress declared war on Mexico, appropriated ten million dollars and called for fifty thousand volunteers.

Though diplomats still discussed it, the Oregon dispute was not yet settled. If the belligerent 54-40 stance prevailed, war with England could be expected, Albert Gallatin pointed out in his treatise "The Oregon Question." The ever-westward tide of American home-seekers had swirled at last to the edge of the continent. There was a surge of citizen feeling: the breadth of the continent must belong to the United States. But the nation had neither the time nor strategic means to hold out at the bargaining table for the area which would become British Columbia. In a treaty which some declared was primarily to keep the British out of the Mexican War, the north boundary of the Oregon country was fixed at the 49th parallel.

"GREAT BATTLE! GENERAL TAYLOR VICTORIOUS" —"Arkansas Gazette," May 25, 1846. Dispatches rushed by couriers to newspapers caused government officials to complain that the public learned of events before they did. After the early May assault by the Mexicans, Zachary Taylor rushed to Point Isabel to re-enforce his supply base, then turned back towards Fort Texas. Along the way, he routed Mexican troops at Palo Alto and Resaca de Palma. The small garrison at Fort Texas, across the Rio from Matamoros, had survived a week of bombardment, but among the casualties was Major Jacob Brown, lately Bonneville's fellow officer at Pass Christian. Fort Texas was renamed Fort Brown; the later city there became Brownsville.

President Polk brevetted Zachary Taylor Major General, and named him to command the Mexican campaign to the chagrin of General Winfield Scott, nominal head of the Army. The War Department ordered the Navy to blockade Mexican Gulf and Pacific ports, with special instructions to take possession of San Francisco Bay. General Stephen Watts Kearny prepared to march his dragoons overland to the California coast by way of Santa Fe.

"Mr. Polk's War" appealed to the adventurous, especially in states bordering Texas. Young Arkansas men joined units like "Van Buren Avengers" for which the town mothers were asked to make uniforms and banners. Enlistments were accepted for as little as three months, which reduced the idea of war service to something of a lark. Besides his enthusiasm, the volunteer furnished his body, such as it was, and his courage, if any. The Army supplied him with "arms, accoutrements, ammunition, knapsack, canteen, camp equipment, subsistence, medicine and transportation," the "Arkansas Gazette" reported. Headlines about early victories raised visions of American troops marching triumphantly through Mexico. The officers, particularly those who had served in the Florida War, were aware that a toll of human lives would be levied. In keeping with the custom before a campaign, officers made their wills and arranged family affairs. Most wives and children returned to relatives. Ann Bonneville and Mary, almost three years old, perhaps added brightness to the household in Carlisle comprised of Ann's mother and aunts.

With the call for volunteers, politicians and civilians flocked to Washington to vie for positions as officers of the new troops. President Polk was said to dislike "West Point aristocracy" so the officers of the regular Army expected—and received—few important assignments. The President's law partner, Gideon Pillow, and other party stalwarts were among the overnight generals superimposed at the top of the regular Army structure. "Promotions in the Army, we see, go like kissing—by favor and not by merit," quipped the "Arkansas Gazette."

General Scott wanted to train men at home, sail to Vera Cruz and march overland to strike Mexico's capitol. The administration brushed him aside and devised a chase into northern Mexico, General Taylor from Matamoros, and General John Ellis Wool into Chihuahua from San Antonio.

The March From Arkansas to San Antonio

Major Bonneville was ordered to march a battalion of Sixth Infantry, First Dragoons and Arkansas volunteers from Fort Smith to join General Wool at San Antonio.

Fort Smith staged a resounding send-off on July 13. By way of Shreveport, a well-beaten road led toward San Antonio. Summer rains had swollen the creeks, and trails were boggy. Bonneville's battalion ferried the Brazos River at Washington, Texas, the village where the independence of the Lone Star Republic had first been declared. Bonneville's regulars arrived at San Antonio de Bexar on August 27. One soldier wrote home that the men were "fat, hearty, happy" and "pretty sure there will be no more fighting," since General Zachary Taylor had already whipped the Mexicans, the "Arkansas Gazette" reported.

Stone and adobe buildings clustered around the plaza in San Antonio. The Governor's Palacio, a few ancient barracks and the Catholic missions bespoke a more prosperous era. All were pocked with cannon-ball scars from scores of pitched battles as Indians and Spaniards and Yankees had struggled for supremacy. Padres supported by Spanish military had built missions at this site of an Indian pueblo at the close of the seventeenth century. Don Antonio de Villasenor laid out a town; his name persisted, embellished by de Bexar to honor a Spanish nobleman. The missions, like the vanished pueblos, had passed their days of glory and in the 1840's stood mutely crumbling while a rowdy new people scorned their era. Mission San Juan's roof had fallen in. The steeples and carved facade of Mission San Jose bore bullet scars; it had been converted into a granary. The soldiers were most interested in the Alamo, the mission which had become a monument to Texan bravery. Almost two hundred men had died there—frontiersmen, young adventurers, and some sympathizing Mexicans. Ann Bonneville's brother, William Irvine Lewis, was among the dead. According to family tradition, someone sent Ann's mother a stone from the Alamo and it was fashioned into a cemetery marker bearing his name.

Captain John M. Washington's artillery rumbled six brass cannon into camp on September 4, nine weeks overland and by boat from Carlisle, Pennsylvania. The Second Dragoons arrived, and two regiments of Illinois volunteers, whose commander John J. Hardin had been a congressman; his place in the legislature had been taken by lawyer Abraham Lincoln. Through a balmy September, Bonneville and other officers drilled their troops, helping Brigadier General John Ellis Wool to shape his expeditionary force, the Army of Chihuahua. Wool drew criticism as he tackled the job of making soldiers out of volunteers and their politician commanders. Said to be a strict disciplinarian, Wool was called "old womanish" by some, while others, hard put for wit, ridiculed his name. Lt. Col. William S. Harney sputtered harsher epithets after being placed in arrest for making an unauthorized foray to the Rio Grande.

Most of the supplies came by boat to Port LaVaca; quartermaster personnel freighted over one thousand loaded wagons to San Antonio. The Engineers fashioned pontoons and timbers to be transported to the Rio Grande for "flying bridges." Captain Robert E. Lee joined General Wool's staff on September 22. A personable officer and capable engineer, Lee had good connections, including being a distant relative of Zachary Taylor. He was a cousin of Richard Bland Lee, who, like Bonneville had overstayed his leave in the Rockies.

Destination: Chihuahua

Overflowing San Antonio, Wool's three thousand-man-army began to move in late September. Col. Harney, forgiven, commanded the dragoon van, followed by Major Bonneville's battalion of Sixth Infantry plus a regiment of Kentucky volunteers. Other units left on subsequent days. Past Castroville, Hondo and Sabina, General Wool hustled his men through prairies and groves of oak, and on October 7, crossed a dry ridge and descended to the Rio Grande. At Paso de Franco ford, the Engineers went into action with their flying bridges, and men, animals and wagons crossed the river.

If the soldiers harbored any notions of riotous living in Mexico, General Wool quickly set them straight. "We have not come here to make war upon the peasantry of the country, but to compel the government of Mexico to render justice to the United States," he declared. All supplies would be paid for. Citizens were not to be molested or interfered with and depredations on persons or property would be severely punished. Wool enforced these orders.

Most of the residents of the little town on the Mexican side of the river had fled their stone and adobe houses and hid in the mesquite-covered hills. Carrying a flag of truce, the alcalde offered friendship, and informed Wool that the Mexican troops had departed. He also said that the important interior town Monterrey had fallen to Zachary Taylor, and that an armistice had been declared.

Brigadier General James Shields arrived from Camargo and confirmed the news of Taylor's occupation of Monterrey, and of a temporary truce. Though Shields had been a civilian until appointed by the President to command the Illinois Volunteers, General Wool placed him in command of the "right wing" of the Army of Chihuahua, which included Bonneville's Sixth Infantry.

General Wool decided that the truce did not include Chihuahua, his destination. The truce was due to expire in a few weeks, and Wool's army could do little perched on the border. Chihuahua lay several hundred miles west, but mountains barred the way, making necessary a circuitous route. Armistice or not, General Wool began to march on October 16. Bonneville's battalion led out.

Along the once-important Camino Real to Monclova, farms were weed-grown and houses deserted in mute evidence of Indian and bandit raids unchallenged by an unstable government. A Norther chilled the sparse prairies as the columns skirted little villages into cactus-studded hills. A panorama of the Sierra Madre filled the western sky; it was evident that the road around the mountains to Chihuahua was a long one. Desert vegetation crowded close, and the soldiers began to say that every plant in Mexico produced thorns. Past Santa Rosa del Sacramento the road mounted a maguey-grown plateau then dropped to reach sugar, cotton and corn plantations. At Monclova, the General marched the troops through the streets to the strains of "Yankee Doodle" and bivouacked on the far edge of town. The American flag was unfurled over the Governor's Palace, and General Wool made his headquarters there.

The command had behaved well, marching over two hundred miles inside Mexico with no reports of violence. Some diarists complained that General Wool was kinder to the Mexicans than to his own men—one of the edicts especially galling was the command for each soldier to shave every day, whether he was old enough to grow a beard or not. There was talk that the war was over, and the soldiers would be recalled before they reached Chihuahua. Rumors had it that General Kearny's Army of the West had already conquered Chihuahua.

Move to San Luis Potosi

Considering alternatives, General Wool sent an express to General Taylor at Monterrey, asking if it would not be wiser to remain east of the mountains. While waiting for a reply, Wool ordered drills and repairs and polishing. The "Arkansas Gazette" received word that the men were sick, homesick and disgusted.

General Taylor agreed with General Wool that Chihuahua was not destined to be a scene of action. The armistice had produced no surrender and intelligence indicated an attack might be expected at San Luis Potosi; the Army of Chihuahua was ordered to move there. In a chill and dusty wind, Wool's army set off up the valley. The temperature dropped and tents blew down atop a plateau, but soon it was so hot some of the draft mules died. The columns plodded past Venadito, Soledad and other small villages, reaching Parras the first week in December.

A persistent rumor had it that Mexican General Santa Anna was collecting thirty to forty thousand troops at San Luis Potosi. General Worth, at Saltillo with only a thousand men, heard the same rumor. On December 17, he sent a frantic express to General Wool asking for quick help. Within two hours, the First Dragoons, Major Bonneville's Sixth Infantry and Captain Washington's Artillery clattered out. Volunteers followed as front and rear guard for over three hundred wagons carrying ammunition, hospital stores and rations. Wool steered through the mountains, taking a short-cut in order to put his army squarely in the path of the expected Mexican onslaught and preclude his being cut off from Worth. Marches began at 2 or 3 a.m. and continued until long after dark. Wool's army reached the Saltillo-San Luis Potosi road in three and onehalf days.

It was a false alarm—"Worth's Stampede," some jeered. But the critics had not yet battled the Mexicans, while Worth had given good account of himself at Monterrey. Wool halted his supply wagons at La Encantada and stationed the troops farther south at Agua Nueva. When reconnaissance confirmed that no enemy was approaching, Wool and his officers rode into Saltillo to confer with Worth.

General Zachary Taylor, too, had galloped into Saltillo at Worth's summons. If Taylor seemed more irascible than usual, there was a reason: most of his plans had fallen apart. His lofty military standing had just been diminished by the War Department in Washington. President Polk had decided that the war could not be won in northern Mexico after all, and that the United States must strike Mexico City through Vera Cruz. This had been General Scott's original idea, and he had been awarded command of the expedition.

General Wool was uneasy at Agua Nueva. There were alarms: numerous campfires, which proved to be those of shepherds, an encampment of white tents, found to be sheep in a meadow. Wool moved his forces to Buena Vista where approach of enemy forces could be challenged, if, indeed, behind all the false reports, there really was an approaching enemy.

To the Mouth of the Rio Grande

On January 9, new orders scrambled Wool's tidy encampment, and Taylor's entire command as well. General Scott issued orders to the units he wanted: Major Bonneville's Sixth Infantry, Col. Harney's Second Dragoons, and some of the Engineers from Wool's army, plus the Fourth and Eighth Infantry—all to be commanded by General Worth and proceed to the mouth of the Rio

Grande to join Scott.[1] Bonneville hustled his Sixth Infantry out of Buena Vista promptly. Down off the plateau, they reached Saltillo to join Worth.

Within hours of receiving their orders, Worth's newly-organized division marched toward the Rio Grande. Lionized as the commander who had finally won the Seminole War, General Worth had spent the past several years in Florida, feted at balls and cruising the coasts on tours of inspection. A steamer was named in his honor, and when his regiment moved to Corpus Christi, his supplies came on the "General Worth." In the encampment there, quarrelling had been one of the quieter pasttimes; in a dispute with David E. Twiggs, Worth resigned in a huff, but reconsidered at the urging of General Scott. Bonneville, commanding the Sixth Infantry Battalion, served in Worth's division for the remainder of the Mexican War.

The road from Saltillo cut through farms and orchards, past cotton fields and plantings of maguey, the cactus from which was distilled the Mexican drink "mescal." Some of the ranches were abandoned, for besides past harassment by roving bandits, land-holders had lately suffered at the hands of the invading Americans. Unlike Wool, Taylor had permitted plunder and destruction, diarists noted in dismay. Past Monterrey, scarred with bullets from the September capture by the U. S. Army, Worth's columns tramped north-eastward over a dry and rocky road. From Punta Aguda the sand grew deeper, and the water holes scantier and fouler. General Worth was "nervous, impatient and restless," Quartermaster U. S. Grant would remember when he wrote his "Personal Memoirs."[2] From Camargo, Worth pushed the men over eighty miles of sand and chaparral to Scott's encampment at the mouth of the Brazos.

Bonneville found General Winfield Scott in a mightier frenzy than General Worth. Time snapped at his heels, for he must get his invading army across the Gulf and past the coast before warm weather, lest disease, not Mexicans, defeat him. No advantage of surprise was left to him, for letters had been intercepted. In addition, American newspapers were publicizing troop movements.

Subsistence, ordnance, transports—all were agonizingly slow to assemble, while Scott planned and fumed, and tried to deal with political and military criticism. In Washington, Daniel Webster and others decried the whole war effort. Taylor protested that Scott had robbed him of all his men. General Scott wanted William S. Harney's Second Dragoons, but preferred a more stable commander. In the ensuing dispute, Harney was court-martialed then restored by the harried Commanding General.

An Amphibious Landing at Vera Cruz

Chafing at delays, Scott and his staff sailed for Tampico in February to pick up more troops, leaving Worth to ship out soldiers as fast as transportation arrived.

Merchant vessels of every size and age were pressed into service. It was the season of Northers, and the small craft tossed in choppy waters as men tried to board. Designed for cargo, not passengers, the vessels were overcrowded. On February 25, General Worth's fleet moved down the coast; Bonneville and his battalion sailed on the "Elizabeth Denison." They moored at Lobos Islands, chosen for a point of rendezvous. Shiploads of volunteers from the States had already arrived, but because of a smallpox outbreak, some were not permitted to disembark.

General Scott agonized over the tardiness of his siege train and landing boats, but decided on March 3 he could wait no longer, and led the flotilla south toward Vera Cruz. Northers sent the sailing vessels skittering across the Gulf, and in three days the Army's two hundred transports anchored off Anton Lizardo Island. Navy frigates, sloops-of-war and brigs hovered near.

A howling Norther delayed the landing by a day. At dawn on March 9, the troops were ferried to the shelter of Sacrificios islands three miles below Vera Cruz. Muskets ready and bayonets fixed for charging, eighty men crowded into each landing craft, and in two long columns were towed into place for landing. At a signal, lines were cut loose and the crews rowed for shore. As soon as the boats reached the shallows, the men leaped into the surf and raced up the slopes. Major Bonneville's Sixth Infantry battalion reached the beach first. The remainder of Worth's division were on their heels, and shortly the Stars and Stripes whipped from the crest of the dunes. Picturesque mountains silhouetted the western sky, and cathedral spires rose above the city walls where citizens of Vera Cruz crowded to watch. There were other spectators: British, Spanish and French warships rode at anchor nearby to observe. Before ten p.m. the Army and Navy had landed ten thousand troops without a loss.

On the following day, choppy Northers wrecked thirty of the brigs and schooners unloading the tons of materiel. The horses were dropped from the vessels into the sea to swim and flounder through the surf. Many were lost. General Scott planned to encircle Vera Cruz and attack it from the surrounding hills. He extended his lines under harassment of guns from the city and severed the water lines.

The heavy artillery had not arrived and it would be foolhardy to attack without it. Rumors did arrive: five thousand Mexicans were ready to defend Vera Cruz; a great army was on the way from Mexico City where Santa Anna had collected formidable new columns. It was hard to pin down the truth, for Santa Anna had announced to his people that he had soundly whipped Zachary Taylor at Buena Vista. Official reports to Scott soon revealed the truth. Taylor and Wool, with the troops remaining to them had repulsed Santa Anna on February 22 at Buena Vista and sent his broken columns streaming south. But the rumor could be true that Santa Anna had indeed mustered another army and was ready to do battle. The self-styled Napoleon of the West had duped Americans during the early months of the war. Out of favor and exiled by his government, Santa Anna claimed that if he were assisted to return to Mexico an amiable treaty would soon follow. On orders from President Polk, Santa Anna was allowed safe passage through the blockade. Now he commanded the Mexican army and proclaimed himself to the Mexicans as their savior.

Warm winds swept in. General Scott weighed his possible loss of men in a quick assault and decided instead to soften the city's defenses with bombardment. The Navy loaned heavy artillery, and ferried to shore three long 32-pounders and other large guns, and lugged them within eight hundred yards from the city wall. On the morning of March 24 this great battery fired in relays, in addition to all the explosive power the Army could muster. American shells shrieked into Vera Cruz, gutting a portion and blowing a hole in the city wall. Roofs collapsed. The ground shook until the church bells rang, while flames raced through woodwork and wall hangings, to leave stark stone skeletons of once-beautiful buildings. In the night a Norther fanned the burning sections to blood-red.

On March 26, an emissary carrying a white flag emerged from a defense post. Articles of capitulation were signed the following day. Major Bonneville's battalion, with the rest of the Army, marched into the city up Avenue Independencia to the great plaza. More than five thousand surrendering Mexican soldiers laid down their arms before assembled ranks of Army, Navy and Marine fighting men of the United States. The Americans had lost nineteen soldiers with sixty-three wounded, the Mexicans slightly more.

General Scott issued a broadside in Spanish assuring citizens of their safety, and explaining that the United States was interested only in protecting her new state, Texas. He pointed out that Santa Anna had usurped the Mexican people's hard-won constitutional rights and directed the slaughter of citizens, most especially in Texas.

In the three hundred years since the Europeans had invaded the land of the Aztecs, Vera Cruz had known countless indignities. Cortez had launched his conquests here, and when Spanish-seized treasure flowed from the interior, seaborne robbers hovered like jackals to snatch the cargoes and sack the town. After the long years of struggle for Mexican independence, Spanish ships had made a shambles of the city as a last farewell. As late as 1838, the French navy had also shelled Vera Cruz for alleged Mexican misdeeds.

Battle at Cerro Gordo Pass

It was now April and time to move to the highlands before fevers began to take their toll. Scott could wait no longer, though he would travel short of artillery because he had not enough animals to pull the wheeled pieces. David E. Twiggs—Old Bengal Tiger Twiggs, as he didn't mind being called—led out his column of dragoons and artillery on April 8, setting a killing pace for the pack-burdened men following on foot. One of the brigade commanders was dapper, young General Gideon Pillow, President Polk's law partner, and, it later developed, his Excellency's private spy in Army circles. Bonneville's Sixth, with other troops still in Vera Cruz, worked to put together teams and wagons for the siege train. Rumors persisted that Santa Anna had assembled another great army, so monumental efforts were made to get the rest of the invading troops on the march.

Scouts rushed in with word that Santa Anna and six thousand men were marching to meet the Americans head on. General Scott was on his way to the front in minutes; Worth's columns, which included Bonneville's battalion, quickly followed. Out of Vera Cruz, the first thirty miles of sand and palmettos were littered with equipment the preceding troops had thrown away. The regulars believed only volunteers could be so foolhardy, and quickened their steps so they would be on hand if real fighting must be done. At Plan del Rio, Scott found Twiggs feverishly preparing to push his division out to do battle with the Mexican forces known to be in the boulders and brush of nearby Cerro Gordo Pass. The road here wound steeply up between embankments of the high hills, Atalaya and El Telegrafo. General Scott ordered a delay until reconnaissance could show the strength and placement of the enemy.

Santa Anna, though soundly defeated by Zachary Taylor's army at Buena Vista, had grandly proclaimed himself the victor. He was hurrying an army of twelve thousand men eastward from Mexico City to meet the American challenge. Deciding to make his stand at Cerro Gordo, he placed his forces in the rocky defile, with batteries on the road, on a plateau on his right front, and on the peaks Atalaya and El Telegrafo. His lancers had revealed his army's presence by peppering shots at an advance detail of Twiggs' division. Except for that circumstance, Twiggs would have met the Mexicans head on in the pass. Still unaware of the size of the opposition, Twiggs was preparing to march when General Scott arrived.

Engineers ferreted out the Mexican batteries and the possibilities of flanking them. Planning the assault, Scott ordered Twiggs' dragoons to charge the peaks. Pillow was ordered to advance on the plateau. Bonneville was assigned, with Worth's other battalions, to circle around and cut off a Mexican retreat. Early in the morning, the troops moved off the road and up the rough paths. The artillery had to be pulled piece by piece "over chasms so steep that men could barely climb them. Animals could not," Ulysses S. Grant remembered.[3] Mexican batteries on Atalaya opened fire, but Twiggs' men were able to seize the hill, though with considerable loss of life. With darkness, firing ceased, but the Engineers worked through the night to place 24-pounders atop the captured Atalaya.

At daylight the troops moved forward. Dragoons assisted by the battery on Atalaya charged Telegraph Hill. Men rushed in, and in hand-to-hand fighting the battery was taken and turned on the Mexicans as they fled. Twiggs and Worth pushed their men in pursuit. The Mexican cavalry tried to charge, but failed as Worth's column advanced. White flags fluttered and hundreds of Mexicans surrendered, but Santa Anna and half his men sped back up the road, with Worth's division peppering their rear.

Cerro Gordo was a victory for the Americans, but sixty-three Americans lost their lives; over three hundred were wounded, including young Joseph E. Johnston, recently appointed Lt. Colonel of a regiment of volunteers. General Pillow reported himself "shot to pieces" though he is recorded as only having received a slight arm wound. The dead were buried; the wounded collected in tents. Mexicans received equal care, their own records note. Writing his reports, General Scott praised all his officers and men; he was especially generous to Robert E. Lee. A fellow engineer, P.T.G. Beauregard, was said to be peevish at being overshadowed by Lee, claiming it was he who found the path around the peaks, and then been laid low with fever while Lee led the troops to glory.

General Scott moved his invasion army out quickly toward Mexico City. The road ascended toward blue snowcapped mountains, and in a few hours the troops marched into the brick streets of Jalapa. Low stone houses sat in frames of foliage and flowers, and townspeople lined the streets to watch, while church bells rang in salute. A public bath, a laundry and other delights of civilization invited the troops to linger. General Scott stayed, but ordered Worth's division to proceed to Perote.

The cottages and fields were soon left behind as Bonneville and his battalion, with Worth's division, tramped up the ancient highway through broken hills to the bluffs shouldering the continental backbone. The road became steeper, hewn out of the face of the mountains. The men camped at the summit; at daylight they marched on to Perote. At this oasis on the high plain the moated Castle of Perote dominated the town. A Mexican officer delivered the stone fortress to the conquerors. While troops toured the countryside to buy supplies, Worth and his staff, together with Col. N. S. Clarke's brigade—which included Bonneville's battalion—occupied the castle. General Worth wrote that the fighting was probably all over, since the Mexican army had been dispersed and almost all their arms captured. At about the same time, General Scott was writing from Jalapa, "Mexico no longer has an army."[4]

Puebla Occupied

Early in May, General Quitman arrived in Perote, bringing his division of volunteers and orders from General Scott who was still in Jalapa waiting for ordnance. Scott directed Worth to proceed to Puebla, ninety miles closer to Mexico City. Quitman also brought the news that since the twelve-month volunteers' terms were expiring, Scott had sent a large group home. For reasons not yet apparent, General Pillow had decided to go with them.

Worth's columns moved out promptly, passing villages and grain fields fenced with maguey. At Tepeahualco, at the foot of bare granite cliffs, a crumbling church spoke of more prosperous days. Near here ruins indicated inhabitance by a forgotten people, perhaps ancestors of the furtive, almost naked brown families who peered out of caves and rock-shelters. From Vireyes the road climbed to table lands. Now there were small corn patches nourished by streams, with villages clustered around their churches. The road climbed higher and the volcanoes of Puebla came into view.

"Captured a few prisoners in the affair at Amazoque," Bonneville noted, many years later. General Worth's division had reached Amazoque village at noon. An excited drummer boy ran in with the news that Mexican cavalry was approaching. Quick reconnaissance confirmed a force of horsemen swooping out of Puebla. Col. Clarke pondered whether to form a square to meet the assault, "whereupon Major Bonneville shouted loudly 'Lord, Colonel, back up to this stone wall, and we can whip six thousand of them!' " according to the official reports.[5] General Worth directed the Second Artillery and Sixth Infantry under Major Bonneville to "take the enemy in the flank" and after "a rapid and effective fire" the Mexican column broke and fled. "We took some prisoners and found a few dead," Worth wrote. It was learned later that Santa Anna had tried in vain to persuade Puebla citizens to defend the city. Disappointed, he had sent his infantry back to Mexico City and rode out with his cavalry to test the strength of the American columns. Met with force, he rode on.[6]

Cautious, General Worth ordered the men to spend the night in their battle positions. It began to rain, and by morning the mud was ankle-deep. A deputation from Puebla arrived and tendered the city's surrender. Mud-spattered and weary, the soldiers marched between the rock pillars of the garita through a linden-shaded alameda to the plaza.

Puebla, City of the Angels, took pride in its trees, fountains and array of churches, belled, steepled, and domed. Piled in the market place was a bounty of fruits, and superior cloth, leather goods and porcelain. But rumors flew, and Worth saw scarecrows, according to his critics. He issued a circular warning of a plot by Mexicans to poison the food.

General Scott was not pleased when he arrived in Puebla. He disavowed the poison-food circular, declaring that it was an insult to the Mexicans, and that it might also give them ideas for future action.[7] General Scott had ample reasons to be irritable. Equipment, reinforcements and money to pay the soldiers and buy supplies were overdue. Guerilla bands harassed the line of communications from Vera Cruz. Adding to the confusion, President Polk had decided to settle the war by negotiation. His emissary enraged Scott with lofty airs of secrecy, then enlisted his support in a plan to bribe Santa Anna into surrendering. Santa Anna had emerged the winner with the ten thousand dollars in cash.

Four thousand troops arrived from Vera Cruz to join the forces at Puebla. They brought pack and riding animals, over five hundred wagonloads of supplies, and a quarter million dollars in coin to pay the soldiers. The newcomers were under the command of newly-promoted Major General Gideon Pillow, whose visit to Washington had been a triumphal one. He had displayed his wound and dispensed his version of the battles of Vera Cruz and Cerro Gordo. Rewarded with advancement from Brigadier to Major General, he now outranked everyone except Scott. Old line officers who had worked and waited for decades for promotions were not pleased with Pillow's quick ascent, and would have been even more disgruntled had they known the extent of his biased tattling to President Polk.

More troops were expected to join, so the Army waited, and the Army does not wait with grace. A court of inquiry sifted through details of Col. John McIntosh's difficult journey from Vera Cruz with an unwieldy column of recruits and wagonloads of money. He had lost thirty-two men in repulsing a band of hijackers. General Worth still smarted from the dressing down he received for his management of Puebla. He demanded a court of inquiry and was further deflated when the court recommended a reprimand.

The Battle of Churubusco

General Scott's plan to take Mexico City was daring. Reports indicated the defending army far outnumbered American forces, and even if defeated, the Mexicans could scurry into the countryside to regroup. Among distant kibitzers, Britain's Duke of Wellington predicted disaster for General Scott.[8] The American army numbered eleven thousand men, though over two thousand had to be left behind in Puebla—eighteen hundred sick, plus a garrison to look after them. Generals Worth, Quitman, Twiggs, and Pillow each commanded divisions. Worth's, designated the First Division, was composed of two brigades—John Garland's Fourth Infantry and Second and Third Artillery, and N. S. Clarke's brigade of Fifth, Eighth and Sixth Infantry, the latter commanded by Major Bonneville. The siege train of a thousand wagons loaded with supplies, guns and ammunition had attracted a rabble caravan of camp followers: gamblers, jobbers, male and female adventurers. Soldiers or civilians, all were confidant they could batter down the gates and "sleep in the halls of Montezuma" as they were fond of saying.

The divisions set out at one-day intervals, marching briskly through countryside fresh with summer rain. The road was uphill, and wound around the base of Ixticcihuatl, white-tipped with snow. Off to the south, towering above its supporting range, Popocatepetl wafted smoke. A steep climb brought the troops to a camp beside Rio Frio, where frost glistened on alpine mosses and twisted pines. Llano Grande, a narrow plateau almost eleven thousand feet above sea level marked the summit, and soon a turn in the road brought into view mists floating over the valley of Mexico, and Montezuma's splendid city.

Mexico City lies in a basin, a jewel of architecture and foliage set in a filigree frame of lakes and marshes. In Montezuma's time, it was a paradise of lagoons and floating gardens, with paved causeways leading to gates in the city walls.

As the centuries passed and the lagoons ebbed, overhead aqueducts were constructed to carry water into the city. In 1847 when American troops looked down from the heights, the valley spread out in a patchwork of villages and fields, each hamlet sheltering churches and convents.

The highway led sharply down from the rim. At the edge of the valley, Scott spread out his camps for miles. Major Bonneville's Sixth Infantry, with General Worth, camped on the shore of Lake Chalco. Mexican forces hovered just out of artillery range, scouts learned; there were a few skirmishes. In one, Bonneville sent Captain William Hoffman and four companies to assist a dragoon action led by General Scott's aide, Lt. Schuyler Hamilton. Hamilton suffered severe wounds and a dragoon officer was charged with cowardice. Major Bonneville, bristling in defense of his men, appended a report commending the actions of Captain Hoffman and his command. It was an obscure episode—except that the wounded Hamilton was a grandson of Alexander Hamilton, and the story received wide coverage.

Scouts learned that a northern approach to the city around Lake Texcoco was long and well-defended. A direct push was hazardous because of heavy guns fortifying the red butte El Penon, squarely blocking the road. Possibly it was just as well the Americans did not know how well all the other approaches were fortified, not by single installations, but by successive posts. By way of causeways radiating like spokes from a wheel, Santa Anna's army could quickly reenforce any position along the protective rim of the city.

After a deceptive feint to the suburb Mexicalcingo, General Scott sent the entire army around Lake Chalco to approach the city from the south and west. Early on a cloudy August 15, Worth's division led out, with the other troops close behind. The narrow road threaded between the marshy lake and rough foothills into meadows, marked off with dikes planted to lombardy poplar and mimosa trees. Bonneville's troops camped in a cornfield. A march next day brought the columns past San Gregorio to St. Agustin, nine miles from the city. On August 18, Scott ordered Worth's men to advance, to see what could be learned of the fortifications at San Antonio, on an ancient toll road leading to the city gates. There were acres of marshes on the right, too soft for artillery, and on the left a lava field, a pedregal. Batteries were hidden in pepper trees at San Antonio, scouts found. They did not learn that even stronger firepower nestled in the walled San Mateo convent off to the side, and at a bridge over Churubusco River, two miles further on the causeway. Bonneville's Sixth, with Worth's division camped in a drizzle of rain.

Looking for a way to bypass San Antonio, General Scott sent troops to widen a path through the lava field to accommodate artillery wheels. Enemy fire from Padierna hill beyond the pedregal slowed the efforts. General Scott kept his engineers and officers busy during the night, probing, moving into position, and at daylight, American troops surprised Padierna from the rear. In seventeen minutes the Mexicans retreated. The quick rout was only the beginning of action of August 20, 1847.

To take San Antonio, General Scott planned a wide pincer movement from the sides to precede a challenge to the center. Impatient to send his men into battle, Worth ordered Garland's brigade to proceed toward San Antonio on the road, and dispatched the infantry on a rough trail through the lava field to circle around the village. Bonneville's Sixth, in the lead, found tedious marching, mostly single file, which scattered the companies. Garland's men found no resistance, for the Mexicans were scurrying from San Antonio toward Churubusco River. Rear guards covered their withdrawal. At this time the Sixth was emerging from the pedregal.

"Hearing the heavy firing, I directed myself so as to reach their flank. I advanced over fields of corn, deep canals, and upon my appearance the firing of the enemy ceased, and they rapidly retreated. I then made a rapid movement parallel to them, determined to pursue the advantage," Bonneville reported. At this point, Mexican cannon swept the Sixth with grapeshot.

"I intended to extend my command to the right and left of the road to cover themselves and hold this position until the brigade came up . . . However it was learned that the enemy had their ammunition wagons just in front, defended by only a few pieces of artillery . . . by a consideration of the advantages to be gained by preventing the enemy from getting their ammunition, and hoping too that the brigade would be in time to support me in the effort, I gave the command to charge, the bugle sounded the advance, and the colors of the regiment were in front."[9]

Mexican cannon, artillery and musket fire shrieked through Bonneville's charging columns. Men went down with ghastly screams when they were hit. What Bonneville and his superiors did not know was that Churubusco tete de pont and San Mateo convent were armed with heavy artillery and that Mexican regulars stood shoulder to shoulder in every available spot, supported by large corps of cavalry and infantry reserves. "Santa Anna had gathered here the whole of Mexico's remaining forces for what he intended to be a fight to the finish."[10]

Sgt. Frances Fox: "While we were charging . . . there was a crossfire upon us . . . I jumped the ditch . . . I looked back and saw the Major still advancing on the road, with his sword raised as if in the act of encouraging his men."

Sgt. Downs, with the color guard: "The companies then broke to the right and left of the road; all the companies in front went on to the wagons. One man was shot dead, and nine wounded at the wagons."

Lt. Simon Bolivar Buckner pointed out that the crossfire was coming from the convent. Bonneville ordered the men into the corn. The scant cover there did not stop the bullets and served only to disorganize the companies. Several men fell dead or wounded. Bonneville sent Buckner to give Hoffman, the color guard and other advance companies the order to take cover.

Captain Hoffman: "I found myself there with a very small force, and seeing no more of the regiment, I sent Lt. Buckner back to report to Major Bonneville where I was, and that I wished to be supported or recalled. We were in the presence of a very overpowering force of enemy and exposed to a very heavy fire."

Wounded in Battle

Out on the causeway, Major Bonneville was struck by grape—a cluster of cast-iron balls used as a charge for cannon. The shot went through his left sleeve and tore through his coat into articles covered with thick leather in his breast pocket. The impact caved in two of his ribs and blew him into the ditch. He was able to clamber out, dazed and in shock by the time Lt. Buckner came from the cornfield.

Lt. Buckner: "I searched for Major Bonneville and was told that he had fallen or was knocked into the ditch; I soon saw him coming out of the ditch and reported from Captain Hoffman. He said 'we must fall back.' The point where I found Major Bonneville was two hundred yards in advance of the point where I left him. He was alone at the time."

Lt. Buckner, returning to Captain Hoffman in the cornfield, found him also alone. Two or three men joined them, and they made their way back to the road. The regimental colors, directed by Hoffman off to the right were lost somewhere in the cornfield, no one could say exactly how or where. From the sides of the road where they sought the scant cover of ditches and brush, men and officers began to draw back from the deadly fire.

Captain Hoffman: "I continued to fall back. It was reported to me about this time that Lt. Bacon was wounded and lying in a ditch alongside the road."

Lt. Bacon, mortally wounded, was moved to the doorway of a small house. He beckoned to Lt. Buckner and asked for the Major. Bonneville, still dazed, crossed the road and stayed with Lt. Bacon "five or ten minutes" according to Buckner. General Worth, in the rear and unaware of the overpowering fire the Sixth had faced ordered them to charge a second time.

Lt. Buckner: "As the remnants of the Sixth moved to the road and met the reinforcements approaching, General Worth's messengers, on horseback, brought the command to join the attack. We faced about; Major Bonneville gave orders to charge and we advanced."

Major Bonneville: "The second charge was made with the same success as the first, with the same results, except that supported by the remainder of the brigade, the different parts of the regiment did not fall so far to the rear."

Captain Hoffman: "We had not advanced a great way, under direct enemy fire and a cross fire from the left when a round of shot passed through the column killing and disabling from six to eight men. At this, the column as if by common consent moved to the right, crossing the ditch into the field adjacent of the causeway. I was left on the causeway, and seeing that it was impossible to recall the men, I followed them. They sheltered themselves under some buildings."

Reserves advanced and found themselves in a storm of crossfire, with grape round shot and musketry sweeping the ground. Dead and dying men lay on the road and beside it.

Lt. Buckner: "We advanced through the cornfields in the direction of the enemy's work . . . we had but few men with us." The second rebuff was temporary, for by this time Scott had moved in with the rest of the Army. He sent Twiggs to assault the convent to stop the crossfire. Twiggs' forces charged, but had to fall back again and again before the fire. Generals Pierce and Shields, trying a flanking movement, ran into Santa Anna's reserves near Los Portales and suffered the loss of a third of the men, killed and wounded.

The Mexicans began to falter. Americans in great numbers were moving closer. Supported now on both sides, troops rushed the tete de pont once more. This time the defenders gave way, and the Americans entered the work. They managed to seize one of the big guns and turned it on the convent, making it possible for troops on the other side to storm into it and complete the capture.

The Sixth, still in the cornfield, advanced with the supporting regiments. Captain Hoffman and the men he commanded made a wide swing to the right. Closer to the road, Major Bonneville, with a fragment of his command moved forward through the shattered cornstalks.

Lt. Buckner: "The cry was raised that the enemy was in retreat. Major Bonneville and a few men entered the fort." Lt. Johnson's company and other stragglers joined.

Sgt. John Miller: "When I came into the Fort Major Bonneville was in command of part of the regiment. He was forming the regiment at that time, and soon afterward he marched on the road toward Mexico."

Sgt. Downs: When we were on the bridge Col. Harney passed with his dragoons and we had to stop to let them pass. At this time I noticed that Major Bonneville appeared very feeble or exhausted. Then we marched up to where the regiment encamped for the night. The Major ordered a list to be made out of the absent and missing, and a detail to look out for the killed and wounded . . . We were then dismissed. I went and set down on a bank, and Major Bonneville came soon after, and finding a seat about 3 yards from me sat down. I saw his coat was torn on the left breast."[11]

Bonneville apparently said nothing of his injury. Perhaps there were too many dead and dying to fuss about being blasted into a ditch. When he died, though it was many years later, his doctor certified that the cause was "Phythysis Pulmonalis," a wasting disease of the lungs "caused by a grape shot wound in the left side, fracturing two ribs."

Bonneville's Sixth spent the night along the causeway, numb with exhaustion, and shivering in torrents of rain. August 21 was burial day. There was no time nor heart to pay honors, only a grim haste to dig into this alien soil and make a sanctuary for the shattered bodies. One hundred and thirty-nine Americans were killed on August 20, and many more died later of their wounds. The First Artillery, with Twiggs, suffered many killed, including Lt. Satterlee Hoffman, young brother of Captain William Hoffman. The Sixth totalled nine men killed, eighty-three wounded, including Lt. Hendrickson, severely, and Major Bonneville, Captain Hoffman and Lt. Buckner, slightly.

Major Bonneville was ordered to move his battalion to Tacubaya. There it was learned that the garrison at San Mateo convent had included fifty American deserters. They were captured, and were slated for execution. Col. Harney's cavalry, which had clattered past the Sixth on Churubusco bridge, had chased the Mexicans to the city gates, where Captain Philip Kearny had pretended he didn't hear the "recall" and rode on until he lost an arm.

At his headquarters in the Archbishop's palace at Tacubaya, General Worth congratulated his subordinates. He shook Major Bonneville's hand and said he didn't know he had been wounded, or he wouldn't have ordered him to lead the second charge. He told Bonneville to report himself wounded.

Bonneville shrugged off the injury. He had received "a fracture in the flask" he jested, for among the articles in his breast pocket was a small canteen.

The officers hurried off their reports. Major Bonneville concluded his account: "I cannot but feel proud of the manner in which the regiment advanced until literally cut to pieces," and gave generous credit to his officers. Brigade Commander Clarke condensed the Sixth's efforts: "Major Bonneville, coming up as rapidly as ground permitted ordered an advance . . . gained the road after sharp musketry and pursued the Mexicans." Col. McIntosh who took command after Clarke was wounded, added "their list of killed and wounded will testify to their being in the hottest of the fight." Bonneville's hasty and successful, though costly charge to keep the Mexicans from salvaging their ammunition wagons was not acknowledged either in the official reports or later. It was noted, however, by a Mexican government official. Jose Fernando Ramirez wrote of Churubusco that the Mexican troops "held back the enemy at the bridge . . . But the burning of an artillery ammunition wagon, the command to retreat, and an enemy column which outflanked them determined the outcome of the struggle. Everything, everything was lost."[12]

An epidemic of quarrels ran through the regiments, as if the festering bullet-wounds and fevered broken bones spread infection from tent to tent. The Sixth was not immune from the bickering, as later it would be most painfully apparent. Mulling over the day's disasters, Bonneville may have scolded his juniors. Why did they not all follow him in the first charge toward the wagons? One company officer retorted, later, that they were ordered to advance before they were ready. Others said they could not hear the orders. Captain Hoffman in particular mounted a seething resentment: Why had he been told to take cover in the cornfield and then not supported or told to retreat? Bonneville's answer was that he told nobody to retreat "nor did they await any such orders." He could have countered: Why did Hoffman on the second charge make such a wide detour that his men found it unnecessary to fire a single shot at the enemy? Still, Captain Hoffman suffered a special grief in the death of his brother, only months out of the military academy. Another brother had died in the Florida War. His father Col. William Hoffman, who had commanded the Sixth preceding Bonneville, died at Corpus Christi as the Mexican War began.

Mexican emissaries asked for an armistice. Scott, weighing a negotiated peace against the loss of many lives, assented. While the soldiers marked time in the suburbs, their wounds and tempers festering, negotiators exchanged pleasantries in what soon became apparent was a stall for time while Santa Anna regrouped. Mexico's war for independence was fifty years later than that of the United States, and the fledgling nation had never known stability, for it had inheirted from its European landlord examples of gouging and favoritism which were not easily rooted out. Tacubaya, where Worth's division was quartered, personified the whole of Mexico to many of the Americans. It was luxurious and it was squalid; it was a garden of fruit and flowers and ancient trees, and a ruin of weed-choked fields and crumbling stone walls. Beautiful houses, graced with fountains and jasmine arbors belonged to owners whose names and culture were strictly Spanish. Poor huts housed "common Indians . . . very plain, with a humble mild expression of countenance, very gentle and wonderfully polite in their manners to each other," according to a contemporary visitor.[13]

Less than a mile north of Tacubaya lay Chapultepec Park, said to have been a favorite retreat of Montezuma, though it was the conquering Spanish who built the palace on the hill at one end of the park and on the other the Molino del Rey, and a square powder-house, the Casa Mata. Rumors flew, among them the story that the Mexicans were melting down their church bells and casting them into cannon balls inside El Molino. Not part of the rumor, but all too true was the fact that powerful weaponry was nestled inside the stone walls, with Mexican soldiers eager to trap the Yankees.

Battle of Molino del Rey

Scott had been duped by the armistice. On September 7, Mexican troops could be seen pouring out of the city to bolster defenses at Chapultepec Park and other posts on the outer rim protecting the city gates. Now, with the mockery of the armistice ended "we have all our fighting to do over again" Captain E. Kirby Smith wrote, and added "tomorrow will be a day of slaughter."[14] He spoke truly; he was slain.

General Worth was ordered to take El Molino and Casa Mata. He planned to soften the objectives with artillery, then take them with infantry muskets. Garland's brigade would storm the Molino. Bonneville and his Sixth with Clarke's brigade would seize the Casa Mata. Astir at 2 a.m., the men were in battle formation by dawn. Bombardment began. But Worth, impatient, did not wait for adequate shelling, and ordered the infantry to advance. The siege guns had to stop shelling to keep from hitting their own men. Col. Garland's brigade, attempting to storm the Molino, staggered back under a deluge of bullets which felled eleven of the fourteen officers and a like number of men. As the remainder of the troops retreated, the enemy surged after them, murdering the wounded on the battle ground.

Col. John McIntosh, commanding Clarke's brigade, fared no better. In Bonneville's Sixth, Captain Hoffman, whom Bonneville had designated field officer of the day, got off to an early huff when he arrived on horseback and had to send the mount to the rear, since orders were for the attack to be made on foot. The battery had scarcely opened when Worth ordered the brigade forward. After a few shots over the heads of the infantry, the battery had to cease. The Sixth advanced on the open plain toward the Casa Mata, where the enemy was completely protected by breastworks. The only cover for the Americans was a slight ridge of maguey just thirty yards from the Mexican line. Mexican fire peppered the plain.

Sgt. Lewis Bates: "I saw the Major in front of the battalion saying 'Forward, Sixth Infantry' with his sword up."

Sgt. John Miller: "The regiment received a great many cannon shot from the enemy . . . the regiment marched forward, Major Bonneville in front."

Sgt. McCann: "Major Bonneville was in front marching to where the enemy was behind their breastworks. He gave the orders several times to keep cool and dress on the colors."

The men wanted to answer the artillery fire, though their muskets were hopelessly out of range. The officers had to stop this and urge the lines forward to where their shots would be effective.

Sgt. Miller: "I saw Major Bonneville and other officers using every endeavor to rally the men forward. When the regiment made the charge every man was for himself for the little breastwork." In the doubtful shelter of the maguey, the Sixth opened their musket fire.

Captain Hoffman: "The low embankment was just sufficient to protect one lying close to it; several of the men were shot while lying down, and others through the head while in the act of firing. I saw Col. McIntosh lying upon the ground killed or wounded . . . Col. Martin Scott had been shot dead at my side a moment before. I told Major Bonneville that he was in consequence in command of the brigade. He replied that we were as well off there as anywhere."

Major Bonneville: "I had no idea of retreating, as I knew that a great many more men would be killed in the retreat, and that it was not by any means necessary. I saw the Fifth falling back. I was astonished and gave the word Halt as loud as I could three or four times, but it availed nothing."

Their Col. Martin Scott dead, the mangled Fifth was disintegrating. Other regiments too began to rush to the rear. The wounded Col. McIntosh raised himself on his elbow and gave the order to halt the retreat and rally on the colors.

Sgt. Steinecke: "Major Bonneville apparently did not hear it. Someone ran up and told him, then he immediately gave the word 'Halt and rally on the colors' and repeated the command again and said 'Damn it to hell why don't you halt!' "

Sgt. McCann: "Major Bonneville gave the order several times to halt. He halted but the regiment continued to retreat under enemy fire. The Major appeared cool in retreat and there were not more than six men in the rear of the Major."

Major Bonneville: ". . . the colors did halt, but the men and officers were still going to the rear and it was impossible to rally the regiment . . . which was of utmost importance to check the enemy sallying from his works."

The enemy sallying from his works whom Bonneville tried so desperately to stall, were swooping out on the battlefield to bayonet and strip the American wounded. The failure of the brigade to make a stand to protect their fallen comrades would forever haunt the survivors, though a few valiant attempts were made to rescue the wounded. Major Bonneville reported that Lt. Edward Johnson and two sergeants of the Sixth carried the dying McIntosh to the rear under severe fire.

As soon as the infantry withdrew, Casa Mata could again be shelled, and the bombardment continued until the defenders streamed out the back in retreat. General Scott had now taken charge. He ordered Major Bonneville to lead the Sixth and Eighth regiments to bolster the faltering Molino assault forces. Reinforcements from Twiggs' division arrived and helped batter in the Molino gates, though stubborn Mexican rear-guard action continued. Inside the Molino, the Sixth destroyed the gun-making foundry. But it was a hollow victory, for Mexican guns on towering Chapultepec castle still commanded the gates of the city.

One-fourth of the Americans in the day's battle were killed or wounded. Over one hundred dead were buried in a trench at Tacubaya. The wounded were gathered in wagons and taken to hospital tents. The Sixth suffered twenty-one killed and fifty-one wounded, including Lt. Rudolf Ernst, severely. In his report Bonneville praised all his officers, with special mention of Captain Hoffman and Lt. Ernst. General Scott gave the victory scant attention in his reports, possibly because it accomplished so little.[15] General Worth had wanted to continue the charge from the Molino to Chapultepec castle. Scott refused, preferring to plan, regroup and bombard first. In recriminations, Worth's supporters accused Scott of misleading Worth as to enemy strength. Scott's spokesmen pointed to Worth's negligence in taking too little time for bombardment before sending out the unfortunate infantry. In the continuing verbal disputes, no division or officer escaped criticism. Beauregard thought Lee was getting more than a fair share of the praise, and the rest of the Army thought the Engineers were all being flattered too much. Diarist Robert Anderson wrote that Army doctors treated his wound with a bread-and-milk poultice; there seemed to be not even a folk remedy for the mounting fever of disputes in command circles.

Mexico City is Captured

The United States Army camped at the gates of Mexico City. There could be no reinforcements, nor could the Army stay long where it was. The great city was the beating heart of the nation; its citizens numbered over two hundred thousand. Santa Anna's army outnumbered Scott's two to one. Moreover, the Mexicans were at home, while the Americans had only scant knowledge of the strength or location of the inner defenses. Mexican resolution to resist was evident. The fields between the causeways leading to the capitol were flooded, and numerous additional guns were wheeled into place at the gates and along the city walls between them.

In a council—which General Worth was too peeved to attend—Scott told his officers that he had decided to make a feint at the southern approaches while wheeling his main strength to attack the western gates at Belen and at San Cosme. First he would take Chapultepec hill. The Army already had a bitter taste of the guns entrenched in the castle, but Scott felt it would be foolhardy to bypass such a stronghold.

Scott planned to batter Chapultepec castle as he had Vera Cruz. If the bombardment did not produce surrender, Pillow's and Worth's divisions would come out of the Molino and charge through a cypress grove and up the hill. Storming parties with ladders were assigned to go over the walls if the castle gates could not be forced.

Batteries took positions on Saturday night. All day Sunday, September 12, shells flew at Chapultepec, but there was no sign of surrender. The divisions moved into position. Pillow was reported miffed over the arrangements; Worth was quoted as muttering about defeat and even Scott was said to have misgivings.

At dawn on Monday, September 13, American siege guns opened fire. At seven-thirty, the batteries concentrated grape and canister on the grove to clear it of enemy before the infantry charged through to assault the castle. After a five-minute lull, Pillow's forces moved out but were pinned down under cannon fire from the castle. In the scant cover of brush they were partly sheltered because they were so close under the hill the enemy guns could not reach them. But they had left the ladders behind. Frantically, Pillow sent for "Worth's whole division." Worth sent the Eighth, Sixth and Fifth Infantry, in that order, out of the Molino to rush up the hill.

Enemy fire raked them; several soldiers were killed or wounded in the grove as the men ran through the woods to gain shelter under the hill. Captain C. S. Lovell of Bonneville's Sixth remembered that the move through the woods was made in a run to get out of enemy fire. But Captain Hoffman grumbled "The advance was very rapid . . . there was no occasion for us to move so fast."

Major Bonneville: "I crossed rapidly, as the Eighth had done before me, in order to save my men as much as possible from the fire of the enemy, and arriving at the foot of the hill, I ordered them to take advantage of every obstacle to cover themselves."

The breath-catching interval was short. General Pillow was helped to the rear with an injured ankle. General George Cadwalader was now in charge at the foot of the hill, and ordered the Sixth to follow the Eighth around the hill to assist the assaulting party. Major Bonneville ordered his battalion to form for the charge.

Sgt. Frances Fox: "I saw the Major at the head of the regiment . . . I heard him call out for the companies in rear to close up." But Captain Hoffman had other ideas; he told the men to lie down. Later he would say he did not know General Cadwalader was there. Major Bonneville pointed out that at the base of the hill, the enemy fire was over their heads, and ordered the companies into battle formation. Before the last two companies were formed, Captain Hoffman gave the order to advance. Later he said that Lt. R. S. Ripley, Pillow's aide, told him to. The lagging companies, in the mounting noise and excitement, charged up the hill instead of around the base, and were separated from the battalion the remainder of the day. Or perhaps Lt. Edward Johnson and Lt. Lewis A. Armistead preferred to go in that direction and mount the parapets. They made a happy choice, for they received special mention in General Worth's report, though they disobeyed division, brigade, battalion and field-officer orders.

It was a heady interval, and all the hot-spur officers were looking for opportunities to enhance their reputations. Lt. R. W. Kirkham, Clarke's aide, shouted for the Sixth to go up to the castle. He led away, without orders from superiors, several of the regiment. Bonneville was furious at having his command scattered. "It was my intention to wait until my regiment was formed and then advance to the point designated in obedience to my orders. There was no necessity for interference." Bonneville still had with him, however, his contrary field officer, Captain Hoffman.

Captain Hoffman: "We were conducted by a staff officer around the base of the hill . . . We remained there but a few minutes before the work on the hill was carried . . . the officers and soldiers who were on the works waved their swords and hands to move forward." In retrospect he called Bonneville "dilatory" in moving cautiously while awaiting orders more authentic than those shouted by eager lieutenants.

It has been said that both the Americans and Mexicans attached far more importance to Chapultepec than its military value justified. That may be why, when the assaulting parties finally scaled the walls and battered down the doors to clamber up on the parapets and raise the flag, the intoxicating scent of victory was in the air. Regiments and companies of diverse divisions mixed and mingled as officers and men hurried on toward the final goal.

Major Bonneville: "One of General Cadwalader's staff directed me to turn the hill by the north to prevent the enemy from escaping. As I approached the road, the enemy were retreating and dispersing in all directions. I immediately gave pursuit with the portion of the regiment with me at that time." Not far from Chapultepec was a hacienda, part of which was used as a Mexican hospital. Bonneville placed sentinels over the enemy wounded and their surrendering attendants. "General Quitman overtook me at the hacienda and ordered me to collect the portions of the different corps as they advanced."

Quitman's forces, moving around Chapultepec hill had heard the shouts go up that the castle had been taken. Joined by some of Pillow's command and Bonneville's battalion they swarmed forward, intent on reaching the Belen gate. The causeway was centered by an overhead aqueduct, whose arches offered illusory protection from the garita batteries which were spitting defiance. The men inched along from arch to arch. Captain Drum advanced his battery, and supported by other artillery gained a foothold in the garita. The infantry was ordered to wait.

Major Bonneville: "The fire of the enemy now became extremely severe from the batteries in front and on the flank. Several charges were made by the enemy . . . I advanced the portion of my regiment, placing them flat upon the breastwork and around it." The Sixth were footsoldiers with muskets, but ready to add their strength to the artillery and cavalry if need be. Inside the garita, Captains Drum and Benjamin both had been killed, but their crews continued to return the Mexican fire. The investment forces held.[16]

As the Sixth crouched in the shelter of the sandbags at the garita breastwork, Major Bonneville remarked to Captain Hoffman that Quitman's forces were advancing too far for safety and might run out of ammunition. Twilight began to close in; the Belen battle looked like a stalemate. Hoffman chafed. Quitman had been ordered only to threaten the Belen gate, while Worth was to have the privilege of entering the city first, at San Cosme.

Lt. Buckner: "As I remember, just about dusk, Hoffman proposed to the Major that he should join the rest with General Worth; if we remained where we were we would have no opportunity to do anything, that General Worth was penetrating into the city, and that by being with him we would have the opportunity."

Sgt. Steinecke: "The Major spoke to General Quitman about joining the remainder of the regiment, but as near as I could understand the conversation, the general refused."

Major Bonneville: "The enemy fell back, and toward sunset the firing ceased. I now suggested to General Quitman the propriety of my uniting with the other portion of the regiment under General Worth, and between 2 and 3 a.m. he consented for me to do so, which I did about daylight."

Bonneville led his remnant of Sixth toward the San Cosme garita. There, to the dismay of Captain Hoffman and the others who still hoped to do something spectacular, the battle was over. The San Cosme garita had fallen, and by the time Bonneville and his Sixth caught up, Worth's division began to march through the city streets to the National Palace.

Meanwhile, at the Belen gate, Quitman had indeed run out of ammunition, as Bonneville feared he might. More firepower was brought forward, with plans to renew the assault at daylight. But Santa Anna moved first. He gathered his depleted forces and departed, leaving the civil government to deal with the invaders. White flags flew, and Quitman's jubilant division marched to the grand plaza and hoisted the American flag in the morning sunlight. Worth's division was only moments behind, escorting Major General Winfield Scott astride a magnificent horse, and arrayed in full dress, complete with gold epaulets and white plumes. Regimental bands blared triumphant anthems; troops cheered. The Americans were in possession of the Halls of Montezuma.

General Scott declared strict martial law and detailed military police to work with Mexican authorities in putting down disturbances. An assessment was levied on the city to provide blankets for sick and wounded soldiers.

Many of the wounded died, including Bonneville's Lieutenant Rudolf F. Ernst. On October 2, an earthquake crumbled some of the buildings. Mexicans rushed to the streets and fell on their knees to plead for safety from this new terror.

Recriminations After the Battle

In October, 1847, Bonneville fought the cruelest battle of his career. He won less than complete victory and was sentenced to be "admonished" for partial guilt in three of ten charges brought against him.

The period following the fall of Mexico City was a grim one in Army circles. Opportunities for military glory were past, and most of the disgruntled shrugged off their disappointment or mumbled their complaints to friends, in continuing Army tradition. A few, however, were not content to let their real or imagined slights wither.

Captain William Hoffman brought charges against Major Bonneville. By his own testimony, he had enlisted a number of Bonneville's junior officers to sign one or more of the specifications. Several of these officers reneged under cross-examination, and some refuted the accusations of others which they had not signed themselves. Abundant testimony upheld Bonneville—that of the remainder of the Sixth's junior officers, non-commissioned officers, and officers from other regiments who had battled by Bonneville's side. Hoffman's overriding personal ambitions were pointed out in the court martial: not the battles, not the regiment, not the rest of the Army was important, but "I," Captain Hoffman.

It has been suggested that the death of Hoffman's brother at Churubusco was somehow Bonneville's fault, but that tragic event occurred not "before Hoffman's very eyes" as some claimed, but on the opposite side of San Mateo convent where Satterlee Hoffman served with the First Artillery. Hoffman was guilty of disobedience and disparagement, yet no one brought charges against him. Perhaps it was in self-justification that he pointed an accusing finger at Bonneville. The venom he spewed to make a scapegoat of his superior officer was unworthy of his past and future record as a soldier.

The court-martial of Major Bonneville convened in the stone Convent of San Francisco. Captain S. C. Ridgely of the Fourth Artillery was appointed judge advocate. The Sixth had fought heroically in heart-breaking assignments, but a sorry list of grievances was paraded before a panel of bored judges for more than three weeks. Scores of hand-written pages of testimony in the case are preserved in Record Group 153, National Archives.

Like all specifications of courts martial of the era, those against Bonneville were damning in their rhetoric. Lumped under the insulting term "Misbehavior before the enemy" their charges were that Bonneville:

1. "Failed at Churubusco to give orders during battle and when regiment was broken, failed to take measures to reform." The verdict of the court: "Not Guilty."

2. "Ordered battalion to charge the enemy's work in columns when battalion was in much confusion and while three or more companies were too far in rear to hear orders and take part." "Guilty," the court concluded concerning this effort to plunge rapidly into battle at Churubusco to capture the ammunition wagons.

3. "Ordered battalion to advance, suffering a small portion to remain in the presence of an overpowering enemy force while remainder under his orders fell back without supporting or recalling the advance party until requested to do so." This was when Hoffman and his detachment had moved into the cornfield at Churubusco. It was at this moment that Bonneville had been knocked into the ditch by the grapeshot. Lt. Buckner, sent by Captain Hoffman to request that he be supported or recalled testified that he saw Bonneville climbing out of the ditch alone; the troops had retreated without waiting for orders from their fallen commander. Nevertheless, the court said "Guilty" on this count.

4. The fourth specification revealed the depth of Hoffman's animosity; "Separated himself and secreted himself and remained absent when he knew the regiment had been ordered to charge." Col. Clarke's aide, Lt. Kirkham, and General Worth's aide, Capt. Pemberton, had signed this charge along with Hoffman. Lt. Kirkham admitted under cross examination that the accused "moved as required" after receiving the orders. Though Lt. Buckner was one of Hoffman's witnesses, his testimony revealed that Major Bonneville was present giving orders except for the brief time when he was blasted into the ditch, plus the "five or ten minutes" he spent in the shack with the mortally wounded Lt. Bacon, and he "made no effort to conceal himself" as he crossed the bullet-sprayed road to reach the wounded lieutenant.

Bonneville's courage was stoutly defended by other witnesses, particularly the non-commissioned officers, Sgts. Downs, McCann, Steinecke, and others. Sgt. John Miller called the Major "very cool." Lt. H. M. Judah of the Fourth Infantry and Major Montgomery of the Eighth were among those vouching for Bonneville's good personal conduct. Captain T. L. Alexander, Hoffman's brother-in-law, who had signed some of the specifications but not this one, testified that he saw no desire on the part of the Major to conceal himself nor disposition to avoid duties from sense of personal danger or exposure to enemy fire. On this charge the court ruled "Not Guilty."

But General Worth, angry as he was over the whole Mexican campaign, apparently felt that here he could win one small skirmish. He and his aides had signed the fifth specification: "Failed to join the regiment when ordered by the commanding general of the division to charge enemy batteries, though within hearing distance, and was informed that the regiment was about to advance" at Churubusco. This was after the first disastrous charge, which Worth never acknowledged, and after Bonneville had been wounded. General Worth had apparently forgotten his words to Bonneville at Tacubaya after the battle, or chose not to remember them. Lt. Buckner testified, "Major Bonneville gave the orders to charge, and we advanced" but Bonneville himself said frankly of the order for the second charge "I did not hear it, nor did I see the portion of the regiment, and if I had heard it I was not capable of joining it." Bonneville's admission of physical failure during those moments no doubt contributed to the verdict of "Guilty," though the panel considered also the prestige of the complainant, General Worth.

Specification 9 claimed that Major Bonneville had made discouraging remarks at Belen gate about General Quitman having advanced too far for the safety of his troops. Captain Hoffman appeared to be the only one discouraged; others testified they were not and the panel agreed. Specifications 6, 7, 8, and 10 were general complaints: the accused did not whisk his battalion to spots better situated to give opportunity for glory to all the junior officers. The testimony of the complainants themselves confirmed that the Major had faithfully followed orders from his superiors. The court voted "Not Guilty" on these four specifications. Ironically, officers who had blatantly disobeyed orders—including the Sixth's own Lt. Edward Johnson—had found excitement and honors.

Selective deafness and amnesia emerged in individual testimonies. Few heard orders given to himself, but each had heard orders given to others. In cross examination, testimony of some of the accusers bordered on the apologetic. Neither Col. Clarke nor General Worth would acknowledge Bonneville's first quick charge on the Mexican ammunition wagons; to do so would air the questionable generalship of sending the Sixth Infantry armed only with muskets to challenge unreconnoitered Mexican fortifications. Hoffman's vindictiveness bordered on the comic: Bonneville set the pace too fast and he set it too slow. He ordered the men to take shelter or he did not order the men to take shelter—every move was wrong, according to Hoffman. Then, in spite of his lengthy testimony of faulty orders, Hoffman insisted throughout the trial that Bonneville gave no orders at all.

Some of the testimony may have assuaged Bonneville's pain and humiliation. The statements of some that they heard no "charge" order at Churubusco were refuted by the sworn testimony of Sgt. Downs of the bugle sounding, and the "charge" order given by Bonneville and repeated by Captain Hoffman and most of the other officers. Most of Lt. Buckner's testimony supported Bonneville though he had signed some of the complaints. Captain Alexander, too, had second thoughts: "I did not discover anything from his manner or appearance that induced me to suppose for a moment that he was under the influence of fear at all . . . I did not hear any order to retreat, only to advance."

But the testimony was cruel, too: ". . . heard that Major Bonneville was wounded, but it was spoken of so lightly . . . ." As witnesses droned on in conflicting pettiness for days, the court-martial resembled a shabby Roman holiday, with a lone, short, bald-pated officer for quarry. Bonneville sensed this, when he said in his closing remarks, "A victim was necessary on the ruin of whose reputation the foundation of others were to be laid . . . It is with deep distress that a time when the Army and our country are exulting in the success of our arms I have seen myself and through me my regiment arraigned before this court; its every action as a body has been sifted, and its voice has spoken its own condemnation . . . I hope they will unite with me in an effort far more creditable to restore the reputation of the regiment . . . ."

Regardless of the "not guilty" verdict of seven specifications and "guilty" of three, with the explanation that by "guilty" the court implied "only a want of due exertion and activity," the judges decreed that the accused should receive the slap "to be admonished in the Army's general orders." Bonneville suffered a hurt far worse than that in his aching chest. It was a vote of no-confidence from some of his peers, an insult to his competence as a commander, and a threat to his standing in the Army. That was exactly the goal Captain Hoffman had set out to accomplish.

By December, William Hoffman began to realize what he had done to the Sixth Infantry regiment. Reports of the battles were printed at great length in American newspapers. There was little mention of what the Sixth had accomplished, and against what odds they had been ordered. In a long letter to Army headquarters, Hoffman attempted to set the record straight: "The first gun that was fired at Churubusco was fired upon the 6th Infantry . . . the fire upon us was terrible, both direct and from the convent on the left . . . with the small force that we had, unsupported, it was impossible that the attack against the tete de pont could be successful."[17] Hoffman wrote much more, but his attempt to recapture the luster that had been the Sixth's availed little, for most veterans would remember that regiment as the one in which the officers trampled their own glory in the dust.

In another footnote, when brevets for meritorious service were handed out, the junior officers of the Sixth Infantry received a generous share. Major Bonneville had recommended each for brevets, Captain Hoffman for two.

Chapter Six
1848-1855

Stateside and Columbian River Commands

Return from Mexico to Fort Gibson

On November 1, 1847, Major Bonneville left Mexico City in a convoy bound for Vera Cruz. Columns of wagons and men extended for miles, and included the wounded who had recovered enough to go home. Because Mexican guerrillas continued active, the caravan could travel only as fast as the slowest units, adding to the fatigue and disenchantment of war's end.

November winds chilled the plateau and whined through the forests lining the road toward Rio Frio pass. At Puebla the Mexicans were less cordial than they had been in summer. Pueblans had good reasons for being edgy; in September, after leaving Mexico City, Santa Anna had harassed the American garrison there for weeks. The road skirted villages into the pass of LaHoya. Past Jalapa's fruit and flowers and through the battlefield of Cerro Gordo, the great wagon train creaked at last to the sands of Vera Cruz.

Josiah Gregg was in New Orleans as the steamer "Alabama" from Vera Cruz docked on November 24. He wrote of the arrival of Generals Quitman and Shields, Col. Harney and Major Bonneville, allowing them the adjective "gallant" and noting the "great stir" made to welcome them home. He conceded that this attention was merited, but scoffed at the fuss over Zachary Taylor, now frankly a candidate for president of the United States.[1] A reception at the St. Charles hotel honored Quitman, Shields and Harney, according to the newspapers. Bonneville was not mentioned. He may have hurried back to his family.

Margaret Bonneville lay in Calvary cemetery in St. Louis. She had died on the day Bonneville marched with Wool's army into Monclova, October 30, 1846. The "St. Louis Daily Union" reported the death "after a long and painful illness, Madam Margaret B. Bonneville, a native of France, at a very advanced age. Madam Bonneville has been a resident of the city for many years, and is well known for her excellent qualities, for kindness and charity . . ." After Marie Therese Chouteau's death, Margaret had lived at 8th and Walnut Streets. What disposition was made of her possessions and literary materials is not recorded.

Ann, her little daughter, her mother and aunts were living in Philadelphia, and it was not a light-hearted season for them. Archibald Campbell had died, leaving Ann's sister Agnes Elizabeth with two children, Robert G. and Mary. Soon after Bonneville arrived, Ann's mother Mary Irvine Lewis "died suddenly," according to family records. The Irvine Philadelphia home was at 431 Market Street; Ann's grandparents had lived for many years in this neighborhood of the sturdy red-brick Pennsylvania State House known, since 1776, as Independence Hall.

Bonneville was still ailing from his wound, and wearied from his journey. The cloud on his reputation arrived home almost before he did; a busybody contemporary saw to that. The "Arkansas Intelligencer" of December 22, 1847 reported "We have been furnished with the proceedings of a general court martial held in Mexico City in which Major Bonneville was tried for misbehavior before the enemy. He was found guilty of the charge, the court understanding it to mean only a want of due exertion and activity and sentenced to be admonished." What part of the "proceedings" did the tattler furnish? Not all the scores of handwritten pages, obviously, since of the ten charges, Bonneville was found wanting in only three. The Van Buren editor did not completely swallow the story, for he added "Major Bonneville is well known to our citizens and has always been regarded as a brave and excellent officer."

Bonneville's discomfiture was overshadowed by more momentous military quarrels. During the autumn, letters belittling General Scott and extolling Generals Worth and Pillow gained wide circulation in stateside newspapers. Scott was outraged at "such despicable self-puffings." Pillow and Worth sputtered in return, and General Scott placed them in arrest. Courts of inquiry into the charges and countercharges were pending.[2]

General Kearny's Army of the West, too, emerged with more publicity of the quarrels of the command than of the fact that they had won for the United States the area later comprising Colorado, Utah, New Mexico, Arizona, Nevada and the glittering prize, California. As ordered, General Kearny had led his men to Santa Fe and across desert country to the coast. Major Philip St. George Cooke, also in Kearny's army, commanded five hundred volunteer infantrymen, the Mormon Battalion, who trudged in the dusty wake of the horse-soldiers, and when they arrived on the coast had completed the longest infantry march in history. Released from duty in California, most of the Mormons set out over the Sierras for Salt Lake desert country, where disciples of the slain Joseph Smith were attempting to gain a new foothold.

The Navy had helped seize California, and Commodore Robert F. Stockton considered himself in command of the prize. General Kearny disputed Stockton's claim, particularly his appointment of thirty-four-year-old John C. Fremont as governor of California. General Kearny, as Fremont's superior, ordered him back to the states, and there accused him of mutiny, disobedience and unsoldierly conduct. The court-martial, in session as Bonneville returned from Mexico, enjoyed wide publicity.

> Major Bonneville, U. S. Army, arrived on Tuesday last, on his way to Fort Gibson to take command. Major Bonneville will accept our thanks for the packet of papers he brought up for us. — "Arkansas Gazette," February 23, 1848.

Companies of dragoons and Sixth Infantry comprised the garrison at Fort Gibson, and the post had been improved since Bonneville left it. A visitor wrote, ". . . a pretty place, the fort itself with its blockhouses, the palisades with their heavy wooden gates, all newly whitewashed. Within this enclosure was a little burying ground carefully protected and tastefully adorned with trees and shrubs."[3] The cemetery had been augmented by victims of the late war, for the government lost no time in exhuming the dead and shipping them home. The bodies of Lt. John D. Bacon and Lt. Satterlee Hoffman had arrived by steamboat in December, according to the "Arkansas Gazette." Bonneville's friends could be forgiven if they concluded that the report of Bonneville's court-martial presented to the Van Buren "Intelligencer" in December was delivered by the escort of deceased Lt. Hoffman.

Post-War Events; A New Bonneville Proposal

"Court of Inquiry Finds Fremont Guilty of Disobedience of Orders," the "Arkansas Gazette" headlined in late February. It had been the bitterest military trial since General Wilkinson was charged with treason for trying to sell the Mississippi Valley some decades past. General Kearny found himself vilified and slandered while defendant Fremont was pictured as a far-visioned patriot by his father-in-law, Senator Benton. Nevertheless, the court found Fremont guilty of all charges and sentenced him to be discharged from the Army. President Polk ordered Fremont released and reinstated. The family's pride salved, Fremont resigned his commission.

The "Arkansas Gazette" quickly dropped the Fremont affair and turned to current news. Steamships were crossing the Atlantic in fifteen days. Minor heroes pounded the lecture circuits detailing the conquest of Mexico. France had writhed in another revolution and was trying again to be a republic. John Jacob Astor died in New York, ending the era of fur-trade empire building. He bequeathed half a million dollars for a New York City library; Washington Irving served as director. Trapper-turned-Oregon-citizen Joe Meek made headlines when he arrived in the Washington, D. C. with news of an Indian massacre of missionary Marcus Whitman and his family near Fort Walla Walla. Among the victims were his own half-Indian daughter, Helen Mar Meek, and also Mary Ann Bridger, daughter of Jim Bridger.

It was election year, but ailing James K. Polk declined another term. Stocky, be-wigged Lewis Cass was the Democratic nominee, though his chances were diluted by Martin Van Buren's come-back try. Zachary Taylor won the Whig nomination. His chief rival, Winfield Scott, had been ordered to face charges in the Pillow affair. Almost lost in the clashes was the fact that the Treaty of Guadalupe Hidalgo made its way through negotiations and confirmations. It gave back to Mexico the occupied capitol and all the territory south of the Rio Grande, officially ending the Mexican War.

In early 1848, few citizens appear to have grasped the potential of the vast tract won in the Mexican conflict. One who did was Major B. L. E. Bonneville, still ailing but commanding at Fort Gibson. "Here I brought to notice that the best route to cross the continent was from Fort Smith up the Canadian to Santa Fe," Bonneville wrote.[4] He had probed the Canadian River and was knowledgeable about the trade route from Fort Smith to Santa Fe. He also knew that Kearny's army marching to southern California had encountered no mountain passes. Foreseeing a migration of homeseekers, Bonneville urged development of a Fort Smith-to-Santa Fe road as the best and straightest way to the Pacific. It may be that the urge to walk to the west was beginning to beset him once again. But he would need first to recover his health, and also to reach a wider, more influential circle for a new dream beginning to take shape.

Recuperating in the East

"Major Bonneville, U. S. Army, arrived on Saturday from Fort Gibson. He leaves today for a tour of the east for the good of his health," the "Arkansas Gazette" of June 21 reported. In July and August, Bonneville reported to the Army from Carlisle, and his health apparently improved in his family circle. Carlisle Barracks overflowed with cavalry recruits training for duty in the vast new areas of the nation. Major Philip St. George Cooke, recovering from his march to the Pacific with General Kearny and his harsher ordeal as Kearny's "co-defendant" in the Fremont court-martial, commanded there. The paths of Cooke and Bonneville had crossed a number of times; now both officers were struggling to regain their resources of body and spirit, for the future in their profession appeared to hold considerable promise.

The Bonnevilles traveled to Monroe County, Virginia, in early autumn. Besides the advertised curative powers of its mineral springs, this verdant area was Ann's birthplace where Grandfather William Lewis had built a fashionable spa. Like other popular resorts in the area, Sweet Springs Spa's mineral waters were touted as cures for "all varieties of Fever, Plague, Dyspepsia, Die-of-anything, Gout, Gormandizing and Grogging . . . and all other diseases and bad habits except smoking, spitting and swearing."[5]

Business, politics, gossip and fashion were fully discussed at the vacation resorts. In the late summer of 1848, wild rumors added new and exciting dimensions to the plans of many. It was said that gold had been discovered in California, not just a trace, but fabulous quantities of nuggets lying about for the taking. Always intriguing to the adventurous and land-hungry, California had enticed Americans even while it belonged to Mexico. Now, with news of a rich gold strike, almost everyone wanted to get there.

Disappointment: Arbuckle Gets Even

Scores of pioneer caravans had followed the trapper trails to Oregon; the Mormons had veered off to their new promised land, Utah. Bonneville knew better than anyone that the Oregon Trail was a summertime road, and the formidable Sierras barred the way to California, though a few companies had taken wagons through. The sea route around the Horn took six months; Central American passages held tropical dangers. In spite of its desolate stretches, General Kearny's road to California via Santa Fe was the most promising. Some gold-seekers thought the government should help them, and Bonneville's promotion of a Fort Smith-to-Santa Fe-to-California road took wings with the notion that he could stake out the road westward. Disabilities put aside, he plunged into action. From Carlisle he wrote letters to Fort Smith's newly launched weekly the "Herald" and other newspapers enumerating the advantages of a route west from Fort Smith.

"It is shorter, more level . . . can be traveled earlier in spring and later in fall. The Canadian River affording quantities of sweet cottonwood rushes and winter grass enables parties of size to travel at all seasons. Even when the prairies are burnt, the Canadian bottoms are always safe . . ."[6]

From the Cavalry Training School at Carlisle, Major Philip St. George Cook also wrote public letters endorsing the route, citing his successful trek, with wagons, as part of Kearny's army. General Kearny could not add his appraisal for he died in October. General Matthew Arbuckle, in one of the few non-negative pronouncements of his career, added his support; John Rogers spearheaded the efforts of Fort Smith boosters.

Arkansas Senator Borland plumped for a federally funded highway from Fort Smith to Santa Fe, and also pointed out that a transcontinental railroad could be easier built at lower latitudes than the one being promoted from Lake Michigan to Oregon. With such dedication to his home state, he won reelection easily in November. Zachary Taylor won the presidency, chiefly on his military reputation, for it was widely believed he had never lost a battle. His critics opined that his victories had all been accidental including the three-way contest which gave him the presidency, but many saw him as a homespun leader who could handle any situation. President Polk, in his last message to Congress in December, 1848, officially announced the rich gold strike in California. Actually, the find had been made almost a year previously by James Marshal, at Sutter's Fort. The gold rush had already begun.

Armed with a memorial from the Arkansas legislature requesting aid for their California road project, Bonneville and Senator Borland tackled Secretary of War W. L. Marcy at Washington, D. C., and before long the Senate committee of military affairs recommended a survey of the route. Bonneville's hopes soared when he received this order: "Sir, you will report to Fort Smith, perhaps for special service. If not, rejoin your regiment."

Bonneville wrote, many years later, "Went to Washington City—with the assistance of Senator Borland obtained a small escort to establish my long cherished idea and was ordered to report to General Arbuckle for that duty."

Bonneville hurried to Arkansas where California-bound gold-seekers already overflowed Fort Smith and Van Buren. At night, campfires glowed in tent-towns and excitement mounted as the days lengthened and spring winds blew in.

General Arbuckle was informed in early March that Congress had indeed appropriated money for the road survey. Possibly, too, Arbuckle received other instructions, or possibly his next moves were his own idea. He sent for Captain Randolph Marcy, nephew of the retiring Secretary of War, and awarded him the special service of commanding the military escort and the survey.

"He gave the command to Captain Marcy," Bonneville wrote, and added, "Dr. Bailey asked if I would permit him to see General A. on the subject . . . I told him no. I would not beg for what I had originated and brought thus far successfully. I had started it, and now if he determined to give the feather to another he could do so. I would not petition for what was mine . . . ."[7]

Residents of Arkansas presented a memorial asking that Bonneville be named commander of the expedition. It was to no avail. An editorial printed in several newspapers protested: "The hopes and wishes of the people of Arkansas have been dashed to the ground by the apparent fact that Col. Bonneville was not appointed to command the expedition . . . But the devotion of Col. Bonneville to the interests of Arkansas, his long residence among us, and above all his promotion of the route pointed to him as qualified in every respect, but the fates are against him. Bitterly and sadly goes he from us now, keenly stung with disappointment. May his pathway be bright, and his future career brilliant and honorable, and long will he be cherished in our memories as a gallant soldier and sincere friend."[8]

A New Assignment: Fort Kearny

Bonneville reported to regimental headquarters at Jefferson Barracks and was shortly on his way to a new assignment, Fort Kearny on the Platte River. Commanding three companies of Sixth Infantry, he set out from Fort Leavenworth on May 10. To Bonneville, the road west was a far cry from the trail of seventeen years before. Now, hundreds of people with wagons and herds of cattle churned up the prairie. As of old, small bands of Indians watched from the horizon, weighing their chances of levying toll. There were remembered streams, the Vermilion and the Blue; all the creeks now had names, including one called Wyeth. Littering the way were broken axles and bones of horses and oxen, and as the trail lengthened, cast-off furniture and baggage—debris marking disintegrating dreams. There were graves at almost every camping spot, some partly dug out by wolves, some carefully heaped with stones and bearing pathetic inscriptions. There were a few returning travelers, faint of body or spirit or resources, creeping contritely back home.

Rough ravines flattened to plateaus, and from a ridge, the Platte Valley came into view. The meandering river with its belt of cottonwood trees and numerous islands appeared to have no beginning and no end. Fort Kearny's mud-walled buildings blended into a stark panorama of wide blue sky and endless brown earth. The first Fort Kearny, many miles to the east (Nebraska City) had been abandoned and the name given to this post at the head of the

Grand Island of the Platte, a better location to serve Oregon Trail travelers. There were two adobe and two sod buildings, plus a storehouse and stables. On the night Bonneville and his companies arrived, May 29, a near-typhoon flattened hundreds of camps along the Platte.

Lt. Col. W. W. Loring and a sizeable corps of Mounted Rifles arrived. They were assigned to travel the Oregon Trail to the Columbia. Quartermaster Osborne Cross and artist George Gibbs both wrote journals of their trip, though their commander did not; Loring had lost an arm at the gates of Mexico City. Loring's Mounted Rifles were "most hospitably received by the officers," George Gibbs wrote, though he added that the turf-walled quarters were "almost uninhabitable in wet weather." Quartermaster Osborne Cross wrote, "While at Fort Kearny I had occasion to converse frequently with Col. Bonneville the commander of the post. He had been many years ago among the Indians in the Rocky Mountains and had obtained while there much valuable information . . . I found it, in more than one instance before reaching the Columbia River, of great importance."[9]

Almost six thousand wagons passed Fort Kearny during the spring of 1849. Most of the travelers were greenhorn gold seekers; the post area looked like a huge dumping ground of broken and discarded gear. To lighten their loads, some even threw away food, and when wood became scarce, they used their bacon for fuel. Some of the sojourners were so innocent of the country ahead they disdained counsel, but most were eager for advice. The *Adventures of Captain Bonneville* was used by some as a guidebook, though Irving's reputation as a teller of tales had shed a fictional glow on the volume. Oregon settler Joel Palmer had published a journal; Mormon pioneer William Clayton's guide was detailed and accurate. John Charles Fremont's reports of his western expeditions contained trustworthy information of mileage and terrain, and provided a glimpse of the young officer as a careful pathmarker rather than a brash opportunist rushing to glory. In the glory department Fremont had fared well in spite of the court-martial. He was off on another expedition to explore the Colorado Rockies, financed by businessmen who envisioned a transcontinental railroad straight along the 39th parallel.

Captain Howard Stansbury wrote in his journal, in June, "Called on Col. Bonneville, whose adventures among the Rocky Mountains are so well known to the world. He received us very courteously, offering us every facility in his power in furtherance of our progress." Stansbury, with a detachment of engineers was assigned to survey the Great Salt Lake and its valley.[10]

Incoming travelers brought news of a disastrous fire in St. Louis. A steamboat burned, and fire spread to other vessels moored along the docks. Flames leaped to freight stacked near and raced westward up Locust Street to Market Square, destroying fifteen blocks. Years later it would be reported that many of Bonneville's records, mementos and perhaps even the original manuscript of his western journal were destroyed in a warehouse fire in St. Louis. Which St. Louis fire took his property is hard to guess; there were many. There was other news: James K. Polk had died of cancer. Death thinned Army officer ranks too. In a bleak Texas encampment, cholera claimed Major General William Jenkins Worth. Assigned to command the southwest frontier, he had reached the forks of the Trinity River and had begun to build a post on the bluffs. The post and the city there later were named Fort Worth.

Promotion to Lt. Colonel of the Fourth Infantry

Mail from the Adjutant General's office brought Bonneville notification of his promotion to Lieutenant Colonel in the Fourth Infantry and orders to report to headquarters. Army headquarters in 1849 were in New York City instead of Washington, D. C. for the reason that General in Chief Winfield Scott preferred to maintain distance between himself and his erstwhile subordinate, President Zachary Taylor. Like many, Winfield Scott returned from the war sick, weary, and disillusioned. After the military tribunals had finished sweeping the Pillow affair under the rug, General Scott took his headquarters staff to Fort Columbus on Governor's Island. New York society healed his scars and the city's press gave proper coverage to his ideas, applauding, in 1849, the notion that since the British parliament was mistreating the Canadian provinces, they might, with proper encouragement, join the United States.

Bonneville's new assignment was command of Madison Barracks at Sackett's Harbor on Lake Ontario. One company of Fourth Infantry, a chaplain, a surgeon and a few junior officers comprised the garrison, a total of sixty in a spacious brick and stone post designed to accommodate one thousand men. In the hindsight of 1816, Madison Barracks was built on a bluff overlooking the bay to bristle her guns at intrusions from Canada across the lake. The last action there had been in 1812 when one American vessel turned back five British warships. The land forces—farmers and lumbermen—old-timers remembered, had only 24-pound cannon balls for their 32-inch "Old Sow," so they wrapped them in carpeting to make them fit and drove out nine hundred soldiers who had landed from British ships.

The village streets of Sackett's Harbor were wide and shady, with homes of brick or stone, for as in most saw-mill towns, fires had destroyed the frame buildings. Fragrant smoke from the saw-mills floated through the trees, and a plank road led eleven miles eastward to Watertown. Winters were frosty and glistening, with sleigh-rides and checkergames for recreation, according to a contemporary quartermaster, Captain U. S. Grant.[11] Ann and Mary probably joined other officers' families at Madison Barracks.

To the surprise of some, President Zachary Taylor declared a national day of prayer because of epidemic fevers. The President had matured on his new battlefield. As his grasp of national affairs developed, so, too, did his determination to control the forces that had begun to splinter the nation. Admirers of the sturdy warrior have ventured the opinion that his firm hand might have guided the opposing factions into settlement before their passions led them into civil war. But history is full of might-have-beens. Zachary Taylor died of an "intestinal ailment" on July 9, 1850. Millard Fillmore became President.

Letters from California gold-seekers to the folks at home began to appear in the newspapers. Some acknowledged homesickness; one wrote sourly that San Francisco was cold all year. But even the most barren of western spots seemed to have potential: the Mormons displaced from Nauvoo, Illinois, had reportedly developed farms and a thriving city on the shores of the Great Salt Lake. The new Mormon leader, Brigham Young, urged stateside members and new converts arriving from Europe to gather in this newly created Zion. "Persuade all good brethren to come, who have a wheelbarrow and faith to roll it over the mountains" the "Arkansas Gazette" quoted Young as saying in October, 1850. Many of the Mormons did just that, pulling their belongings over a thousand miles in two-wheeled "handcarts" drawn by manpower, and, presumably, faith.

A New Post: Wisconsin's Fort Howard

In the spring of 1851, Lt. Col. Bonneville was ordered to Fort Howard on Lake Michigan at Green Bay. It is likely that he traveled to his new station by water because Green Bay, Wisconsin, had only lately been conveniently accessible in any other manner. It is likely, too, that his family accompanied him for the pleasant journey. Passenger vessels were all steamers in the 1850s, fitted out for comfort with salons and dining rooms. From Sackett's Harbor, the New York shores were wooded, with clearings for wharves at small towns like Oswego. Leaving Lake Ontario, vessels by-passed Niagara Falls by way of the Welland Canal on the Canadian side and followed the long southern shore of Lake Erie. Detroit, originally the Frenchman Cadillac's trading post, belched smoke and steam and bustled with Great Lakes traffic of farm produce and lumber. The French had built a post in the river waterway into Lake Huron and in 1851 narrow water-front farms still lined the shores. It was said that the Yankees told the French farmers that the first steamboats were pulled by sturgeon, and that the Frenchmen believed it to be true. Fort Gratiot, built in 1813, pointed its guns toward Canada.

Lake Huron, named for a vanished Indian tribe, had been an important waterway from French Canadian settlements to the heartland of French America. At the Straits of Mackinac the deep channel between Lake Huron and Lake Michigan washes sharp-faced cliffs where gales smashed many ships against the rocks in the scores of years since Nicolet's crew paddled through to what they thought would be China's shores.

On June 24, Col. Bonneville arrived at Fort Howard on a western arm of Lake Michigan. Here, too, one company and officers lived in a post designed to accommodate whole regiments. Like other forts on the Great Lakes, the site on the west side of Fox River had first been a French fur-trade post, then had belonged to the British until the Americans pre-empted it in 1816. Because access by boat was not strictly convenient for moving household items, departing officers had left furnishings, and the quarters resembled a curio shop of past commanders. Townspeople remembered that some were pleasant, while some quarreled with local leaders. In 1817, Zachary Taylor had entertained with dinners, balls and concerts. David Twiggs was a martinet; Hugh Brady attended balls in full dress, but with silver spurs on his boots. George Brooke's wife sponsored religious functions but frowned on theatricals.[12]

The transition from fur-trade paradise to leadmine bonanza to farm-land prosperity had swept Wisconsin to territorial status in 1836 and statehood in 1848. Shiploads of lumber, wheat and meat steamed out past the stone lighthouse. In the bustle of commerce, Indian threat or British invasion seemed ludicrous, and the Lt. Colonel with his company and a half in the rambling fort an anachronism. Nonetheless, Bonneville began at once to repair and tidy up Fort Howard. Teamsters, woodcutters and carpenters augmented the military in refurbishing the works, according to post returns.

This was a choice interlude for Bonneville, Ann, and eight-year-old Mary. Little girls wore ruffled and beribboned dresses in the middle of the 19th century, with peek-a-boo pantaloons and crinoline petticoats in imitation of the billowy skirts of the ladies. A proper schoolgirl wore a snood to keep her hair neat, and an apron over her dress. Schoolchildren in the 1850s learned to read in the delightful *Illustrated Reading Books* published by William McGuffey. The lilting song *Oh Susannah* was on the lips of young and old. It had been written by a young Cincinatti bookkeeper, Stephen Foster, whose images of a lively Southern style of life became more appealing after Congressmen Henry Clay, Daniel Webster and others hammered out a solution to the slavery arguments between Northern and Southern states. Called the "Compromise of 1850," the measure settled the slavery question, many proclaimed.

At Fort Howard, few military tasks remained. In October, a detachment traveled to Lake Powaygonnee to preserve order at annuity time, though except for the use of white men's vices, the Menominees had a reputation for peace.

Transfer to the West Coast

In May, 1852, Bonneville spent two weeks at a court-martial at Fort Gratiot. On his return a letter from Army headquarters awaited him. To the delight of most of the Fourth Infantry, the entire regiment was ordered to the west coast. In a matter of days, Bonneville had Fort Howard boarded up, ordnance put in storage. With subsistence supplies for the steamship journey to New York, Bonneville, his sixty-eight men and a citizen physician embarked on the "Julius D. Morton," bound for New York City.

At Fort Columbus, Bonneville found heavy responsibilities. Col. Whistler, apparently one of the few people who did not want to go to California, had secured a leave of absence, and Bonneville as Lieutenant Colonel inherited the task of shepherding the regiment to the Pacific coast. He was handed Whistler's letters of instruction—some of them weeks old—and began the task of securing transportation for seven hundred men and officers, including two dragoon companies. While he tried to fill demands already made, Bonneville received more instructions, some conflicting with previous orders. He must requisition the necessary transports. No, a steamer had already been chartered. The steamship line would furnish subsistence for the men. No, you will see that the requisite supply of Army rations be provided. More changes: "Six or seven companies of the regiment will proceed to California via the Isthmus of Panama . . . The remaining companies and Dragoon recruits will proceed via Cape Horn."

In view of the cholera situation, a crossing of the Isthmus in July was foolhardy. Some felt that General Scott would not have approved such a journey, but he was busy as Whig candidate for President of the United States. Dr. Charles S. Tripler, medical chief of the Fourth, warned the surgeon general that the trip would be murder. He was assured that there was no danger because the soldiers would move too fast for the disease to catch them.

Bonneville's arrangements for his family can only be conjectured. Ann's cousin, Dr. William Irvine, maintained a home at 190 Second Avenue in New York City for his young daughters; the Bonnevilles may have said their goodbyes there. Without a doubt, Bonneville would not even consider taking Ann and Mary across the steaming Isthmus. Bonneville was fifty-six years old. Perhaps he thought this would be his last far-away assignment, and he could have a permanent home. On June 18, 1852, he purchased from Louis Chouteau Smith a building lot on 6th Street in St. Louis. He "erected a double residence on the lot having a single center wall, each residence having about 12 rooms in 1852."[13] If this information is correct, the arrangements were made by mail, since post returns show Bonneville was not absent from his Army duties in 1852.

More problems surfaced at Fort Columbus. The men had not been issued promised supplies of clothing. In answer to Bonneville's complaint: "The General in Chief is astonished to learn that you have not been supplied . . . The want of clothing must not, however, delay the departure . . . you will embark with the portion of your regiment that proceeds by Panama on the 5th inst." Captain U. S. Grant served as regimental quartermaster; if the fault was his, the records do not show it. Grant, like Bonneville, was leaving his wife behind. The Grants had a son, and were momentarily expecting another child.

Cholera in Panama

Bonneville's final orders arrived by "Telegraphic Dispatch." In a last minute change, transportation was on the Aspinwall side-wheeler "Ohio." Quartermaster Grant complained that the old ship had already secured a full complement of passengers and the "addition of over seven hundred to this list crowded the steamer most uncomfortably."[14] Some found the voyage exciting. Delia B. Sheffield, the sixteen-year-old bride of a sergeant, remembered "I was wild to go . . . separation seemed an eternity to me then, and besides I wanted to see the wonderful West."

"The weather was delightful during the voyage from New York. We were very pleasantly entertained each evening by the concerts given by the 4th Infantry band. We also had dancing and card playing and during the day we watched the whales that follow the ship. Lt. Col. Bonneville, the commandant of the 4th Infantry, although a most gallant and experienced officer was of a somewhat testy temper . . . a small man . . . in the habit of pacing the deck, cane in hand, during the greater part of the day . . ."[15]

Blue hills appeared in the south on July 13. The "Ohio" steamed into Navy Bay—Columbus had named it Bay of Ships, for he believed it big enough to hold all the vessels of the world. At Aspinwall history was current. New York businessman Wm. H. Aspinwall had secured a concession from the government of New Granada, Colombia, to build a railroad across the Isthmus. With the discovery of gold in California, Aspinwall's small dream became an important project. Aspinwall, later renamed Colon for Columbus, was built on stilts over a swamp. Swarms of insects attacked nose, mouth and eyes; Captain Grant, wrote "I wondered how any person could live many months in Aspinwall and wondered still more why anyone tried."[16]

The reason was gold fever, searing hot in the early 1850s. Scores of workers had died on the railroad project—a life for every cross-tie, it would be said. In 1852, the track reached only twenty miles up the Chagres. Before they were put aboard a train to carry them to the end of the line, Dr. Tripler warned all personnel not to drink native products and to avoid personal contacts with inhabitants. The first miles of railroad bridged Black Swamp where tons of boulders had been dumped into the mire to form a roadbed. From the thatched-roofed village Gatun, the railroad followed the Chagres—Columbus had named it River of Crocodiles. Besides the crocodiles and the profusion of monkeys, early travelers found other jungle denizens; the chilling night cries of puma inspired the naming of Lion Hill and Tiger Hill along the river's courses. There were bright-plumaged birds and "brilliant butterflies . . . like blossoms blown away," according to an 1850s visitor, Bayard Taylor.[17]

In a riverside cottage near Bohio Soldado lived John L. Stephens, a partner in the Aspinwall railroad company. Stephens had been sent by President Van Buren in 1839 to Central America to look into the possibilities of a canal to connect the Atlantic and Pacific. He reported the Chagres valley route the most likely, then tarried a dozen years to write about the ruins he explored in Chiapas and Yucatan. When Aspinwall needed an influential partner for negotiations with the Colombian government, he persuaded Stephens to become president of the railroad company. Stephens secured generous terms and stayed on to assist in the monumental task of building a railroad through the jungle.

Past Stephens' cottage the train reached the end of the line, and the Fourth Infantry was deposited on the bank of the river. Leaving Captain Henry

Wallen's company to escort the fifty or so women and children and travel at the slower pace of Quartermaster Grant's loads of gear, Bonneville hurried the other seven companies upriver in bungo boats. Each boat carried thirty to forty passengers, and were poled against the current by near-naked natives. Here the Chagres valley was enchanting. "The river, broad, and with a swift current . . . winds between walls of foliage that rise from its very surface . . . the gorgeous growths of eternal summer . . . jungles of cane and gigantic lilies, cocoa . . . superb palm . . . blossoms of crimson and purple and yellow . . . streamers of fragrance," Bayard Taylor wrote.

At Gorgona, Bonneville hustled his men out of the bungo boats and up the trail to Panama. Balboa was said to have gone this way on his journey to the mountain-top where he saw the Pacific. There had been a cobbled road—the King's Highway—across this waistland of the continents and it was said that the conquistadors sent more gold over it than all Europe possessed. Now the Camino was crumbled, like the Spanish empire itself, and the moss-grown stones were brown with long-spilled blood. Many of the natives, black people called Cimarrones, were descendants of slaves who had picked up their chains and yokes silently and escaped into the jungle while their whip-masters slept. It was said the Cimarrones would not go near the trail at night because it was haunted by the ghosts of slaves who died there pulling carts of gold.

The spectre that pursued the Fourth was cholera; rumors flew of the dread plague, and Bonneville urged his soldiers over the trail so fast that some of them discarded their bedrolls and knapsacks. From Cruces to Panama the twenty-eight-mile trail led over a rocky backbone. On the landward approach to Panama village a stone wall with fortifications of a forgotten day opened at a city gate. Adobe huts lined rubbish-strewn streets, but some of the great houses of the past had been converted into hotels. Gambling houses and grog shops overflowed with raucous adventurers passing the time until a ship could take them to California. Bonneville ordered his troops to camp on the waterfront; from there they were ferried to the steamship "Golden Gate" as soon as it anchored. Several men died, including Lt. John Gore.

Meanwhile Quartermaster U. S. Grant, with Wallen's company and the women and children, traveled by bungo boat to Cruces. Grant had the task of moving the equipment—tents, mess-chests, and also all of the regiment's arms, for according to treaty, no soldier was allowed to carry a gun on the Isthmus crossing. The contractor who had bargained to move the regiment across the Isthmus hauled more lucrative civilian loads while Army baggage waited. Worse, the cholera epidemic began to sweep along the trail. The beleaguered quartermaster mustered enough mules for the women to ride, and sent them ahead with Wallen's company.

"In the afternoon of the day of our arrival, we went aboard barges and were towed out to the steamer "Golden Gate" lying at anchor about two miles from the city," Delia Sheffield remembered. But cholera had caught up with the Fourth. The "Golden Gate" was quarantined.

"Strong and healthy would be attacked by it and would die in a few hours. We did not know who would be the next victim, and it grew to be a common sight to see strong men, walking along the deck, to be taken with cramps and die in a short time," Delia Sheffield recalled. She remembered the death of only one woman, whose husband also died; their three children were sent to the U. S. consulate to be returned to the states. "The surgeon said that the immunity of the women and children was owing to the fact that they did not use liquor," Mrs. Sheffield wrote.

At Cruces, Quartermaster Grant waited in vain for transportation. At last he hired natives at exorbitant prices to pack the baggage and the sick to Panama. "About one third of the people with me died, either at Cruces or on the way to Panama," he remembered bleakly.[18] Rather than add Grant's ailing detachment to the regiment on board, arrangements were made to convert an abandoned ship in the harbor to a hospital station, and to this was brought the sick from the steamer as well. Some were quartered in hospital tents on Flamenco Island. Delia Sheffield said one hundred and fifty died; Dr. Tripler said eighty-seven. Brandy with capsicum and chloride of sodium, mustard, camphor, calomel and quinine comprised the available remedies.

The sickness abated on the "Golden Gate." Captain Patterson ordered all the passengers ashore while he fumigated the ship. He permitted only the well and convalescent to reboard, and steamed away on August 3. The sick were left behind on Flamenco Island in the care of Surgeon Tripler and one company.

Destination: Oregon

Aboard the "Golden Gate" it became known that the Fourth's destination was Oregon. It is doubtful if this assignment pleased the soldiers who thought they were being transplanted to California. For Bonneville there was irony. It had been just twenty years since, eager and younger, he had scouted and mapped the mountains and rivers of Oregon country, probed the British strongholds and teased their partisans. Confidant of his country's position and his own ability, he had offered to take immediate possession. For his efforts, he had lost standing in his profession and earned only a grudging pardon from his superiors. The froth which Washington Irving added in the publication of his journal brought more fame to the writer than to the leader of the expedition, obscuring the solid purposes. Now, however, he was assigned to command the United States Army in Oregon. Bonneville at no time asked acclaim for his service to his country. Still, he may be pardoned if in his innermost thoughts he acknowledged a measure of pride for his part in winning the Oregon country.

On August 18, the steamer approached the barren headlands of San Francisco Bay. Past the swift deep currents of the narrow passage—the Golden Gate—the great bay opened out serene and island-studded. Oak-grown hills rimmed the water, and on the Presidio bluff the Stars and Stripes flew from a tall staff. The "Golden Gate" anchored for several hours while Bonneville conferred with Ethan Allen Hitchcock who had recently moved into his Pacific Division Headquarters in the busy town. Only five years before, San Francisco had been a tiny Mexican village named Yerba Buena. The Americans renamed the town and the streets, and built wharves and warehouses beside this most admirable harbor in the world as some called it. The gold rush produced a shanty-town growth, swept away periodically by fires, but promptly rebuilt, still squalid. By 1852, the population had reached 36,000.

"Very few of the soldiers were allowed to leave the steamer for fear they would desert in order to go to the gold fields, where, we were told, fortunes were being made every day," Delia Sheffield wrote. The "Golden Gate" steamed through the strait of Carquinez into Suisan Bay, and docked at Benicia Barracks, temporary post for the Fourth Infantry.

News of the Fourth's agony of cholera had already reached California. A steamship line official issued a statement to the "Sacramento Union" newspaper describing the epidemic which had stricken the regiment. Asserting that the soldiers were "allowed to find their way across the Isthmus as best they could" he appeared most anxious to clear his company of any possible recrimination.

The weekly San Francisco "Alta California" of August 21, 1852, carried this item: "The Golden Gate brings the Fourth Regiment of U. S. Infantry, under command of Col. De Bonneville, consisting of 434 privates. The officers of the regiment are Col. Wright, Major Alvord, Capt. Wallen, lady and 3 children, Capt. Grant, Capt. McConnell, Lt. Underwood and lady, Lt. Collins and lady, Lt. Slaughter and lady, Lts. Montgomery, Jones, Russell, Scott,

Withers, Bates, Morris, Hodges, Mr. Alvord, Mr. Camp. There are also twenty-one women and twenty children belonging to the soldiers of the regiment. Invalids were left on the island of Flamenco in the Bay of Panama in charge of Lts. Boneycastle, Huger and Surgeon Tripler."[19]

Captain Patterson put in his word, stating that the company had put one of its ships into use as a hospital and that there had been but sixty-seven deaths from cholera, sixty-five among the troops because of their imprudence while marching over the Isthmus.

Bonneville's Fourth Infantry left Benicia for Oregon on September 14. Heavy gales tossed the steamship "Columbia" all the way to Astoria. Almost everyone was seasick, but at the elusive mouth of the Columbia the captain brought his ship safely into the main channel. High on a wooded bluff, Lewis and Clark and their men had spent a rainy winter. A few log cabins at the water's edge comprised Astoria, the town which grew around the Fort Astoria of 1811. Renamed Fort George, the post still functioned as a Hudson's Bay Company trade store, though most of the buildings had crumbled. The United States maintained a customs office there.

The air carried the smell of pungent pine as the transport steamed up the Columbia. The vessel docked at Portland, Oregon; smaller boats carried the Fourth across the river to the spacious post which would be their home for a season. On low bluffs sloping up from the shore, Columbia Barracks consisted of soldiers' quarters, kitchen, bakery, guardhouse, storehouses and officers' housing, all built of sturdy hewn logs. The ground floor of a large house on officers' row served as headquarters for the regiment. Commandant Bonneville's living quarters were on the second floor. (This, and some of the other buildings are preserved by Fort Vancouver Historical Society.)

Major J. S. Hathaway and one weary company of First Artillery had occupied Columbia Barracks since 1849. They had arrived by steamer to build a post adjoining the site of Hudson's Bay Company's fur-trade capitol, Fort Vancouver. Plagued by desertion of men to the California gold fields and by continuing ill health, Major Hathaway was listed "sick" on Bonneville's first post return from Columbia Barracks. The return noted also that the regiment lost a bugler when Army headquarters, perhaps at the request of a distracted family, ordered release of John Buckley on grounds that he was only fourteen years old. Two privates also gained civilian status because they were under age.

Autumn along the Columbia River is mellow and languid, scented with berry-laden shrubbery and bronzing oak and maple leaves. The firs hold the morning mists, and the midday sun glows amber. Life at Columbia Barracks settled into a pleasant routine of morning drills and cleaning of habitat and burnishing of equipment, with time too for hunting and for rambles in the woods or forays across the river to Portland. Delia Sheffield remembered that "all the furniture was rude and home-made . . . the easy chair that Captain Wallen made out of a barrel and upholstered with calico stuffed with moss was the envy of the whole garrison."[20] Captain Wallen was assigned to the Dalles and took his company upstream to the post where the Columbia swirls through the gates of the Cascades. The regimental quartermaster, too, paid an early visit to the Dalles. Captain Grant wrote his wife that he had made arrangements to purchase "quite a number of oxen and cows" at the Dalles. He hoped to augment his income so he could sent for his Julia. Later, he wrote that he had netted three thousand dollars on his livestock venture, but lost half of it in a bad loan to a fellow officer.[21]

On November 7, 1852, Father J. B. A. Brouillet of St. James Catholic Cathedral at the post baptized "Michael Kelly, 6 wks. old son of Sgt. Michael Kelly of the 4th Infantry and May Hogan." It is apparent that the baby was born only a day or two after the Fourth arrived at Columbia Barracks. Another baby boy, George Henry Laherty, son of Sgt. John Laherty and Emeline Stevens, born a week later, was also baptized at St. James.[22]

Because of the criticism of his regiment for the Isthmus crossing, Bonneville asked early in November for a court of inquiry into his own conduct as commander. Before that request could reach headquarters, orders came demanding that "the officers who accompanied this detachment report on their conduct in abandoning their commands . . . and the property for which they were accountable." In compliance, Bonneville required each officer to submit a report.

Finding civilian prisoners housed in the post jail, Bonneville complained to territorial officials. He expected to have need for the facilities, for California gold fields and other opportunities beckoned. Advertisements in the "Oregon Statesman" offered rewards for deserters; the bounty for absconding soldiers had not changed since 1824 when the "Arkansas Gazette" offered $30. Within a month, according to post returns, detachments were afield in pursuit of deserters; later returns showed soldiers serving sentences for their attempts to leave military life.

The officers' quarters were heated by fireplaces, and when December rains fell, fragrant fires crackled to ward off the dampness and chill. Delia Sheffield and her sergeant husband moved into one of the houses on officers' row where

Delia presided as housekeeper for a number of the officers. Those who had brought their families were the envy of the others, who could only wish for now-and-then mail. Ann Bonneville spent Christmas, 1852, in Philadelphia with her sister Mary Leiper and other family members, according to a family letter.

From Pacific Division headquarters in San Francisco, Colonel Ethan Allen Hitchcock wrote that Bonneville's "request for a court of inquiry about his management of the Isthmus debacle was refused as entirely unnecessary." It was a vote of confidence from General Scott, or possibly by that time it was apparent that the primary error lay in ordering soldiers across the Isthmus in July. General Scott had lost his bid to be President; too aloof to campaign, he had carried only four states. Elected was Franklin Pierce, who had been one of the instant generals in the Mexican War.

The rains turned to snow and severe cold. Diarist George Gibbs wrote of "snow to the depth of over a foot . . . The Columbia is frozen nearly across." After his trip across the continent with Loring's Mounted Rifles, Gibbs had tried mining. A windfall appointment to be collector of customs at Astoria brought him to Portland to arrange for bonds. He also visited Columbia Barracks. "Damn," he wrote, "it does me good to meet an Army man."[23]

Lt. August Kautz joined the regiment; he had been wounded helping volunteers bring arms and ammunition to Rogue River settlers besieged by Indians. Rev. John McCarty of the Protestant Episcopal Church was added to the roll as chaplain and schoolmaster. Bonneville sent a company to garrison Fort Steilacoom on Puget Sound, and dispatched a company to march up the Willamette and over the mountains to Indian-threatened gold diggings in Scott valley.

An Encounter with Peter Skene Ogden

To resolve "a constant source of irritation," Bonneville wrote to headquarters asking confirmation of the four-square-mile military reservation at Columbia Barracks. Hudson's Bay Company had allowed employees to stake out homes near their post. Newly arrived settlers presumed equal rights, showing disdain for the British holdings, and only slightly less for the Army's claims. Coincidentally, Peter Skene Ogden had recently visited Washington, D. C. making a plea for British rights.

"Short, dark, and exceedingly tough," a contemporary described Peter Skene Odgen during the heyday of the fur trade.[24] In March, 1853, when

Odgen returned to Oregon after a year's sojourn in the east, he was fifty-nine years old, totally white-haired, and mellowed to the point that he was planning to publish his memoirs. Canadian by birth, Ogden preceded Bonneville into the intermountain area by almost a decade and made six Snake country expeditions for Hudson's Bay Company, carrying out instructions to strip the country bare of fur to discourage American encroachment. While Bonneville was in the mountains, Ogden was expanding the Honorable Company's holdings in British Columbia. He succeeded John McLoughlin at Fort Vancouver. Ogden had lost favor with settlers when he hosted British emissaries in pre-treaty maneuvers, but won considerable respect when he rescued survivors at Waiilatpu after the Indians had hacked the Whitman family to pieces.

Bonneville and Ogden met for the first time, most probably, in 1853. "Bonneville was in command at the old headquarters of the company that had helped in his failure twenty years before," wrote historian Edmond S. Meany. "Some of the Hudson's Bay Company officers were still there, and toward these Bonneville manifested a kindly courtesy that speaks well for the native gentility of the man."[25]

There was no stockade around the Army's Columbia Barracks, but Hudson's Bay Company's old Fort Vancouver nestled inside a high log palisade near the river in Columbia Barracks' front yard. This was the fortress over which John McLoughlin presided for so many years and from which he sent the directives which thwarted Bonneville in his attempts to reach the lower Columbia. The fur trade post was no longer a feudal manor, but some of the old traditions persisted; the gates of the stockade were locked each night and flung open at dawn. Workshops, office, store, arsenal and gentlemen's quarters lined the walls, surrounding an open court where trappers had bartered their furs. Peter Skene Ogden lived with his family in an imposing house within the stockade. His wife was a Flathead—Salish. Julia, a queenly woman, was taller and older than Ogden, and his good companion for over thirty years. During his recent visits to New York City, Ogden had bought fine dress materials for Julia and their grown daughters. There were Ogden sons, too, Peter and Charles, whose Cree mother, Mary, was Ogden's first wife, and Julia's sons Michael and Isaac, all in the fur trade.[26]

Oregon teemed with promise. It was a time and a place for unbounded ambition, for staking out farms or building sawmills or loading river and ocean vessels. Army men could be but bystanders, watching the bustle of a burgeoning empire, envious of those who were free to participate, homesick for families and friends, and bored with the lack of military action they might have expected. Whenever there was an Indian scare, the militia rushed off in fine frenzy, returning with braggart tales of the justice they had dealt to the original claimants of the hills and valleys. The regular Army was a show of force, a supplementary power marking time against an uprising by the Indians in such numbers that the Oregon volunteers could not slay them all, or the unlikely event of an attack by a foreign power. The post was, however, of utmost importance because of the stores and ordnance maintained there.

Oregon had been invaded, but it was by families trudging the hundreds of miles across barren high plains, their livestock stirring clouds of dust and their wagons stacked with tools and high hopes. They traveled many of the trails Bonneville followed in the 1830s when the United States was still uncertain whether this choice tract of the continent could be wrested from the British. The forests and highlands north of the Columbia had been slower to fill, but by 1853, there were so many settlers Congress agreed to divide Oregon and create Washington Territory.

The steamer "Fremont" arrived in May, 1853, bearing Congressman Joseph Lane traveling with family and staff members. Col. Bonneville sent the Fourth Infantry band to Portland to greet the party, though as Oregon's first territorial governor, Lane, like most political appointees from the east was not revered by the settlers. Longtime residents saw their claims usurped by more aggressive newcomers and Lane himself acquired John McLoughlin's sawmill at the falls of the Willamette.

Dr. McLoughlin, who in the 1830s had slammed the door to Oregon against Bonneville, had, in the 1850s become a man without a country. Loyal to his company and to the British government, McLoughlin kept Americans out of Oregon as long as he could. Next, he tried to deflect the incoming homeseekers southward in the hope that the area north of the Columbia could be kept British. Still, when destitute immigrants arrived he provided food and shelter. For his pains, he became persona non grata to his company and found it necessary, in 1846, to retreat to his long-claimed holdings at the falls of the Willamette. He filed citizenship papers to qualify for legal ownership but his claims were denied. Some of his property went to private interests, while the rest of his estate was confiscated for the establishment of a university. In 1853, old, sick and embittered, McLoughlin resided in Oregon City.

A detail of Army railroad scouts arrived in the spring of 1853; Lieutenant George B. McClellan debarked from a steamer with orders to requisition gear and supplies from Columbia Barracks' depot for his assignment: to find a pass over the Cascades from Puget Sound, and to meet the main overland railroad survey party enroute from St. Paul, Minnesota. Isaac I. Stevens, one of the bright young engineers of the Mexican War headed the many-faceted survey. On his post-war assignment, Stevens campaigned vigorously for Franklin Pierce, defying a reprimand from the Secretary of War. His efforts paid off with a triple-sweet political plum: Governor of the newly-created Washington Territory, Chief of Indian Affairs, and director of a transcontinental railroad survey. With ample funds, Stevens left overland from St. Paul with a force of over one hundred men. To resupply his survey party enroute, Stevens ordered rations taken from St. Louis up the Missouri River to the terminal of navigation, Fort Benton (Montana), and other supplies from San Francisco to the Bitterroot Valley.

Twenty-seven-year-old McClellan's assignment appeared to be the easiest. He had only to cover a few hundred miles eastward from the coast. His detail numbered sixty-six, including a surgeon, a geologist and a civil engineer. George Gibbs, already fired from his customs collector job by the new regime, accompanied McClellan and submitted the reports, in addition to serving as interpreter. Red-haired McClellan and Quartermaster U. S. Grant disagreed sharply during the preparations, according to one officer, but on July 16, all was ready and the cavalcade set off toward Puget Sound.

General orders in August announced the change of name from Columbia Barracks to Fort Vancouver. Some settlers were less than delighted with the large post on the Columbia, manned by regular Army personnel. They preferred the militia system with pay and instant commissions from the federal government but with local option as to raids and reprisals. However, the territorial governor appealed to the Army in August for help in Rogue River country. Col. Bonneville obliged, sending a howitzer "with its caisson containing a good supply of ammunition under charge of an officer and six men . . . very competent to work the howitzer. Lt. Kautz has charge . . ." Bonneville wrote the governor. In a confrontation at Table Rock (Medford), "a howitzer borrowed from Col. B. L. E. Bonneville, did much to awe the natives into submission" and a peace treaty was signed with a coalition of Indians. Lt. Kautz presumably was able to exact a measure of vengeance for his wound of the preceding winter.[27]

Captain U. S. Grant left Fort Vancouver in September for a new assignment at Fort Humboldt, north of San Francisco. Delia Sheffield wrote that Grant had planted a patch of potatoes which was flooded out by late-melting snows. Bonneville loaned Grant money for the endeavor, according to one Grant biographer. Grant confided to Delia Sheffield that he despaired of getting ahead in the Army and thought he might go into the lumber business.[28] Other officers shared his feelings. In San Francisco, William Tecumseh Sherman of the Third Artillery resigned to become a banker; Joseph Hooker entered the California land business.

Reunion With Mountain Men

Bonneville took a 20-day leave in October; he may have elected to see areas which were denied him in the 1830s. Upstream from Vancouver are tree-grown canyons and intervening highlands on the river's north side. On the south, narrow waterfalls cascade from high bluffs, creating fern-grown bowers. Multi-colored rocks nourish lichen and moss, and in places boulders have tumbled into the Columbia, creating rapids and holes where Indians for centuries have fished for salmon. At the Dalles—"the gates"— the river passes through the Cascade mountains and swirls with elemental power in its headlong rush to the sea. "Bonneville was deeply impressed by the mighty stream, and particularly the value it held for the nation. During his command at Vancouver, he often pointed out the potential value of the Columbia's controlled waters . . . though his associates considered his ideas visionary in the extreme," Ida Wilcox Howell has written.[29]

In the Willamette Valley, Bonneville's unrealized goal of two decades back, farms and villages lined the river. The gentle moist climate and deep black soil made farming easy. There were thick stands of trees for buildings and boats, and the fishing and hunting provided fine subsistence for those who chose to do no more than that. Mountain men found in the verdant Oregon valleys a satisfactory compromise between their love of nature's wild beauties and the comfort of permanent homes. Robert Newell made his home at Champoeg. Doc had left the fur trade in 1840; he claimed to be the first to take a wagon from Fort Hall to the Willamette. By 1853 he had served in the legislature, undertaken peace missions to the Indians, and spearheaded civic movements such as importing a printing press for the "Oregon Spectator." Flamboyant Joe Meek was farming, more or less, on the Tualatin Plain. After his little daughter was killed in the Whitman massacre and Joe made a dramatic horseback ride to Washington D. C., he secured a commission as United States marshal. As such he had hung five Cayuse chiefs for their part in the Whitman murders. Stephen Meek, too had claimed a farm, but he preferred a more mobile life as guide for immigrant trains. On one disastrous trip he lost his way seeking a route through central Oregon—perhaps the trail he had traveled with Bonneville in 1835.

Tom McKay was dead. After Bonneville treated him to the honey-and-liquor refreshments in 1834, Tom had built Fort Boise to compete with Wyeth's Fort Hall—this strategy most likely devised by his stepfather, John McLoughlin. When the trapping era faded, Tom, too, tried farming. In 1853 he was sleeping the long sleep on his farm near Scapoose. Tom McKay's neighbor there, Courtney Walker, had come west with Nathaniel Wyeth in 1834. At that time Wyeth still thought he could outwit John McLoughlin, and devised the ruse of having Walker join Hudson's Bay Company as a spy. In Oregon, Walker farmed, taught school, and held early territorial offices but like other old timers found himself out of favor when more aggressive settlers arrived. The new breed managed by 1852 to move the territorial capitol from Oregon City to Salem, forty miles up the Willamette.

Legend has it that Portland, Oregon, might have been Boston, Oregon, except for the flip of a coin by two New Englanders. As early as the 1820s French trappers had built cabins in the dense green trees at the mouth of the Willamette, but it took Yankee enterprise to launch a shipbuilding industry at this promising site. Joseph Gale, who had trapped for Bonneville, headed the ambitious settlers who built a 48-foot sailing vessel, "The Star of Oregon," and began a brisk trade to Yerba Buena on San Francisco Bay. The notion of a trading center at Portland in competition with Hudson's Bay's monopoly caught on rapidly and soon a smith, tannery, distillery, flour mill and stores served the area. The Columbia Hotel and the Willamette House welcomed travelers well-heeled enough to scorn sleeping in their wagons. In 1853, the "Oregonian" was three years old, a lusty weekly which claimed Equal Rights, Equal Laws, and Equal Justice to All Men but referred to Negroes as niggers and Chinese as celestials. The "Oregonian" carried little news, but served as a lively bulletin board for local and San Francisco advertisements. One dentist offered "Pivot Teeth Inserted with Wooden Pivots" while a competitor's "Artificial Teeth made useful for eating" were "Hammered out of ten and twenty dollar goldpieces upon a blacksmith's anvil."[30] Skiffs plied between Portland and Fort Vancouver; one mentioned by Delia Sheffield was the "Eagle," which also ran to the Dalles. Another was the "Honda Lie."

Col. Bonneville welcomed I. I. Stevens with his various railroad survey detachments who paddled down the Columbia to Fort Vancouver in November, not exactly in triumph, having come to less than satisfactory terms with either the terrain or the natives. Lt. McClellan reported that the mountains east of Puget Sound were rugged and impassable, thus disappointing planners who had envisioned a road in a beeline from Walla Walla to the Sound. Governor Stevens berated McClellan for his timidity in not pushing through Snoqualmie Pass, but Stevens had not found Marias Pass through the Continental Divide, even though the Blackfeet had described it to him. The mountains were still to be reckoned with. So were the Indians.

The Yakimas had eyed McClellan's cavalcade in alarm and resentment. Their chief, Kamiakin, left his cattle and irrigation ditches and launched a campaign to unite the tribes to stand their ground. Rufus Saxton, freighting supplies up the Columbia to meet the overland body, was challenged by war parties along the way. He met the Stevens caravan in Bitterroot Valley. There at the spot where Father P. J. DeSmet had built St. Mary's mission in 1841, John Owens was about to abandon his trading post because of Indian hostility. With an eye to the future, Governor Stevens assigned Lt. John Mullan and a detachment to build a military storehouse there—Cantonment Stevens (Stevensville, Montana). Trying to placate the tribes along his route, Stevens arranged a future council with the Blackfeet and he used this promise of better relations with their long-time enemies to ingratiate himself with the Nez Perces and the Flatheads.

The railroad survey party rested at Fort Vancouver for several days as the guests of Col. Bonneville. The Indian situation was uncertain, and the geography had baffled them, but the explorers bragged about the delicious corn and melons they had enjoyed at Lapwai, where Bonneville's former trapper William Craig made his home among his Nez Perce in-laws. Another pleasant stopover mentioned in the accounts was at Hudson's Bay's Fort Colville, where Angus MacDonald furnished "fifty imperial gallons of extra rations" to entertain the Americans.

Orders came from the Secretary of War to reduce the Army reservation to one square mile; Bonneville began the survey to mark the new boundaries. Col. Wm. Whistler, erstwhile top commander of the Fourth, appeared a few times on post returns as "absent without leave" but managed to stretch his furlough into retirement. Captain Wallen, too, was months overdue. Wallen was under duress: Captain Grant wrote to his Julia that Wallen had lost a child. Delia Sheffield, however, enjoyed living at Fort Vancouver. "Occasionally we would have parties; the dining room would be cleared for dancing to the music of the Fourth Infantry band. We would dance until the wee small hours of the morning. Our guests would come from far and near." She wrote of "private theatricals in our little theatre." Like many other soldiers,

Sgt. Sheffield chose to remain in the West when his term of enlistment ended "and so we lived through all the early pioneer days of Oregon Territory."[31]

Fort Vancouver received no mail in January, 1854, but an assortment of tidings arrived in February. The steamer "San Francisco," carrying the Third Artillery regiment around the Horn, was battered and almost sunk in heavy seas. One hundred and eighty soldiers were washed overboard. Col. John M. Washington was among those lost.

General John Ellis Wool replaced Brigadier General Ethan Allen Hitchcock as Pacific Division Commander. Hitchcock complained that the order was issued by Secretary of War Jefferson Davis, without consultation with General Scott. But the newspapers had been having a heyday with recent Hitchcock actions. Learning that a vessel and crew were about to sail from San Francisco to seize the government of Sonora, Hitchcock ordered them impounded. Many Californians supported the idea of grabbing the Mexican province, but Hitchcock's decision was granite. "Damn public opinion," he is quoted as saying, and battled to a standstill a suit for damages and a citation for contempt by the state of California. At about the same time, the United States acquired title from Mexico to nearly 30,000 square miles of land south of the Gila River in a more acceptable manner, by purchase. The Mexican War treaty had not clearly defined the boundaries; a payment to Mexico of ten million dollars concluded the Gadsden Purchase, named for the ambassador to Mexico. James C. Gadsden was also president of the South Carolina Railroad Company and, like Secretary of War Jefferson Davis, advocated a transcontinental railroad approximating the 33rd parallel of latitude.

> "We have confirmed by consent of Monsignor A. M. Blanchet, Archbishop of Nesqually, Col. Benjamin Bonneville and James Cockerl (called Ryan) J. B. A. B."

This excerpt is from church records of St. James Catholic Parish, Vancouver, Washington Territory, March 30, 1854. "A great friendship grew up between Bonneville and Father J. B. A Brouillet, the snuffy, cheery, good-hearted little padre resident at St. James Cathedral," historian John A. Hussey has written. St. James was not imposing; it was a cathedral by virtue of the residence there of the bishop. In early drawings, the hewn log cathedral could have passed for a country school house except for the cross atop the gabled roof.[32]

May, 1854, brought a reply from Army headquarters to the reports submitted more than a year previously of the troubled Isthmus crossing. Bonneville's classmate, Samuel Cooper, had become Adjutant General, and in his letter to Bonneville, he stated that the Secretary of War considered the reports entirely satisfactory and exonerated the officers from censure. May also brought the Wallens back to the Columbia; post returns noted that Captain Wallen was "absolved from A. W. O. L." In June a company of Third Artillery swelled the ranks at Fort Vancouver. These soldiers were survivors of Col. Washington's sea disaster. In August Inspector General Joseph K. F. Mansfield arrived to appraise Bonneville's command.

"The discipline of this post was good," Mansfield wrote. "The arms and equipment of these troops is in good serviceable order . . . Col. Bonneville gave a handsome battalion drill, and the infantry companies drilled well at infantry and as skirmishers, and the artillery company went through the artillery drill handsomely. Harmony exists among the officers. And Col. Bonneville commands the respect of all."[33] Bonneville remembered, too, that these were good times. Some time later he wrote to his Fort Vancouver ordnance chief, Captain T. J. Eckerson, "I often look back on my Vancouver stretch where I see all as I once saw them . . . your rosey-cheeked and round faced boy . . . Withers' and Forsythe's porch filled with smoking and talkers, then out comes Wallen's buggy and gray horse, drawing he and his wife down the slope . . . Auger leaving Mrs. A. and four healthy young ones on and about the porch . . . the quarters, the church, the Hudson's Bay, and Ryan with his weather-beaten hat and face. I think I hear my old cow lowing, and Raines calling for the Honda Lie and Mrs. Raines calling for the Major. So much for my old picture and all its reminiscences. I think I enjoy the medley now, as much as when I heard it under the three big trees."[34] Though Bonneville must have longed for his wife and daughter, his years at Fort Vancouver were among the best of his Army service. He commanded well. His emoluments were adequate; his monthly paycheck at this time totalled $235. He was also allowed three horses and two servants.[35]

An incident which may have happened at about this time is recounted by Edmond S. Meany: when Chief Lawyer of the Nez Perces came to Fort Vancouver, Colonel Bonneville, speaking in the Nez Perce language asked about an old chief, long dead, and about Chief Lawyer's brother. The Indian did not recognize this "baffling mild-mannered stranger" who finally reached up his hand and removed his wig, whereupon the Chief exclaimed "Bald Headed Chief!"[36]

Bonneville's years at Fort Vancouver may have seemed idyllic, especially in retrospect, but winds of discontent were blowing through the Pacific Northwest, fanning Indian anger. There were reasons: Major Gabriel Raines reported from the Dalles that settlers were locating on Indian land. Indians had scant recourse, since their testimony was barred in court. From northern California, Captain H. M. Judah reported that he had arrived at Fort Jones just in time to prevent whites from exterminating peaceable Indians who had already surrendered their firearms. In San Francisco, General Wool, like his predecessor General Hitchcock, was inclined to favor the Indians. He refused to order the Army to march in a show of force as suggested by some of the Indian agents, and directed Bonneville to offer assistance to the militias only as needs arose.

The Army was thinly spread. The nine companies assigned to the Northwest actually numbered less than 350 men. Vast reaches of the interior lay untouched, a desert to be crossed quickly by homeseekers and goldseekers bound for easier terrain. The great Snake River country lay, as Bonneville described it when he first glimpsed it from the mountains above Pierre's Hole "a sleeping ocean." In the 1850s there were two oases for travelers: Wyeth's Fort Hall, and Fort Boise, where Francois Benjamin Payette, patriarch of a handsome Indian family, preserved the amenities of French hospitality. It was near Fort Boise in August, 1854, where nineteen immigrants were killed by "Snake" Indians as the Shoshoni and Bannock tribes were being called. Another wagon train was attacked ninety-five miles farther east and three whites killed.

The acting Oregon Governor sent a messenger to Bonneville asking for arms, stores, and ammunition in order for the militia to launch a full-scale military operation into Snake country. Bonneville refused, stating that winter operations into the interior were impractical. He promised that troops would be dispatched to the field early in the spring and would use every means possible to secure and punish the offenders. In the meantime, he sent a company to patrol the Oregon Trail for some distance inland.

Something had happened to the once amiable Shoshoni. The herds of buffalo had disappeared, reducing the red men to beggar status. The hungry Indians were short-tempered, but many of the outrages against the whites stemmed from initial offenses against the Indians.

Peter Skene Ogden died in September, 1854. His health had deteriorated during the summer. Thomas McKay's name, too, appeared in Oregon news columns at this time. When he died, he had willed his considerable estate to his Chinook family. In September, 1854, the administrator he had named was found to have embezzled most of the assets.[37]

General Wool wrote to commend Bonneville on his "measures to suppress Indian difficulties." It was an unusual gesture, coming from the crusty Pacific

Division commander. Wool was still irascible, his contemporaries found. When he arrived in San Francisco, he gave Ethan Allen Hitchcock scant hours to clear out his belongings. Then, disapproving of Hitchcock's move to San Francisco, he moved Division headquarters to Benicia. Governor Stevens visited Wool there in October, and recorded quarreling with him about the Mexican War.

Governor Stevens had not enjoyed a good summer. In Washington, D. C. he found that Secretary of War Jefferson Davis had shut off funds for the railroad exploration; Davis preferred a southern transcontinental route. The best Governor Stevens could do for Washington Territory was a commitment for funds to survey a wagon road from Walla Walla to Fort Benton, the head of navigation on the Missouri River. Stevens and his family had crossed the Isthmus in September, and spent weeks in San Francisco recovering from fevers. In early November his party arrived for a two weeks visit with Col. Bonneville. In spite of rebuffs, I. I. Stevens intended to shape Washington Territory into an up-and-coming part of the United States. The Indian problems seemed most pressing, and plans for treaties were discussed around the crackling fires at Fort Vancouver. When he returned to Olympia, Stevens sent messengers to the Yakimas and Nez Perces proposing a spring meeting at Walla Walla. He wrote to Bonneville in March, 1855, requesting that Private Gustavus Sohon accompany the treaty expedition: "His service would be valuable from his knowledge of the Indian country and his ability and taste as a draughtsman and Artist . . . Truly your friend. I. I. Stevens." Private Sohon's service as an artist proved extremely worthy; his portraits of Old Joseph, Red Wolf, Looking Glass, James, and others are classics.[38]

Promotion to Colonel

News reached Bonneville in May that he had been promoted to full colonel and assigned to command the Third Infantry. The Portland "Oregonian" reported in early June that Col. Bonneville was enroute to the states. He traveled by way of the Isthmus, retracing his outward journey.

Past Golden Gate bluffs, Alcatraz Island had received a new lighthouse. Wharves had been extended; sturdy warehouses replaced bayside shanties, and the city had mushroomed up the slopes. Little remained of the grace that had been Yerba Buena. The meadow of mint—the "good herb" which gave the Spanish village its name—was filled with houses. There had been a path through it from Mission San Francisco de Assisi to the Presidio; the

Spanish had established these footholds in 1776, following their pattern of capturing both bodies and souls of the natives.

The Presidio stood deserted in 1855. Surgeon Tripler's wife recalled in her memoirs that they were displeased that General Wool moved headquarters back to Benicia since it interfered with a thriving private practice in San Francisco. Eunice Tripler's views of California were all negative, though she had some justifiable complaints: A partner failed to pay back a large loan, and an embezzler made off with three thousand Tripler dollars.[39] Ellen Sherman also disliked California, though in 1855 she had moved into a new house befitting her position as wife of a leading San Francisco banker. William Tecumseh Sherman had continued to correspond with Ulysses S. Grant, whose move to Fort Humboldt had not been a happy one. Already homesick and discouraged, Grant failed to please his commanding officer and found respite in a Eureka bar. He resigned in 1854, borrowed money for passage home, and in New York borrowed from classmate Simon Bolivar Buckner to reach his family.

Great fortunes had been made, and some quickly lost in land and investment speculations. There were safer, lucrative pursuits. Hubert Howe Bancroft was amassing nice sums of money peddling books which his family shipped around the Horn. Bancroft was aware of history being made in the West, for he began collecting source material of the times and later publishing it, not always with accuracy or lack of bias. For example, his slanderous appraisal of Bonneville, published after Bonneville's death, had no basis in historical fact. His references, as pointed out by historian Dale Morgan, were "peripheral."[40] Bancroft and many writers who followed him ignored the vital role of the Army on the American frontier, paying scant attention to the show of force which made possible the westward push across the continent. Though the Army contributed a generous measure of exploration, treaty-making, surveying, mapping and road-building, Army service, by and large, was anonymous because officers and military units were constantly being shifted.

As soon as he secured passage, Bonneville was on his way. Like San Francisco, Panama City had expanded its docks to accommodate traffic. A three-day celebration in February had marked completion of the railroad across the Isthmus, but those who paid the fifty cents per mile found the journey still hazardous. Engines jumped the tracks on the soft roadbeds; one work-train was said to have disappeared completely in the mud of a swamp. For less affluent travelers, the railroad company furnished cattle cars at half price and also sold the privilege of walking along the roadbed.

Wild creatures had moved back into the forests before the clatter of the trains, and even the gypsy-colored birds had retreated from the noise, but morning fogs still shed enchantment on the tropical lushness of Chagres Valley. At Bohio Soldado, the cottage of John L. Stephens stood deserted, for the explorer, naturalist and railroad president had died of cholera in 1852, just weeks after the Fourth Infantry had battled the same disease.

The docks at Aspinwall groaned under freight waiting to be transported by railroad—tools, food, machinery, manufactured goods, mail, and hordes of people. Trains from the Pacific side brought ore, furs, and a lesser number of people—some businessmen, some disappointed fortune-hunters, and some, like Bonneville, professionals with a task completed and a vision of home and family uppermost in their minds.

In New York City, one new feature thrust its impact on returning citizens. Across the few hundred yards of water from Governor's Island, Castle Garden was being used as a "Landing Depot" for immigrants. Once acclaimed as the most elegant hall in the nation, the auditorium on the tip of Manhattan was growing shabby with the wear and tear of thousands of European homeseekers meeting America. Here they could exchange their money, buy tickets for their destinations or register at the Labor Exchange for jobs. Officials tried to shield the newcomers from the sharpers and swindlers who crowded the Battery in wait for them. The United States government perceived the unprepossessing throngs of families as precisely what most of them would prove to be, the most precious cargo a young nation could receive.

Chapter Seven
1856-1860

Controlling New Mexico Indians

The Journey to El Paso

Bonneville's reunion with his family was brief. When he arrived at Carlisle he found Ann recovering from a long illness. By early September she was able to travel with him to Sharon Springs, New York, and at that popular health spa in the Catskills, her health improved. "She can take daily walks of a mile, with fair promise of soon being able to accompany me to my station Fort Fillmore, New Mexico, where health is said to be perennial," he wrote to a colleague.[1] But Bonneville's orders directed him to march several hundred troops across Texas, a trip for only the robust. No evidence—no contemporary journal or newspaper item or letter—has surfaced to show that Ann and Mary ever went to New Mexico.

As before, it took weeks for the outgoing companies and their officers to assemble at Governor's Island in New York Harbor. After a two-week sea journey, Bonneville's steamship docked at Corpus Christi, prospering as an assembly point for the California-bound. The road from Corpus Christi led northwestward across hilly cattle country to reach San Antonio. Here new American buildings had replaced many adobe structures. The Alamo was being used as a storehouse by the Quartermaster Department; other Army business was conducted in rented quarters. Obedient to orders, Bonneville left some of his charges at San Antonio and at other posts along the way.

From San Antonio, the California road crossed bleak and dusty distances to touch Army posts built after the Mexican War. Fort Inge, at the outer reach of settlements on the Nueces River consisted of tents and a few log buildings with thatched roofs. Beyond lay leagues of low hills, scrubby timber and prickly shrubs. Fort Clark, on Mora's Creek, spread out in makeshift shelters built of upright logs. Situated to protect Texas from Mexican and Indian raids, it was a large post, with a cemetery even larger, for it had become the resting place of many freighters and westbound travelers. From Fort Clark the road veered south to San Felipe Springs, then skirted the eastern banks and scant tributaries of the Pecos River to Fort Lancaster. From this post the route lay across a broad barren mesa, monotonously the same day after day. Comanche Springs, gushing pure water, was a welcome oasis, but only for caravans of goodly size, for Indian war trails from the midwest prairies into Mexico passed through this area.

Westward, the prairie gave way to rolling hills, and the road climbed into the Davis Mountains. From Fort Davis at the top of a rocky ridge, a pass led through the Quitman range and down to the Rio Grande. Cottonwood trees and farms and little villages signalled the end of a very long walk across Texas.

In 1855, Fort Bliss adjoined the trading village of Yankee merchant James Magoffin. Early visitors wrote little about quarters at the post—the Army used Magoffin's buildings for a time—but marveled at the fruits and vegetables, the vineyards and fields of grain in the valley of El Paso. The city on the Mexican side of the river numbered several thousand people. A few plantations dotted the American side.

Bonneville set off north toward Fort Fillmore, headquarters of the Third Infantry. Three or four miles up the Rio Grande, a dam diverted water into canals for irrigation, and to power two flour mills, one owned by Judge Simeon Hart. Here the river had cut a channel "el paso" through the mountains. Cottonwood trees lined the banks of the stream: "Rio Brava del Norte" the Spanish had named it, but except in flood seasons, it ran shallow and sparse, "too thick to drink and too thin to plow." Above the alluvial bottoms, dry mesas rose to the hills.

In Command of the Third Infantry at Fort Fillmore

The Third Infantry band, in all the smartness they could muster, greeted Colonel Bonneville's arrival at Fort Fillmore in January, 1856. "Orders were issued to clean and brighten brasses and otherwise appear in military style," Dragoon Sergeant James A. Bennett wrote.[2] Fort Fillmore stood on a rise above the Rio Grande, and commanded a view up and down the Mesilla valley. Adobe buildings formed three sides of a parade square, which opened to the river. Besides the barracks and other essential buildings, there was a "commodious complex of rooms" for the commanding officer. The setting was deceptively tranquil. Lt. Col. Dixon S. Miles had built Fort Fillmore in 1851, and his tenure had been stormy. Territorial officials berated the Army for failing to rattle swords in ongoing border disputes. Travelers as well as settlers sent a constant barrage of distress calls because of real or imagined Indian raids. Villagers decried the rowdiness of Miles' soldiers, but prospered in the business of supplying subsistence and entertainment.

Within three weeks of his arrival, Col. Bonneville was summoned to attend a court-martial at Taos. He left Fort Fillmore on February 7, and his journey took him northward up the Rio Grande, the great artery through the heartland of New Mexico. Las Cruces, eight miles north, was built Yankee style with a main street, though the name commemorated crosses placed for Mexican freighters slain long ago. Fort Fillmore personnel enjoyed its theatre, dance hall and games of chance. An overnight stop was made at Fort Thorn on the west side of the Rio Grande, where the road to California left the river. Dr. Michael D. Steck, Indian agent to the Apaches, lived near. He was trying against odds to end Apache raids with promises of rations and payment for hunting grounds. Territorial Governor David Meriwether had signed six treaties with the Indians during the past year, one at Fort Thorn. Congress failed to ratify the treaties or to appropriate funds to put them into effect, nullifying Army efforts which had brought the Indians to a bargaining mood.

Near Fort Thorn, where the river begins a bend to the west, an alternate road cut across a ninety-mile alkaline plateau. The "Jornada del Muerto's" sand and snow storms, and Indian and outlaw attacks, had claimed countless lives. Once on their way, travelers did not camp, but hurried on, covering many of the miles by night. One sojourner wrote that on the eerie journey, even the tall weeds looked like Indians.

Fort Craig was a new post, built on tableland on the west side of the river. When Bonneville's party stopped there, a scouting detachment had just returned from a patrol in which hostile Indians were killed, but also, by mistake, a number of friendly Indians. On up the river was Socorro, a purely Mexican village in the 1850s. In a fine valley with clear springs, the site had been an ancient Piro pueblo before the Spanish intrusion. By 1856, the old mission had been remodeled and a new order of land-grant families irrigated crops and vineyards. Dragoons garrisoned a small post at Los Lunas, and twenty miles northward the "Post at Albuquerque," a large supply depot. The rough and crooked trail up the Rio Grande had known Coronado's conquistadors, and for centuries before that, Indian footsteps. Opportunists, colonists, fugitives and missionaries had tramped up and down, but neither commerce nor conquest had brought improvement. In the 1850s, the United States Army was assigned the task to improve the road.

Past farmlands and lava-strewn mesas and solitary buttes, the road reached the meadow which cradled Santa Fe. The mountains and in season the venerable town glisten with snow, for Santa Fe is seven thousand feet above sea level. Already more than two centuries old in the 1850s, it had been a northern bastion of the Spanish empire of the new world. In 1856 there were Yankee touches, the American flag centering the plaza, a new Baptist church, an Odd Fellows hall, and a statehouse under construction. Bakery, apothecary, blacksmith and other shops nestled among saloons. Fort Marcy, overlooking the town, was garrisoned by a company of Third Infantry.

Headquarters of the Department of New Mexico occupied offices back-to-back with the Governor's Palace, appropriately, for the Army was the discipline which made civilian governments possible. The Army, however, was off on the wrong foot from the start in New Mexico. At the beginning of the Mexican War, rumors ran ahead of General Kearny's California-bound expedition, sending some families scurrying to the hills. In Taos, rebels and Indians murdered Charles Bent, the governor appointed by Kearny. This called for punitive expeditions and New Mexico had known scant tranquillity since that time. Army commanders quarreled with territorial officials, citizen militias and Indian agents; abrasive Col. Edwin Vose Sumner had sourly recommended to headquarters that the United States abandon New Mexico altogether. Brigadier General John Garland commanded the department in 1856.

The Governor's Palace, as the Spanish had called the modest quarters, stood between the legislative chambers and the Indian superintendency. A wide portico shaded the whole, and embraced, as it were, New Mexico's three-way problem: disgruntled Indians, Mexican landholders, and Yankee-come-latelies. Many of the sojourners from stateside, judging from the journals they wrote, regarded the Mexicans as ignorant and slothful, but sided with them in the belief that Indians were part of the wildlife to be guarded against and killed if they preyed. Indian affairs had been assigned to the Department of Interior, created in 1849, but the Army retained the doubtful privilege of enforcing orders which did not always reflect good military judgment. Besides keeping peace among the factions, the Army's job was to guard and support surveyors, treaty-makers and railroad route-finders.

Col. Bonneville paid his respects to General Garland and set off northward through mud and snow to the mountain-locked valley of Taos. From Cantonment Burgwin at the canyon corridor, Taos Peak and flanking mountain rose like a backdrop to a multi-storied pueblo, where the Indians, when they chose, drew up their ladders so no intruder could scale the blank walls.

Fernando de Taos village clustered around a plaza and a small adobe church; ruins of a large mission crumbled in the sun. Taos had been a trade center for centuries where Indians of many tribes met and bartered. An unwritten truce prevailed during the trade rendezvous but exploded at the close, and the Army was hard-pressed to keep order.

The court to which Bonneville had been summoned dealt with a reprisal action against Utes and Apaches. General Garland had bypassed Dragoon Colonel Thomas T. Fauntleroy in the planning. Added to that insult, Fauntleroy's assignment was small, though he was able to ambush an Indian camp and bragged that "the slaughter was beautiful to behold."[3] Trouble awaited him in Taos, however; his dragoons, under the influence of "Taos Lightning," rioted and were jailed. One fact was apparent: the proud horse soldiers resented being subject to the command of Infantry officer John Garland.

His assignment in Taos concluded, Col. Bonneville set out southward in March, a trip from melting snows to tender buds to desert blooms. He assumed command at Fort Fillmore on April 8. The glories of spring in the Southwest are fleeting, and hot weather comes early. An unknown officer in the past had left a wealth of books to relieve the monotony for some at the post, but wind picked up billows of sand from the bare parade ground and whipped grit into the quarters. The terrain for all its stark beauty was without water. Congress appropriated money, and Captain John Pope drew the assignment to bore artesian wells. Only artesian wells were feasible because pumps of the day were wood-fueled steam-engine powered. Pope had failed to find water near the Pecos, and in early 1856 was sinking a hole ten miles west of Fort Fillmore. The search for water would prove to be as elusive as the search for peace with the Indians, the Army's task at hand.

In New Mexico, as in many parts of the West, the 1850s saw increasing Indian rebellion against an everclosing noose of white domination. Not that the red men had ever lived in peace. Indian cruelty to fellow Indian had always equalled or exceeded white cruelty to Indian. Plains Indians had chased the Navahos and Apaches into the southwest before the time of Columbus. They in turn dispossessed the ancient Pueblo Indians and whole tribes disappeared. In the Spanish era, colonies usurped the oases along the streams. Anglo settlers crowded the Indians further, and in addition, government planners decided to make Yankee farmers of the nomads, taking "great pains to instruct these people in the arts of civilization," as General Garland wrote in his 1856 report to the Secretary of War.

The twelve thousand or so Navahos in the north-central part of the territory were herdsmen, but cultivated corn and fruits on river bottomlands. The Apaches, said to number five thousand, lived in bleaker areas. Apache segments were named; the mescal eaters east of the Rio Grande were Mescaleros; the basket weavers were Jicarillas. The Mimbrenos, Chiracahuas, Mogollons and Gilas—also known as Coyoteros—took their names from mountains and rivers. Ute Indians lived around Taos and northward. Kiowas and Comanches claimed most of eastern New Mexico, and kept white settlement to a minimum. The term "Pueblos" designated remnants of prehistoric tribes who had lived in communal villages in laddered, blank-walled apartments—the Zunis, Hopis or Moquis, and others.

From Fort Fillmore, Bonneville sent detachments to the field in response to alarms. In an attack the previous year east of the Rio Grande, Apaches had killed several soldiers, and headquarters ordered a post built there. Complying, Col. Bonneville sent a company to Rio Bonito where they constructed Fort Stanton, named for the captain who had been ambushed in the area (about fifty miles west of later Roswell). Apaches protested this new intrusion; there were skirmishes.

In July, Colonel Bonneville was ordered to conduct a court of inquiry at Fort Bliss, commanded, in 1856, by Major Theophilus Holmes. New from West Point in 1835, Holmes had signed the petition at Fort Gibson protesting Bonneville's re-instatement, but in ensuing Army service together the two had become friends. Fort Bliss was popular with diary-keeping visitors who mentioned the relaxed military practice allowed there. Added attractions included Franklin, a new village on the American side of the river, and El Paso, the Mexican town. (Later, Franklin became El Paso and the Mexican city, Juarez.) W. W. H. Davis wrote that El Paso delighted the eye with "Vineyards, flower gardens, orchards and shrubbery loaded with flowers and fruit, and little canals along nearly all the streets," but another visitor wrote that the trade center was a rendezvous for rascals, cutthroats and knaves."[4]

Appointed Commander of the Department of New Mexico

Col. Bonneville returned to Fort Fillmore on August 3 and a week later took an eight-day leave, destination not noted in post returns. Judge Simeon Hart many have invited him back to El Paso; hospitality was legendary at the judge's riverside rancho "El Molino." However, changes were afoot at Department Headquarters, and Bonneville may have gone to Santa Fe. Gen.

John Garland, with whom he had shared General Worth's fiascos in the Mexican War, had given New Mexico his best efforts for three years, beginning with a conciliatory approach to the Indian problems which withered before increased depredation. Garland had inherited a web of problems, including his predecessor's order to launch a war against the Navahos. Now he had come full circle. Though his campaigns against the Utes had been somewhat successful, affairs elsewhere had deteriorated. Advised that any action must be full-scale war, no halfway measures, he began to plan an expedition into Navaho country. But he was ailing, and wanted to go back to the States. Col. Bonneville was ordered on August 30 to replace General Garland as commander of the Department of New Mexico.

Santa Fe was a stained glass panorama of past and present. Abbe Domenich, a traveler of the era, described the scarlet-flowered meadows framing the town, the plaza markets crowded with barrels of Taos whiskey, earthen jars, and baskets of melons, grapes, pimentos, pine nuts, cheese, tobacco and dried meat. Indians brought in venison and wild turkey; rancheros sold bundles of wood, brought to town by burros. Diarist W. W. H. Davis noted that costumes were gradually changing to American styles with blankets being replaced by shirts and coats, though "striking, handsome mounted caballeros" dressed themselves in embroidered sombreros, silver-buttoned jackets and fine serapes. New Mexican women, though mostly barefoot, decked themselves in bright-hued chemises and petticoats, topped with mantillas which might modestly cover the face. Davis was dazzled by the color and verve, but the good Abbe lamented that the women smoked, talked loud, and in the evening after angelus, lounged about the square until time for the nightly fandango.[5]

Governor David Meriwether was no stranger to Santa Fe; he had once been held prisoner there with other Yankee traders. As territorial governor he had achieved good rapport with the Army, a wary stand-off with the Indians, and the uncompromising disapproval of many of the citizenry. In the governor's office of the Palace, bleached muslin covered ceiling beams, and a strip of calico lined the walls. Red muslin draped the platform in the adjoining legislative chambers. The law-making bodies had language difficulty; the most effective members were bilingual. Yankee newcomers were surprised to learn that New Mexicans were not entranced with the 'democracy' which was suddenly their lot. Their traditional ways had enabled them to survive for two hundred years in a land of hostile geography and aborigines. Important families and the clergy possessed most of the property and education and took some care of the others. Family and friendship ties were strong, and wants were few.[6]

Rear rooms of the Governor's Palace served as Army headquarter's offices, but it is likely that personal living quarters of the commandant were elsewhere, perhaps at "La Fonda" adjoining the Plaza and serving as civic center as well as hotel. It was designed with its own interior patio, surrounded by commodious rooms. Visiting officers stayed there.

A change of commanding officers afforded opportunity for face-saving shifting of plans. Reviewing the complexities of his new job, Bonneville "approached the Indian problem with a sword in one hand and an olive branch in the other," historian Frank D. Reeve has written.[7] He cancelled Garland's plan to use civilian volunteers and began to inquire what materiel he could count on. Appalled at what he learned, he requested from Washington an inspection of "the unserviceable quartermaster property at the several posts." The several posts included, besides those on the Rio Grande, perimeter posts at Fort Defiance in Navaho country, Cantonment Burgwin in Taos and Fort Massachusetts north of it, Fort Union guarding the Santa Fe trail, Fort Stanton in the Capitan Mountains, Fort Buchanan in the Whetstone Mountains, and the Presidio in Tucson. Men and officers totalled less than two thousand and included the Third Infantry and portions of the Eighth Infantry, Second Artillery and Mounted Rifles. Bonneville concluded that much planning needed to be done before Garland's war against the Navahos could be launched.

The Apache War

While Col. Bonneville considered which parts of Garland's plans for a Navaho expedition were possible, or necessary, a new development was thrust upon him. An express rider brought news on November 28 that Henry Dodge, veteran agent to the Navahos, had been kidnapped by a band of Apaches. The Governor ordered Apache agent Michael Steck to compel his charges to release Dodge, even if ransom must be paid, adding that this appeared to be revenge for the Army's blunder of killing innocent Apaches. Friendly Mimbres Apache Chief Mangas Coloradas learned that Dodge's captors were Mogollon and Coyotero Apaches, who had joined forces to make war. A little later there was word that Dodge had been killed. Bonneville ordered a detachment to search for the remains. After two weeks of struggling through deep snow, the soldiers found a part of the body of Henry Dodge. The citizenry, egged on by the local press, demanded instant revenge for the Dodge death and for other raids and killings. Editor James L. Collins of the "Santa Fe Gazette" soundly criticized Governor Meriwether's Indian policy; it was said Collins wanted Meriwether's post as Superintendent of Indian affairs. Meriwether's standing deteriorated to the point that he asked for a military guard and slept with a loaded gun. He had long ago been burned in effigy.

Obviously, the Navaho campaign must wait. Bonneville declined also to be pushed into punitive action against the Apaches in the middle of the winter. Planning his campaign against the Apaches for springtime, Col. Bonneville began to mobilize troops and supplies. Projecting a three-pronged sweep, he ordered dragoons to ride from Tucson, Col. W. W. Loring to bring his Mounted Rifles from Fort Union through Mogollon lands and Lt. Col. Dixon S. Miles to march westward from Fort Thorn. Interpreters, packers, teamsters and blacksmiths were hired; Fort Thorn hummed with activity.

Major John Simonsen arrived in a cold rainstorm with several companies of Eighth Infantry and Mounted Rifles. In his command were two young lieutenants whose private journals provide sidelights to the records. Newly-commissioned John Van Deusen Du Bois penned vituperation against all the officers of the infantry and most of his superiors in the cavalry—his dislike being compounded according to the age of his targets, and his witticisms directed at names and physical dimensions. Infantry Lt. Henry Lazelle found occasions to slander Mexicans, Indians, Negroes and Catholics in his journal. Though professing to dislike Du Bois, Lazelle aped the horse soldier's disdain of every plan and every order.[8] The reader can but conclude that both officers wrote to feed their own egos, but can feel sympathy, too, for these inexperienced young men in the hostile arena of an Indian war. Both were just beginning years of faithful service to the Army.

To stock a depot near his area of operations, Bonneville left Fort Thorn on April 30 with a wagon train of supplies and an escort of sixty men. That very night, as if to mock the Army, Apache raiders drove off sixty-five mules from Fort Thorn while the herders slept. A company was dispatched in hot pursuit. On May 1, Col. Miles set his column in motion, designating rifle companies as advance and rear guards. "The infantry companies do nothing," Du Bois complained. He scoffed at "very funny" orders for mounted companies to wash the backs of their horses every night. Miles' command included four companies of infantry, two of mounted rifles and forty Indians, "not a very large force to attack a nation said to have two thousand warriors," Du Bois wrote.

The road westward followed the California trail, skirting the southern flanks of Cooke's range, ablaze at this season with wildflowers. Near Cooke's Spring, Bonneville sent Miles on a sweep south, while he steered the supply train toward a pass to the Gila. After a fruitless search almost to the Mexican border, Miles turned about and headed toward the rendezvous on the Gila. The days were blazing hot. The men suffered from dysentery and ague. "The backs of both horses and pack mules are very sore, raw and swollen" Lazelle wrote, though cavalryman Du Bois, who had scorned washing the animals, did not mention this.[9] From Cow Springs, Miles traveled northwest, scouting the Burro Mountains where Apaches had set fire to the grassy hills, scorching the earth as they withdrew. On schedule, Miles brought his column to the supply rendezvous. Col. Bonneville had chosen a superior location for Gila Depot and his detachment had built tents to house stores, a hospital, workshops and quarters on a bluff in the southern flank of the Mogollon mountains. Later history buffs locate Gila Depot in or near Section 10 R 17 W T. 16 overlooking the mouth of Greenwood Canyon six miles from Santa Lucia Spring, later known as Mangas Spring.

Bonneville intended to scour the Gila and Mimbres valleys, the Burro, Mogollon and San Vincent mountains. He sent Captain Claiborne and fifty mounted men to explore a canyon where Indian guides reported an encampment of Apaches. Lt. Du Bois, chafing for action, was sent with another scouting party and wrote, "We are in the very heart of the rocky mountains, many thousand feet above the sea, surrounded by black frowning mountains, cozy little valleys with vertical sides of solid rock" but his only prey killed was a wildcat.

Col. Loring brought his command to Gila Depot on May 19 after a difficult trip through Mogollon heartland which had yielded nothing. Captain Claiborne returned from his scout to report that he had found tracks of a large herd of stolen sheep. Bonneville ordered portions of both Miles' and Loring's men to pursue the thieves in a pincer movement. Loring found some of the culprits in a canyon; a number of Indians were killed—reports vary—and some captured. Several hundred sheep were recovered, but the most noteworthy news was that one of the Indians killed was the warring Chief Cuchilla Negra. By May 31, Miles' and Loring's columns rejoined Bonneville at Gila Depot. Captain Richard W. Ewell with three companies of dragoons also arrived from Tucson.

Two weeks rest for horses and men, plus additional supplies from Fort Thorn, put the troops in readiness for a push into the wilderness. According to camp gossip, they were heading into an area which no white man had ever passed though, except a Spanish missionary who was shot at with gold slugs. "We are off at last for the Coyotero country!" Lt. Du Bois wrote on June 13. His hopes for quick action were dashed when he was not chosen for duty with Captain Ewell. "One rifle officer, one dragoon officer, and every subaltern infantry officer accompanies him," Du Bois wrote. "I have been ordered to remain, to allow some thin infantry officer to cull all the opportunities he can . . ."

Bonneville traveled with the main column up steep slopes to a rocky mesa, then down a precarious trail to camp in Canon Bonita. Du Bois wrote that Col. Bonneville covered his tent walls with charcoal sketches and added, "among his ideas, some few picked up in his travels as a young man in Oregon are valuable." On Rio San Carlos, the troops saw a deserted pueblo; the Navaho guides reported that they had attacked this settlement of fellow Indians the previous year. On up a steep trail, advance units reported fresh Indian signs. Now Du Bois suffered what he considered the final insult. Though they could join Ewell's advance troops, the riflemen were ordered to leave their horses "dismounted by an infantry colonel and to march on foot." Ewell learned of an Apache encampment but waited until daylight to attack. The Apaches had fled. A warrior yelled in defiance from hidden heights. At this time, to the chagrin of many, the soldiers had to eat horse meat. "Haven't they got plenty of fat mares?" Bonneville is reported to have said in response to complaints of short supplies. It appeared to be wisdom to turn back, but the officers wanted to go on one more day and Bonneville agreed.

On June 27, Captain Ewell led the columns, and this time Lt. Du Bois and his company of rifles, mounted again, rode close behind. Six miles of climbing brought them to a summit commanding a view of Gila Valley. A few miles away dust, smoke and a herd of horses revealed the presence of the quarry. Ewell's dragoons thundered down on one side of the Gila and the Rifles on the other, shooting as soon as they came in range. There was no escape for the Indians on either side of the river, though some tried to hide in the willows. Dust swirled so thick there was danger of the soldiers shooting each other. Du Bois wrote "Balls and buckshot now whistled so thick around us that I withdrew my men." He followed the trail of retreating Indians, "killing one and driving back several others into the midst of the infantry." Du Bois received a bullet though his hat. "It was a perfect stampede," he exulted. "They were all killed. The assembly was blown and we all encamped near the field . . . the whiskey was emptied to our success."

Reports put the Indian dead at two or three dozen, with as many prisoners taken. Nine soldiers were wounded, some from arrows; all recovered. Lt. Du Bois wrote in his diary that one captured brave was executed by a Pueblo guide, and criticized Bonneville for allowing it. No other source mentions the incident. But Du Bois had second thoughts about the whole campaign. "I walked over the field today. I could not avoid asking myself why we had killed these poor harmless savages . . . they had robbed only the mexicans . . ." He was wrong. Apache agent Michael Steck acknowledged that this band of Coyotero Apaches had made bloody raids along the Rio Grande and the California trail; one of those killed in the battle was the very Apache who had killed Henry Dodge.

The troops destroyed Coyotero corn and beans, and gathered up abandoned livestock. When Indians mocked them with yells in the night, some of the soldiers expected another battle. At Rio San Francisco, the command camped near a large Indian village. An Apache messenger came into camp and said he would bring in his chiefs for a talk. Short as they were of supplies and far outnumbered, the Army was not in the best of positions. Nevertheless, Bonneville posted a white flag of welcome. In the night, scattered shots gave the lie to the Indians' peaceful protestations and kept the guards edgy. To the emissaries who finally appeared, Bonneville proposed exchanging his Apache prisoners for Mexicans the Indians held. The Indians agreed, but temporized about arrangements; they were testing the extent of Bonneville's patience, and perhaps waiting for reinforcements. Or, as so many times was the case, those who were willing to make bargains had no real authority to do so, but were waiting for the customary gifts. Bonneville decided to call their bluff. He gave orders to "sound the general" and in short order the Army marched in force down the river. Du Bois thought the movement "absurd" but a Mexican boy who escaped the Indians and joined the camp reported that when the Apaches saw the movement they thought the soldiers intended to surround them and fled to the mountains.

It was time to go home. En route to the Depot the officers celebrated the Fourth of July with a single bottle of liquor which Lt. Du Bois reported they stole from Colonel Bonneville; the rank and file apparently had only the waters of the Gila. The columns struck cross country, avoiding canyons. It was slow traveling and the horse soldiers chafed to separate from the infantry. Bonneville gave them permission to do so, and in a few days all commands were united at Gila Depot.

Early Western Map-making: A Voice From the Past

An express brought word that General Garland had returned to New Mexico and resumed command of the Department. In reporting to him of the campaign Bonneville suggested abandoning Gila Depot. Garland concurred. The Apache war was over.[10] Col. Loring was ordered to look into rumblings in Navaho country, Capt. Ewell and his dragoons headed west, and Col. Miles started his column to Fort Thorn. Col. Bonneville stayed to supervise dismantling the Depot. Some time before he left the Gila, he penned an answer to questions from Topographical Engineer G. K. Warren who was researching early western map-making. The inquiry was like a voice from the past. Bonneville wrote, in part:

"I thank you for your desire to do me justice as regards my maps and explorations in the Rocky Mountains . . . I kept good account of the course and distances, with occasional observations with my quadrant and Dolland's reflecting telescope. I plotted my work, found it proved, and made it into three parts; one, a map of the waters running east to the Missouri State line; a second of the mountain region itself, and third, which appears to be the one you have sent me, of the waters running west. On the map you send I recognize my names of rivers, of Indian tribes, observations, Mary's or Maria's river running southwest ending in a long chain of flat lakes never before on any map . . . On all the maps of those days the Great Salt Lake had two great outlets to the Pacific Ocean: one of these was the Buenaventura River, which was supposed to head there. It was from my explorations and those of my party alone that it was ascertained that this lake had no outlet; that the California range basined all the waters of its eastern slope without further outlet . . . It was for this reason the Mr. W. Irving named the salt lake after me, and he believed I was fairly entitled to it. I gave Mr. Washington Irving the three maps I mention; and as the publication was by Carey, Lea and Blanchard, the originals may, perhaps, be found with them. The earliest editions have maps of my making. The one you refer to me I have no doubt is one of the three maps I made." G. K. Warren commented when he published Bonneville's letter that he could not find the original maps.[11]

In his diary Lt. Du Bois lamented the "degradation of escorting the ox train of supplies and Col. Bonneville." By his reckoning, the command had traveled fourteen hundred miles in the past four months. The hot dust of August hung in clouds over the plodding wagons, and Fort Thorn was a welcome sight for those who brought in the government property. Submitting detailed reports of the expedition, Bonneville enclosed accounts from his officers,

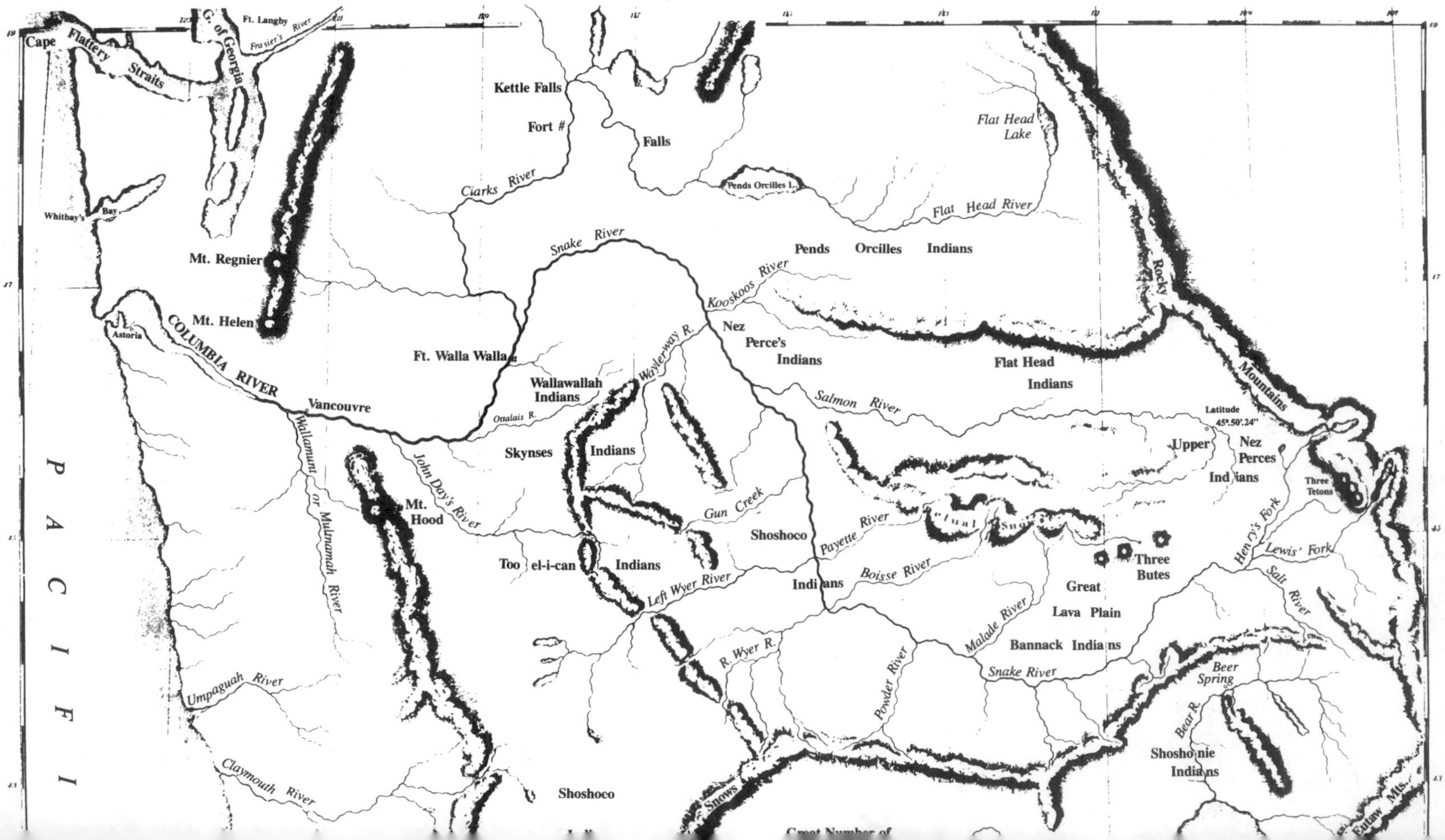

Cape Flattery Straits
G. of Georgia
Ft. Langby
Frasier's River
Whitbay's Bay
Mt. Regnier
Mt. Helen
Astoria
COLUMBIA RIVER
Vancouvre
Wallamunt or Multnamah River
Umpaguah River
Claymouth River
Mt. Hood
Kettle Falls
Fort #
Falls
Clarks River
Pends Orcilles L.
Flat Head Lake
Flat Head River
Pends Orcilles Indians
Snake River
Kooskoos River
Nez Perce's Indians
Flat Head Indians
Rocky Mountains
Ft. Walla Walla
Wallawallah Indians
Waylerway R.
Ottalais R.
Skynses
Indians
John Day's River
Gun Creek
Shoshoco
Salmon River
Payette River
Boisse River
Indians
Too el-i-can
Indians
Left Wyer River
R. Wyer R.
Powder River
Malade River
Snake River
Great Lava Plain
Bannack Indians
Three Butes
Latitude 45°.50'.24"
Upper Nez Perces Indians
Three Tetons
Henry's Fork
Lewis' Fork
Salt River
Beer Spring
Bear R.
Shoshonie Indians
Entaw Mts.
Snows
Shoshoco
P A C I F I

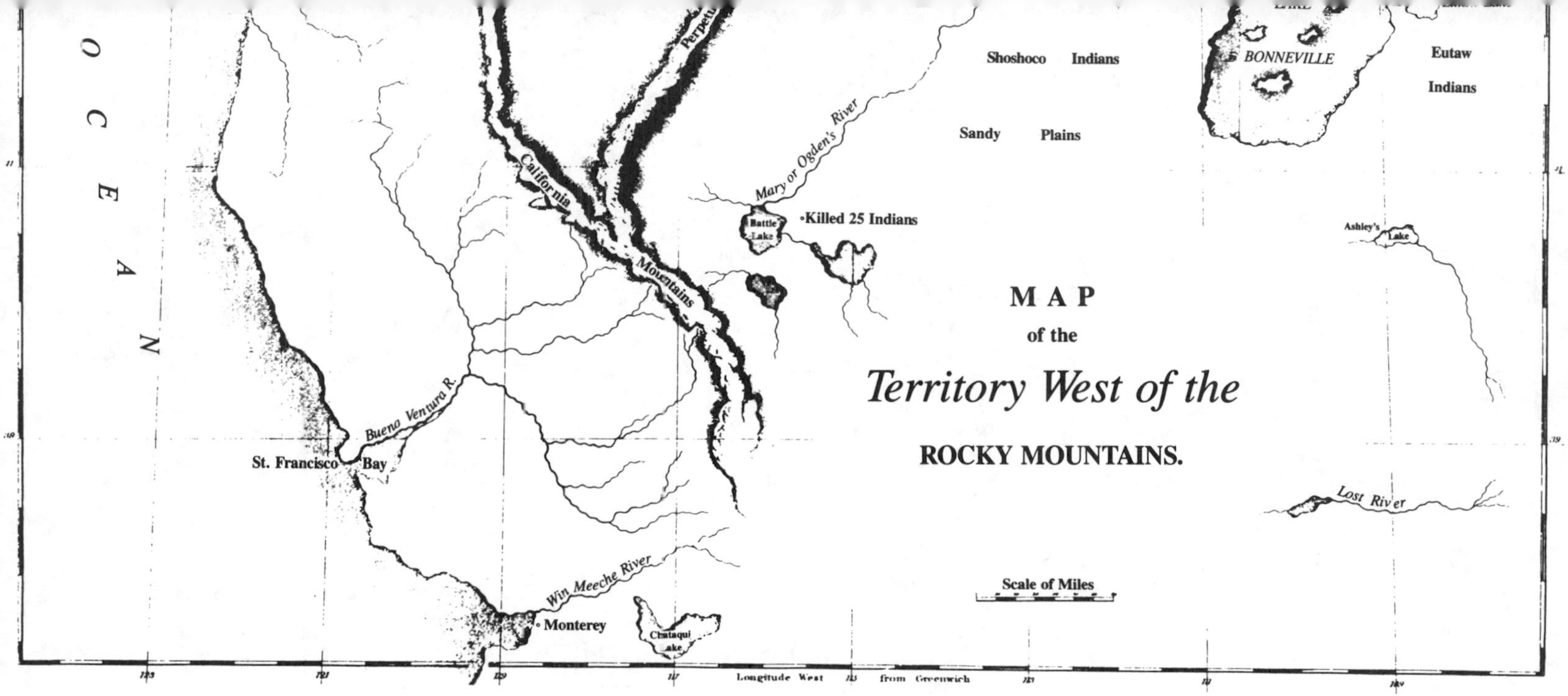

Bonneville's 1837 "Map of the Territory West of the Rocky Mountains" was the first to show the Great Basin without drainage to the sea, the Columbia River sources, the great Sierra barrier and the placement of many Indian tribes. His messengers to California did not report the coastal range; hence it is missing. Names of the geographical features have been typeset and inserted to make the map more legible.

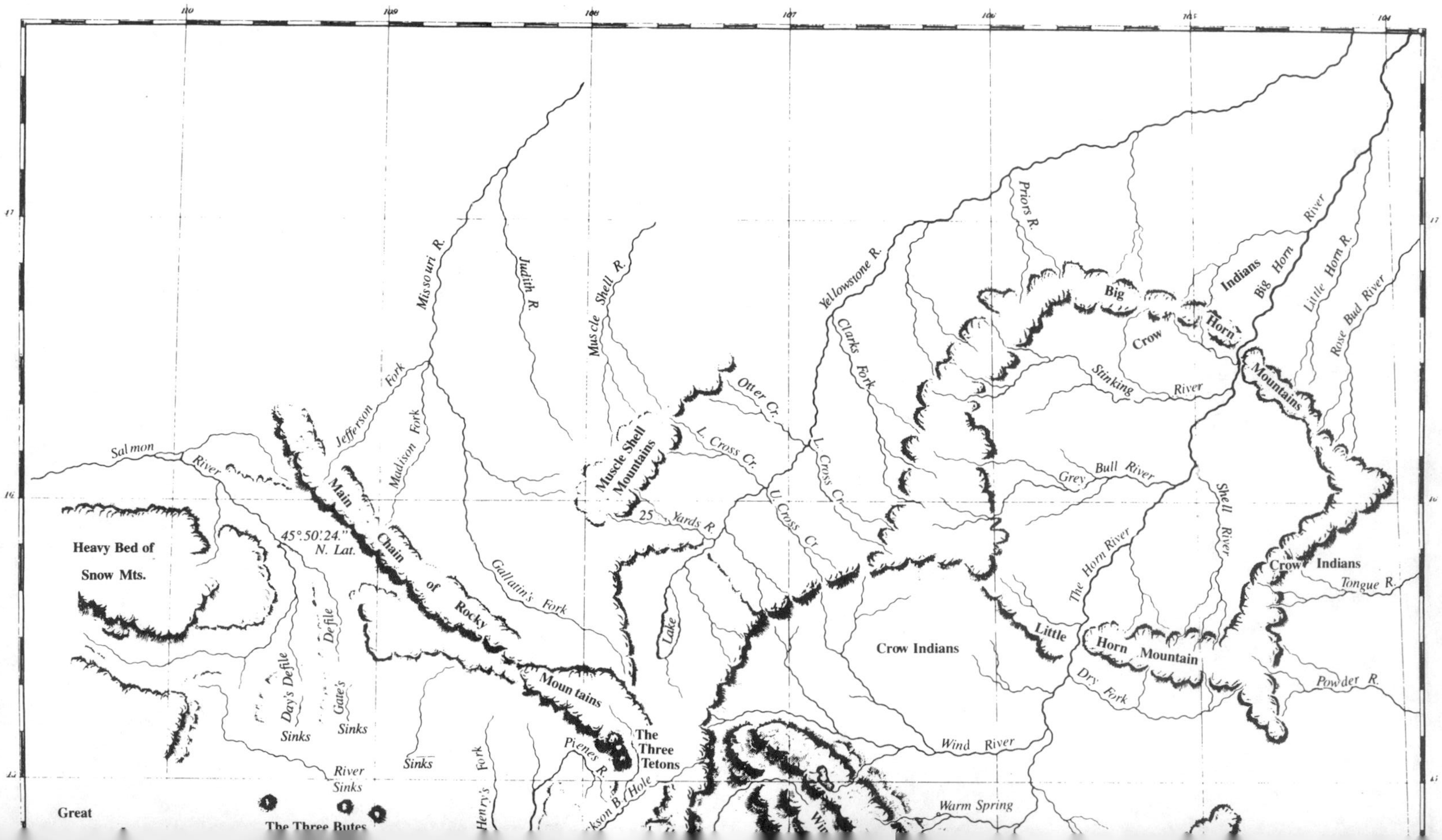

110
109
108
107
106
105
104
47
46
45
Missouri R.
Judith R.
Muscle Shell R.
Yellowstone R.
Priors R.
Big
Indians
Big Horn River
Little Horn R.
Rose Bud River
Horn
Crow
Stinking River
Mountains
Jefferson Fork
Madison Fork
Otter Cr.
Salmon
River
Muscle Shell Mountains
L. Cross Cr.
L. Cross Cr.
Clarks Fork
Grey
Bull River
Shell River
Main
Chain
of
Rocky
Moun tains
45°.50'.24."
N. Lat.
Heavy Bed of
Snow Mts.
25 Yards R.
U. Cross Cr.
The Horn River
Crow Indians
Tongue R.
Gallatin's Fork
Lake
Little
Horn Mountain
Crow Indians
Defile
Day's Defile
Gate's
Sinks
Sinks
Dry Fork
Powder R.
The
Three
Tetons
Pienes R.
Wind River
Sinks
Fork
Henry's
River
Sinks
Great
The Three Butes
Warm Spring

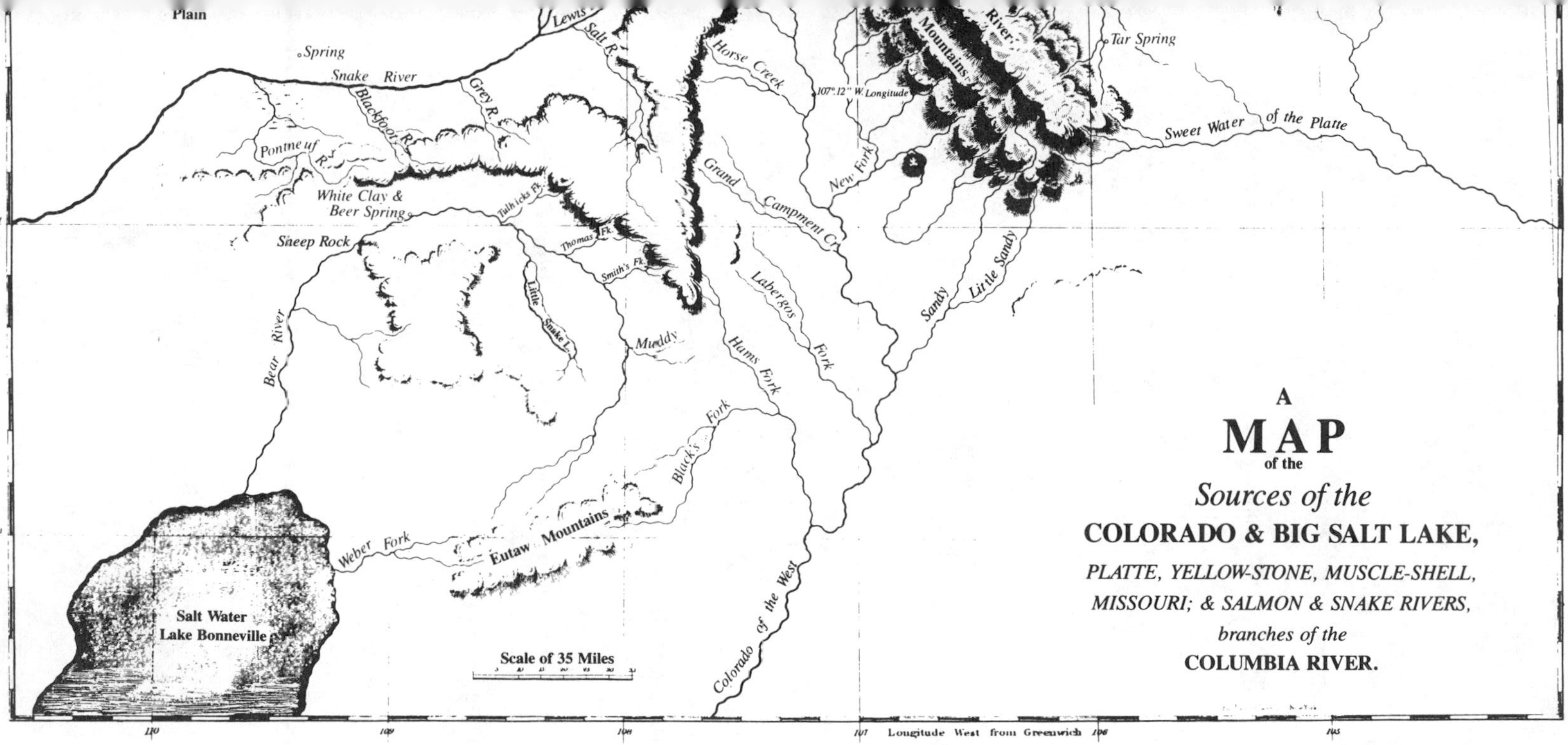

Washington Irving printed two Bonneville maps in his 1837 **Adventures of Captain Bonneville**. *On this reproduction of "Map of the Sources of the Colorado and Big Salt Lake, Plate, Yellow-stone, Muscle-Shell, Missouri; & Salmon & Snake Rivers, branches of the Columbia River," more easily read names of the geographical features have been typeset and inserted.*

and gave full credit to Ewell, Miles, Loring and all the subalterns including Lazelle and Du Bois. The territorial legislature tendered its thanks to Bonneville and the "Santa Fe Weekly Gazette" declared that "the Gila Expedition was the most arduous, trying and dangerous military operation projected since New Mexico became a possession of the United States government."

A delegation of Coyoteros came to the Apache agency and asked for an audience. Agent Michael Steck summoned Col. Bonneville. The Apaches, whose spokesman was Chino Pena, came to ask for peace. After fleeing from the Army on June 27, Pena said, the Coyoteros held a three-day conference and decided to offer all the "mountains, water, sod and grass" in exchange for peace. With Bonneville's approval, Steck replied that the government, too, wanted peace and that the Apaches need not give up their mountains, water, sod and grass, but only their savage habits. Under questioning the Coyoteros admitted their guilt. Nevertheless, compassionate Dr. Steck pleaded for the release of the prisoners taken in the campaign because they were suffering from disease. The harsh truth was that 1857 was a year of severe drought, making existence precarious for the already hard-pressed Apaches. Their unending feuds with fellow Indians and their undying hatred of Mexicans for past mistreatment had left them with no allies and a bailiwick so bleak and bare they had to steal to survive. Mulling their options, the Coyoteros appealed to the government. Besides subsistence, they needed protection.[12]

Proposal for an Apache Reservation

Bonneville had an idea of his own for an Apache solution. Dr. Steck advocated a reserve for the tribe; Bonneville suggested what seemed to him an ideal spot. Prefacing a letter with a summary of his foray into Gila country, he described the "large open country extending from the Burro mountains on the east to the Almoque on the west leading to a valley sixty to one hundred miles long and forty miles wide with finest grazing . . . extensive bottom lands. This valley . . . gives evidence of a former people, agricultural in their pursuits. Though choice and fertile, Bonneville pointed out, the area was too remote for "busy enterprising settlers who seek the great thorofares" ever to want it. His men, on his orders, had mapped the country well. The letter, along with Dr. Steck's supporting one, went to Washington. But though they appear in the annual report of the Secretary of the Interior, no action was taken.[13]

Headquarters Moved to Albuquerque

General Garland ordered Col. Bonneville to move his Third Infantry headquarters to Albuquerque. That ancient village sat centrally among the Army's scattered posts. The "Post at Albuquerque," as it was called, was a busy crossroads, with troops traveling to assignments and supplies being portioned out. One eye-catching detachment passed through in August, 1857: Lt. Edward F. Beale, surveying a road across New Mexico, also trailed along a herd of camels in an experiment to see if they might be suited to army use in desert country.

In Albuquerque, sunshine paints an amber patina on old adobe. In the late 1850s some of the flat-roofed casas were well past the century mark. The Church of San Felipe had been built in 1706, with windows twenty feet above ground level and four-foot-thick walls to withstand Indian battering rams. Other adobe structures encircled the plaza like a barricade; Spanish colonials had corralled their cattle there, and later it became a busy marketplace by day and a fiesta center by night. Casa de Armijo, an elaborate home on the east side of the plaza, was occupied by officers during the Civil War, and may also have been used earlier, when Bonneville was there. There were shops, a hotel, and a weekly newspaper. Some complained that the area was drab, but Albuquerque's vistas included snowy Cebolleta and its mountain ranges on the west, and on the east, the Sandia peaks rising a mile higher than the mesas.

During the autumn, Col. Bonneville was called to Santa Fe to a court martial in which the commander at Fort Defiance stood accused of dereliction of duty. The firm hand of Navaho agent Henry Dodge had kept the tribe under control, and without him the small garrison at the distant post faced a precarious winter. The season had produced little forage for either Indian flocks or for the military's horses and beef. The personal problems of the post's commander added to the difficulty. He was cashiered, but the mounting trouble in Navaho homelands remained.

After two years in New Mexico, Bonneville's initial expectations could have but diminished. But if all was not tranquil in the sunny territory, neither was it in the States, according to weeks-late news. The slavery issue was producing reams of verbiage. A financial panic threatened banking circles. President Buchanan had ordered a sizeable portion of the Army to Utah Territory to stamp out a Mormon rebellion he had been told existed there.

In pleasanter news, Congress authorized John Butterfield to carry passengers and mail overland to the Pacific by way of St. Louis, Little Rock, El Paso and Tucson. Heretofore, travelers had the choice of the Texas "Jackass Mail" or the catch-as-catch-can passenger service of caravans on the Santa Fe trail. This difficulty of travel may have been the chief reason why Bonneville's family did not join him. Apparently they did not, for Ann is never mentioned in contemporary journals, though many officers' wives are. Lt. Du Bois wrote in his diary that on New Year's Day, 1858, he called on Col. Bonneville, "the commandante in Albuquerque." Du Bois did not mention Ann or Mary, which he would have done had they been present. No young woman escaped his notice, and he missed no opportunity, either, to complain about the Army wives he encountered.

With bitter weather, discontent among the red men mounted. Kiowas threatened in the eastern areas; a company of Third was ordered to patrol. New Mexican outlaws attacked a small Navaho band near Albuquerque, and downriver raided peaceable Apaches near Dona Ana. Later, vigilantes calling themselves "militia" raided an Indian camp near Fort Thorn and slaughtered a number of man, women and children; an Army detachment captured these criminals.

Troops Sent for the Mormon War

Major Wm. T. H. Brooks, new commander at Fort Defiance, wrote to General Garland of the almost starving condition of the Navahos. In midwinter, alarms came that Mormons were urging Navahos and Utes to unite with them against the United States government. According to historian Frank McNitt, "Often prejudiced and nearly always exaggerated accounts of the time built a Western myth of Mormon efforts to draw Navahos and Utes into War." But General Garland believed the stories, and fired off letters to Washington and to General Albert Sidney Johnston offering men, supplies and advice.[14]

Snowbound on western high plains, General Albert Sidney Johnston decided he did need help against the Mormons. He dispatched Captain Randolph Marcy with sixty men to seek supplies from the Department of New Mexico. Frostbitten and hungry, Marcy reached Taos in late January. General Garland assembled the requested aid, and in March Marcy moved out with thirty wagons and sixteen hundred animals, and besides his own men, Lt. Du Bois and his rifle company. Du Bois was delighted, writing that he thought the expedition would be "very like romance." Two days later an urgent dispatch from General Johnston asked for two additional companies of infantry and one of mounted rifles. Garland sent Col. W. W. Loring from Fort Union, and ordered Bonneville to send two companies of Third Infantry from Albuquerque.

More Indian Disputes—The Navaho Campaign

In the hindsight of observers, Major Wm. T. H. Brooks' assignment to Fort Defiance in the heart of Navaho country was a blunder. He quarreled with young chieftain Manuelita, and insulted elder statesman Zarcillos Largos. Informed that Indian cattle were feeding in Army pastures, he ordered troops to the field. They killed four dozen Indian cattle plus some horses. Zarcillos Largos came to the fort in the role of peacemaker, but was brushed aside. On July 12, a Navaho shot a fatal arrow into Major Brooks' Negro slave. Brooks summoned Zarcillos Largos, but that once-willing peacemaker rebuffed him. Brooks then issued an ultimatum programmed for failure: surrender the guilty Indian within twenty days, or war would be declared. He wrote to General Garland recommending massive Army action, and that the Utes be urged to raid the Navahos. Garland agreed with Brooks. Fresh recruits were expected soon, he replied, and in the meantime, ammunition would be sent to the Utes to use on the Navahos. Incredibly, this directive had come from Washington: "Should you fail in your efforts to keep the Indians in a state of peace and quiet, then your aim should be to array them against such other Indians as may be found on the side of the enemies of the Government."[15] New Superintendent of Indian Affairs for New Mexico James Collins demurred at the Ute project, but agreed that war was inevitable. However, he commissioned Samuel Yost to go to Fort Defiance to try to salvage the peace.

General Garland chose Lt. Col. Dixon S. Miles to head the expedition. Orders flew from the Department Headquarters in August. Garland wrote that citizen militia might be used, but sent word to Brooks to make no move until reinforcements arrived. Col. Miles, assembling his forces at Albuquerque, sent Captain Geo. McLane and his rifle company in advance. In the last days of August, Col. Miles set off westward for the Navaho War. Enroute, he learned that the ambitious Captain McLane, against orders, had attacked a peaceable Navaho encampment at Bear Springs. Half a dozen Navahos were killed, some wounded and captured. Furious, Miles complained that this stupid action would make the enemy fly in every direction. By two days' forced march he reached Fort Defiance. Here he compounded Brooks' error, thundering that if the slave's murderer was not brought in within five days, he would kill and destroy all the Navahos and that, further, Utes and Pueblos and New Mexicans and Apaches would join him in capturing all the Navaho women and children and in destroying all the flocks and gardens.[16]

General Garland disapproved of Miles' proposed offensive in a communication dated September 9, but on that day Miles had marched with three hundred and fifty troops toward the heart of Navaho country. His outer bluster covered some trepidation, for he wrote to headquarters that since the post commander who departed months before had taken with him every map and sketch of the area, "My march will be like an exploration of an unknown region."

Miles' hasty action no longer concerned General Garland. That aging officer had summoned Col. Bonneville to command the Department, and departed for the States via the Santa Fe Trail. Not explained is the abruptness of his leave-taking. He left on September 15; Bonneville assumed command on the 16th. Miles knew nothing of Garland's departure, for he continued to address him in his dispatches. In any event, whether because of reported ill health or pique at the turn of events, Garland was gone and the burden of the Navaho War fell on Bonneville.

First reports from the field did not please Bonneville. He chided Miles for not supporting Yost's attempts at peace and pointed out that the headlong charge into Navaho country was premature inasmuch as the promised reinforcements had not yet arrived in New Mexico. However, he sent Miles "the best maps within reach, an additional interpreter, quartermaster and surgeon," and permission to hire additional guides. Concluding, Bonneville wrote, "Although it becomes your duty to press this matter by active operations I must insist that you allow no opportunity of negotiating to escape, the moment they manifest a sincere desire to comply with our demands."

The towering, stark red walls of Canyon de Chelly took some bluster out of Miles. Indians mocked the troops from the heights, out of reach of musket fire. In a spooky march through the bottom of the gorge troops and guides killed ten Navahos. From the mouth of the canyon, Miles moved back to Fort Defiance by way of Pueblo Colorado Wash. Navahos followed and harassed them; the bugler and a private were killed by arrows. The troops had captured several thousand sheep; back at Fort Defiance, Miles decided they were a nuisance and ordered them killed.

Miles sent in his report of his week's march, together with a batch of complaints and demands. Bonneville replied that though he was "gratified at the success of the scout . . . I do not desire the destruction of animals you take. All should be sent to Albuquerque; that portion belonging to private individuals should be delivered to them." On another touchy matter he wrote, "In regards to the censure of the late commanding officer of the department, it is an act of my predecessor over which I have no control."

In his reports to Army headquarters, Bonneville voiced his disapproval of Miles' demand "for the assistance of all the surrounding tribes . . . and also for volunteers. I do not consider volunteers necessary at this time," and to reinforce his own views against abetting the Indians in slaughter and plunder, "The superintendent of Indian affairs does not approve of one tribe of Indians being brought into conflict with another." Miles was likewise so informed.

From Fort Defiance, Miles sent scouts into surrounding canyons. Six Indians were killed. Among the wounded, venerable Zarcillos Largos was carried off by the retreating Navaho. The scouts piled "a rich booty of buffalo robes, blankets and saddles" on a stack of wheat and set it afire. Other forays netted warriors, cattle, mules and sheep captured, and camps and food burned. A messenger from wounded Zarcillos Largos offered peace talks.[17]

Bonneville, unaware of the peace overtures, worked to put a second column in the field. Electus Backus arrived with new recruits, and Bonneville directed him to proceed to Fort Defiance by way of Jemez, making every possible exertion to destroy and drive from that part of the country the troublemakers. "I should be pleased if you would furnish me with a map of your route in that part of the country, together with any reliable information you may obtain in regard to it," Bonneville concluded.

Miles' plans to scour Navaho country were too ambitious for the rations his men carried. Winter had already arrived in this high country. Signal fires burned on the ridges, and harassment began. Uneasy, Miles kept his forces together, traveling the mountains north of Canyon de Chelly instead of through it. Mules and horses were dying of hunger and exhaustion. Miles' desire for war waned, and so did Navaho resistance.

"I have had all day appeals for peace," Miles wrote. White flags, one a small cross with a white leaf on it, appeared on the trail the troops were following. "It must have been the work of many, from the footprints around . . . many women and children bare foot . . . "[18]

At the mouth of Canyon de Chelly, the column rested, turned their horses into ripened cornstalks and built fires of hogans. Chief Barboncito came into camp under a white flag and asked for a peace conference. His people were trying to find the killer of the slave, he said. Miles replied that if the headmen would come to Fort Defiance in seven days, peace could be discussed. Major Backus returned to Fort Defiance; he had scouted the ice-blanketed mountains, as directed, past the valley of Los Gigantes to Chinle Wash. Horses were dying and the men cold; when his wide-ranging detachments returned, Backus had turned back to join Miles.

Bonneville's first tidings of what was taking place in the field was the report that the Navaho leaders had asked for peace. Bonneville replied that the chieftains could come to Albuquerque and meet with him and with Superintendent Collins. But at Fort Defiance, Miles and peace-envoy Yost had declared an armistice and spelled out a treaty, including a stipulation that the Navahos elect a head chief to answer for all. Zarcillos Largos obliged, bringing a young man whose name was Huero; henceforth he would be known as Huero Miles, the Navaho said ingratiatingly, and he would act as Chief. Major Brooks demanded to know if he would be paid for his slave; Miles said that some of the captured livestock could be tendered as payment.

At Santa Fe, Col. Bonneville and Superintendent Collins were surprised to learn that arrangements were already made. To save face for the government, they could but proceed with the treaty, amending it so that it would in some measure accomplish the ends for which the campaign had been undertaken. Bonneville had directed Miles to be willing to negotiate, so he did not criticize but Collins was angry. Working together, Bonneville and Collins hammered out a more stringent agreement, and sent word that they would come to Fort Defiance.

Traveling by Army ambulance, they left Albuquerque in the chill of early winter. The military road led westward, rising steadily past red mesas and fields of lava. Towering Cebolleta and its flanking mountains glistened in the north. Toward the continental divide, snows were deeper; the four mules hitched to the ambulance floundered with exhaustion and had to be replaced. Shortly before Christmas, Department Commander Bonneville and Indian Superintendent Collins arrived at their destination.

Fort Defiance bulged at its perimeters with officers and men, civilian supply outfits and scores of "spies and guides," none quite sure the campaign was ended. Some had dug cellar-like shelters into the earth, others had only tents, for the buildings could house but a fraction of the assembled personnel. Agent Yost, smarting from a reprimand from Collins, revealed that Collins had accused the officers of bringing the war to a close because they were tired of it and because Christmas was near. The chill at Fort Defiance was not strictly a matter of weather.

On Christmas Day, 1858, terms of the agreement were presented. Indians were forbidden to travel or live farther east than twenty-five miles from Fort Defiance. The military reserved the right to patrol freely and to build facilities. Fifteen Navaho headmen signed the pact, including the patient Zarcillos Largos, Huero Miles and Huero Backus. Ceremonies concluded, Col.

Bonneville issued "General Order No. 11" announcing the close of the war with the Navaho nation. Major Backus remained to garrison Fort Defiance. Infantrymen and riflemen trudged back to Albuquerque. In his reports to Washington, Bonneville complimented Miles, Backus and other officers, as well as the troops, for their "energy and perseverance under trying and adverse circumstances." Along with the reports Bonneville sent, and noted with some pride, maps of the terrain covered by the patrols. Backus' was late coming in, but in due time, it too was submitted to Army headquarters.[19]

On the whole, 1858 had been a fair year for the nation. President Buchanan made his peace with the Mormons and ordered the Army to withdraw from the long goosechase. Butterfield stages made their first runs through New Mexico and were acclaimed in the newspapers for the record time of three weeks and three days from St. Louis to San Francisco. Prospectors found gold near Pike's Peak in far western Kansas Territory. All the news was late in getting to Santa Fe, of course, but not as late as one event of interest to the Army: in New York City, a second funeral was held for General Worth, dead now for nine years. The always-impatient officer's remains had waited in a vault while city fathers prepared a fitting mausoleum at Broadway and Fifth Avenue.

Indian Commissioner Collins was also editor of the "Santa Fe Gazette." Perhaps because he felt his authority had been usurped, he sharply criticized the Navaho campaign in his columns. He did, however, print a contribution written by Henry Winslow praising Bonneville and Miles, and stating that the once fierce Navaho "now are living as peaceable and quiet as other citizens."

There were others dissatisfied with the past months' activities. Lt. Du Bois, stationed at Fort Union, complained that Col. Loring, instead of being assigned to the Navaho War was sent in the opposite direction—Loring's participation would have included a role for Du Bois. The long weary Utah Expedition had been a disappointment because mediation had prevented bloodshed. Du Bois wrote that Mormon settlers were "vicious looking" and complained about his idol, Loring, being tardy sending in reports: "All my labor thrown away."[20]

Bonneville considered the brief campaign and quick armistice doubtful; he continued to hold two dozen Navahos hostage as insurance for treaty compliance. To strengthen the uneasy peace, he kept a large garrison at Fort Defiance, but alerted other posts to avoid clashes if possible. It was not entirely possible. Mescaleros east of the Rio Grande drove off a herd of cattle from

San Elizario, near Fort Bliss. Lt. Lazelle tracked the fugitives across rough country into the Sacramento mountains. In Dog Canyon, he was ambushed. Forwarding reports to Army headquarters, Col. Bonneville almost made the defeat sound like a victory.

"Lt. Lazelle . . . overtook the enemy, and after sharp conflict was obliged to withdraw, being severely wounded himself, and having three of his men killed, and six wounded. Although this attack appears to have been unsuccessful, it is gratifying to observe it was conducted with vigor and daring . . ."[21]

In peace efforts west of the Rio Grande, Agent Steck found the Apaches wary of promises, for the vigilantes who had killed Indian women and children had not been punished. The Apaches agreed not to disrupt travel on the overland trail, but reserved the right to raid their ancient enemy, the Mexicans. The trail concession was important: John Butterfield's Concord coaches operated regularly, with adobe stations dotting the route across New Mexico.

To the new commander at Fort Defiance, Captain O. L. Shepherd, Bonneville spelled out exactly what he expected: "Your duty is to afford full and ample protection to the settlements near you, and to all citizens passing through . . . Should the Navahos commit any aggressive act, you will not consider it as an offense of the whole tribe, but at once march to the offending band, taking the head chief with you and demand reparation; and if it is refused, chastise the parties at fault on the spot." Bonneville instructed Shepherd to require of citizens seeking redress "affidavits of all the facts and circumstances of the case as to the marks, numbers, and description of animals or other property stolen," since many false claims and accusations were made against the Indians.

Col. Bonneville inspected supply depots at Albuquerque, Las Lunas and Fort Craig, finding them satisfactory. He put detachments in the field in a show of strength. Fifty troops from Cantonment Burgwin visited Abiquiu while the Utes came in for their government annuities. Detachments from Las Lunas traveled into Navaho haunts on the Puerco River. From Fort Craig soldiers made a circuit of Santa Barbara, Rio Mimbres and the copper mines, returning over the mountains. Other patrols continued, their assignments were to scare away harassers, recover stolen property, provide escorts for various surveys, and on occasion to accompany private freighter caravans through risky areas.

Exploration Expeditions and a Circuit of the New Mexico Department

"For the summer's work if no outbreak occurs" Bonneville laid extensive plans. He directed troops from Fort Garland north of Taos to strike eastward across the mountains "to find a good road from that post to the great plains in the direction of the Arkansas" and then "to explore toward Grand River, a branch of the Colorado." In another maneuver, Captain Claiborne was ordered to travel eastward over the mountains from Fort Stanton to the Pecos River, then northward to the Canadian, this to impress the Comanches. A Navaho reconnaissance presented complications. Though the tribes had in some measure filled their obligations, some whites claimed they had not, and wanted punitive measures launched against them. Indian Commissioner James Collins, his initial sympathy gone, growled that the Navaho must be "humbled." Bonneville ignored the clamor and laid out plans for Major John Simonsen to escort a wagon road crew and "continue slowly to explore the country to the northwest, west and southwest . . . to furnish the department with exact information regarding the Navaho country, their bands, numbers, grazing grounds . . . This is not to be a general war," Bonneville cautioned Simonsen, though he would reclaim stolen livestock, "make explorations" and "make a show of force . . ."[22]

Colonel Bonneville had another project in mind, and this one he wanted to do himself. "It is my intention to start on the 2nd of May on a tour of inspection to Forts Buchanan, Bliss, and Stanton, a circuit of about twelve hundred miles, and expect to be absent about sixty days," he wrote to Army headquarters. The circuit encompassed the entire area of the Department of New Mexico from east to west. In his journal of the trip, he expressed his awareness and appreciation of the people, places and endeavors he saw.

With a small staff, Bonneville stopped first at Galisteo. Captain John Pope had wintered there, and was winding down his four-year failure to find artesian wells. Passing Mule Spring and Cooke Spring, Bonneville described the mud hut Butterfield stations which had been built about twenty miles apart along the road to California. Apache agent Michael Steck joined the party at a camp on the Mimbres River near Spanish colonial copper mines. Most of the Santa Rita miners were Mexicans from Chihuahua, suppliers were hard-bitten frontiersmen, and this was also a favorite Apache haunt because the settlers secretly would trade whiskey for cattle stolen in Mexico. Citing a recent clash,

Dr. Steck pointed out the explosive potential. Fort Webster, built to protect the mines, had been abandoned, but Bonneville summoned a detachment to take post there.

Northwest of the Butterfield station at Cow Spring, Bonneville made camp in a meadow at the base of the Burro mountains. On the overland road again, approaching a broad valley "the mirage presented to our view lakes, harbors, bridges, ships and all manner of water scenes changing constantly as we approached." As the party traveled the valley floor, dust rose in clouds about them. Here the stage station employees had to haul water, some a distance of thirty miles, Bonneville wrote.

"We reached Stein's Peak a little before sunset, and the water was so scarce that we did not succeed in watering our animals until near two o'clock in the morning. Here we found about fifty Indians, men, women and children around the station, apparently on the most friendly terms . . . I had a talk with the Indians who appeared to make very fair promises." Turning south with the Butterfield route, Bonneville and his companions wound through rough country to the "valley of San Simon" and on to "Apache pass, a gap in the Chiracahua mountains." At most camping spots water was found only by digging into streambeds.

Leaving the overland road through a pass in the Whetstone mountains to reach Fort Buchanan, Bonneville wrote "On almost every mountain we could see by the fires and smokes that the Indians were there busy preparing their winter's food." Colonel Bonneville was not pleased with Fort Buchanan on the southeast slope of the mountains. The storehouses were but "temporary sheds covered with tarpaulins, and quarters were "of upright poles daubed with mud." The post was too far from the overland road to protect travelers and too far from Tucson to be of value to settlers, yet not close enough to Apache homelands to serve as a depot should a campaign in Indian country be necessary. "The post will have to be rebuilt, and it had better be put in the right place."

From the valley of Sonoita creek, the travelers rounded a point of mountains to Santa Cruz valley where there were farms. At Tubac, mining officials occupied former Mexican barracks, and a town had been laid out to entice settlers. By invitation Bonneville visited the mines at Arivaca and Sopora. "The valley of the river Santa Cruz appears to be a network of mineral veins," he reported. "Silver mixed with copper, and silver mixed with lead, extending, as some suppose, much further west . . ."

Concerning the area northward down Santa Cruz valley, Bonneville noted the existence of "Xavier . . . an old church which is still the admiration of all who visit that part of the country." Of Tucson, he wrote, "a neat little town on the edge of a cienaga, or wet meadow made by the sinking of the Santa Cruz river, and it was refreshing to see the green grass and cottonwood trees . . ." An agent to the "Pimos and Pappagos" assured Bonneville that his charges were friendly and entirely under control. After inspecting a possible site for a new post at the base of the Tucson mountains, Bonneville and his men turned back toward the Rio Grande, keeping close to the overland trail, and making stops in small canyons along the way.

Resupplied at Fort Fillmore, Bonneville set out on the second phase of inspection, "through a pass in the Organus Mountains . . . to San Augustine spring." Thirty-eight miles "eastwardly . . . by digging we found a little water impregnated with sulphur and salt. These sand-hills are remarkably white and extend for miles." The spectacular dunes, drifts and flat expanse would later be named White Sands National Monument. Past the white hills, Bonneville turned north. "Found a small spring . . . this spot gives evidence of having been a planting ground for the Indians during a long period and the canon from which this spring had its source is the place where Lt. Lazelle had his fight with the Apaches. [Dog Canyon] Continued along the base of the mountains, and in six miles passed the San Luz. Here we found Indians tilling the ground." Up the Tulerosa, "a stout stream," Bonneville's party camped with "Mr. Carley, the Indian agent" of the Mescalero Apaches.

"Crossed the Ruidoso and up it, then to Eagle Pass and reached Fort Stanton on the Rio Bonito. Our route lay this day so as to turn the Sierra Blanco by the south and east; it first appeared to us north, enveloped in clouds." Fort Stanton was "judiciously located, healthy, and with an abundance of wood, water and grass. The settlements around the Fort were in a thriving condition . . . The scenery is very imposing; the Sierra Blanco towering far above the others in the south and the Sierra Capitan in the north."

Searches for water marked the journey back to Santa Fe. From Patos Creek, west of the Capitan mountains, there was no water for one hundred miles. At Puenta de Agua there was a meager supply; "the people had abandoned their fields for want of water to irrigate." Returning through Carnwell canyon, Bonneville complimented the Topographical Engineers for "a very fine substantial road."

"I am happy to say that I was pleased with the condition of the troops at the posts I visited, and the apparent care and economy with which the public property was managed," Bonneville wrote to Army headquarters after he returned to Santa Fe on July 3. Among his recommendations: build a two-company post near Tucson to guard Santa Cruz valley, and move Fort Buchanan to San Pedro River nearer the mail route; these two posts would stand between Indian country on the north and developing river valley settlements. For the more pressing need at the Santa Rita mines, Bonneville ordered a rifle detachment of one hundred men to build a post at a site he personally selected at the southeast point of the Burro mountains. There, troops could watch the overland route, the mines and the Indians. With ample wood and water "this point would also be in a proper location for a depot in case of hostilities . . ." The suggestions met with approval. Fort Breckinridge was established at the junction of the San Pedro and the Arivaipa later in the year.[23]

Lt. Edward F. Beale arrived in Santa Fe in August, his roadbuilding work finished for the season because the money was all spent. He reported that the camels he had brought the previous year had wintered well in the western part of the territory. In his travels, Beale and his escort had joined Lt. Col. William Hoffman on the Colorado River to do battle with Mohaves. An interesting sidelight—Hoffman's chief guide in this brush with Indians was Joseph Walker.

From his Navaho reconnaissance, Major Simonsen brought the maps and notes Bonneville had requested. He reported the Navaho were friendly. Albuquerque merchant Henry Connelly took exception to this news, claiming that the Indians were not returning stolen goods and were raiding and killing with increasing boldness. He called for a "war of extermination." "Our relations with the Navahos are complicated," Bonneville countered. "They are a numerous and self-sustaining people, having large flocks of sheep, and cultivating extensively . . . The thieves or ladrones of the nation are beyond control of the remainder. A general war would result in converting at least ten thousand people, who are already endeavoring to sustain themselves by agriculture and stock raising, into robbers, who, concealing themselves in the mountains . . . would be obliged to sustain themselves by stealing from the settlements, or be thrown upon the charity of the government."[24] Henry Connelly was not impressed; his wagons carried supplies to Fort Defiance, though he claimed to represent numerous "outraged citizens." Col. Bonneville ordered Major Simonsen, now commanding at Fort Defiance, to continue reconnaissance of Navaho country, while still pursuing a "kind and gentle course" with the Indians. Complying, Simonsen sent Major Oliver Shepherd and Captain John G. Walker on extensive patrols to Zuni Salt Lake, Canyon de Chelly, Black Mesa and Monument Valley. Both officers reported that the Navahos desired peace.[25]

New outcries were raised with a report that fifty Navaho killed two herdsmen and stole one hundred cattle. Five, not fifty, Indians, and eleven, not one hundred cattle, were found to be the correct numbers. The killings were retaliation for the murder of a chief's brother. Tribal leaders asked why their property was not ever restored, or the murders of their people ever avenged, but they agreed to try to restore recent thefts. The culprits were reported to be in Chusca Valley. One pursuing detachment returned empty handed, and Bonneville ordered a sizeable command to find and punish the guilty Indians. Lt. Du Bois found himself among the companies chosen to go. Major Oliver Shepherd, heading the project, set up an ambush on Pena Blanco Creek which took the life of one warrior. On the return trip, three more were slain. Shepherd reported that he had punished such of the Navahos as could be found. "I was half sorry," Lt. Du Bois wrote. "The war had commenced and the prospect was good for an active campaign."[26]

Replaced as Department Commander

Startling new orders cancelled all planned maneuvers. The edict came from the new Department Commander Col. Thomas T. Fauntleroy. Assigned to replace Bonneville, Fauntleroy was scurrying over the Santa Fe trail to New Mexico when he met an Army-escorted eastbound mail. Proclaiming himself at that instant the Department Commander, Fauntleroy ordered the military escort to abandon the mail wagon, turn around, and accompany him to Santa Fe. There, on the premise that whatever Infantry officer Bonneville had been doing was wrong, Dragoon Fauntleroy cancelled all previous orders. Fauntleroy had been humiliated by the infantry, and now that he was in the saddle, this was his chance to ride over the foot soldiers. He would find, as civilian wrath and Indian problems mounted, that he was astride a very uneasy horse.

Besides salving his injured pride, however, Fauntleroy's abrupt moves as Department Commander may have reflected the apprehension surfacing in military circles that a conflict brewed involving far more than settlers and Indians in remote territories. Orders from Washington were to make no preparations for a general campaign against the Indians while protecting the settlements as far as possible, because a considerable portion of the mounted troops would be required for other service. Still, Fauntleroy found, some control measures were necessary. He reinstated Bonneville's mail escort services through Kiowa and Commanche country.

The civilian faction led by Henry Connelly demanded a militia. Fauntleroy balked. He wrote to Army headquarters that greedy opportunists were behind the move to organize hordes of volunteers and draw support from the government of guns and salaries. He quickly lost favor with Connelly and many civilians, with Indian Superintendent Collins, and even with Territorial Governor Rencher. He moved the Department Headquarters from downtown Santa Fe to Fort Marcy, overlooking the town, and ordered Bonneville to move his Third Infantry headquarters there as well.

Old Fort Marcy was in poor repair—it had been garrisoned only now and then in the past several years. Bonneville added carpenters and blacksmiths to his roster and endeavored to put his post in worthy condition. Sixty-three years old, undoubtedly weary and certainly lonely for a fireside of his own, Bonneville had served four frustrating years in New Mexico. Twice he had been thrust suddenly into command of the Department, and when he could begin to see results of his planning and efforts, was abruptly superceded, this last time with singular absence of grace.

New Mexico had grown to almost one hundred thousand population—not including the Indians. Some wanted to split the vast tract, creating an Arizona territory on the south. Progressive newcomers and long-time residents alike pushed to better the cultural climate. Legislators worked on a public education law which would provide a school for each settlement. There was appreciation too for New Mexico's past. The Historical Society of New Mexico was organized in the closing days of 1859; Bonneville joined the group and contributed historical documents.

Col. Bonneville had a letter to answer, an inquiry about his life's service from Captain Geo. W. Cullum, assembling a record of Army officers. Datelined April 21, 1860, the letter began with an apology for not answering previous requests, "believing it not exactly the thing for anyone to speak of himself." Bonneville outlined briefly his military service, including his years in the fur country. "I explored the Rocky Mountains at my own expense . . ." Of his New Mexico years, he wrote, ". . . organized the Gila Expedition against the Apache Indians . . . Again fell in command of the same department having the Navaho war on hand, which was foretold to be of perpetual duration and as expensive as the Florida War . . . Quieted this formidable tribe in a few months with little expense." Concluding, he wrote, "I would have been more exact in dates but my memory fails me and I have no notes . . . out of the above select what may be to your purpose and put aside the remainder. I am sir, your most obedient servant, B. L. E. Bonneville."[27]

Colonel Fauntleroy's reduction of strength at Fort Defiance was a blunder. With mounted soldiers gone, rebellious factions of Navaho defied the restraints of older leaders like Zarcillos Largos. Cattle, sheep, and mule raids enraged the settlers, who, in turn, organized guerilla attacks into Navaho country. Utes, Apaches and some whites made slave raids, capturing Navaho children as well as livestock and blankets. Angry Navaho warriors swept ever closer to the post and killed four soldiers in an attack on the Army's beef herd. In pre-dawn darkness on April 30, over one thousand warriors stormed Fort Defiance. Though the Indians far outnumbered the garrison, their arrows and old muskets were no match for the arms of the soldiers; in two hours they withdrew. This daring challenge produced new citizen demands for an all-out war. Superintendent Collins laid aside his role as Indian Commissioner and became Editor Collins, frothing for revenge against the savages. Criticism poured over Fauntleroy for refusing unlimited arms and ammunition for the Governor's hastily organized militia.

The Navahos suffered most. Before the summer was over, they found themselves abused on all sides, losing, among others, Zarcillos Largos. It was the beginning of an eight-year period of death and terror for the Navaho. Later, they would have a word for it: "Nahondzod," the time of fearing.[28]

Photo courtesy of Ed Louise Ballman, Fort Smith, Arkansas.

Chapter Eight
1860-1878

"I owe no man"—Bonneville

A March Through New Mexico and Texas

Springtime orders from Washington directed Col. Bonneville to march his regimental headquarters and three companies of Third Infantry through New Mexico and Texas. In his "Journal of the March of a Battalion of 3rd Infantry commanded by Col. B. L. E. Bonneville from the Mouth of the Gallinas, N. M. to Fort Clark, Texas, via Pecos River pursuant to G. O. No. 6, Hd Army" Bonneville's handwritten notes and detailed daily maps delineate the meandering course of the Pecos through Comanche domain; the route had not been previously charted. To prepare for the trip, he spent several weeks at Fort Union, where the Army received supplies by way of the Santa Fe Trail.

On June 3, Bonneville and his staff, Major Oliver Shepherd, Major C. F. Ruff and Lt. Lazelle with their companies began the journey. Arroyos cut through the rolling upper valley of the Pecos; groves of cottonwood appeared on moister slopes. There was good soil in wide bottomlands, "fertile loam with particles of mica." Camp 7 was made at Bosque Redondo and the weather turned searing hot—108 degrees on June 22. "River water brackish; grass dry; salt pool in crater." As the heat continued, "Water decidedly purgative, sulphur-hydrogen besides salts; some holes contain sulphate of soda." The command remained at Camp 13 two nights because of sickness. In a few days, passing "gently undulating hills," Bonneville noted there was no wood, but fair grass and "catfish abundant in river . . . the whole country covered with a thick haze of smoke; signal fires of Indians proceeding on their annual expedition to Chihuahua and Sonora . . . fresh buffalo signs on river bank."

At two hundred miles from Santa Fe, the regiment found good grass and crossed a marsh. In the future this area would prove to be atop an artesian basin—the magic Captain Pope had hoped to find. "Course south southeast . . . hills very rough. Indians apparently ahead, from signs. Old channel of river partly filled up and dry. Gypsum and lime . . . Camp 18." At Camp 22, on Delaware Creek near the New Mexico-Texas dividing line, it was windy and raining, and two hundred and seventy-one miles from the mouth of the Gallinas.

"Struck the mail road to El Paso, supposed" on July 3. Here an unknown sojourner, ahead of his times, had started to build a house. Captain Pope, also ahead of his times, had probed for well-water in the area. Red Bluff Dam, built decades later, flooded Camp Pope with life-giving irrigation water, but in 1860 there was no promise of the treasures this barren earth would yield, nor indication that Pope's dream would ever come true.

"Remained at camp" on July 4. A guide who had been riding ahead saw Indian horsemen watching and "forthwith decided it best for him to wait for the command," for this area was in the path of the Comanche War Trail from the great plains to Mexico. The Comanches were seldom caught in pitched battles either with fellow red men or with whites, and they never came begging for largess. They ranged as lords of a vast sweep of the middle of the continent, living well by levying toll on wildlife and on fellow men.

A comet shone in the clear Texas sky on the night of July 6. The weather turned hot again—108 degrees. "River muddy and brackish . . . salt deposits . . . lizards, one with vermilion spots. Gravelly ridges look red in the distance." On July 9, "108 degrees. One vast plain." Later, "white and red sandstone on some hills . . . passed a waterfall, perpendicular 100 feet" and soon "good grass and water, mesquite becoming taller . . ."

At "Horsehead or Comanche Crossing," Indians had reached the Pecos on their return from horse-stealing raids into Chihuahua. Animals driven in haste between meager watering places often plunged into the Pecos and drank until they died; there were great piles of bones here. The heat continued; many days were well over one hundred degrees. In places it was easier to travel the mesas, but high campsites were without water. "Watered the animals from buckets and troughs" in such camps, presumably from water hauled for emergencies. On July 18, though it was "103 degrees . . . saw a red bird . . . Pecos Spring, very pure water."

On July 19, Bonneville's Third plodded into Fort Lancaster at the junction of Live Oak Creek and the Pecos. Following the overland trail now, the Third left the Pecos and toiled up a steep mesa and across ridges to reach Devil's River. Soon there were "high hills, and cliffs of limestone" and vegetation to delight the eye: "live oak, cedar in ravines, sycamore, hackberry, some pecan, black walnut." Entries in the journal became briefer. "July 24. Leave river and turn out on hills . . . road poor, dusty. Very bad greenish water in pools" and later "painted caves" having pigmented drawings on the walls. In the blazing heat of August, the weary companies trudged into Fort Clark.

"The colonel arrived at his post with his command which came down the Pecos River from Santa Fe . . . He was then quite sick," Army Surgeon W. J. H. White reported. "He had an attack of dysentery . . . great debility . . . a swelling of the legs . . . I recommended a sick leave."

An Insult from Robert E. Lee

Sick as he was, Bonneville confronted another crisis he considered more important than his ailments. General Twiggs, long absent from his assignment to the Department of Texas, was still not on duty. Bonneville's arrival put him in command, according to Army regulations, since as colonel he outranked Robert E. Lee, in temporary command. Lee's biographer Douglas Southall Freeman has explained that Lee was frustrated because of slow promotions and too many old men at the top. Whatever his thoughts or his reasons, Lee flatly refused to acknowledge Bonneville as commander of the Department of Texas.

Bonneville was stunned. To whom could he protest? Lee had long been a favorite of General-in-Chief Winfield Scott. Secretary of War John B. Floyd, like Lee and Scott, was a Virginian. Lee was commanding by right of his brevet rank, and since those honorary promotions were signed by the President, Bonneville laid his distress before James Buchanan as the one who had issued the assignment. Perhaps Lee had implied it. Or perhaps the distraught Bonneville's outrage simply flew to the loftiest target. Datelined Fort Clark, Texas, August 10th, 1860, Bonneville's letter begins with an apology for writing, then plunges into the grievance.

"My character, my dearest rights are affected. Arriving into the Department, I find a junior in command on duty according to his brevet rank . . . My position here is strange anomolous and humiliating. My junior commands me, and it is painfully embarrassing to find myself appealing to the President himself, to be relieved from the degradation . . . Urged however by the duty I owe to myself and more particularly to my regiment, I present my case . . ."

Outlining the history of brevets, Bonneville pointed out that the practice had always been controversial, "greatly to the prejudice of the harmony so necessary to the well being of all armies. The large number of brevets granted since the Mexican War has given them a controlling influence. The law places the command with the senior officer in the line of the Army. The assignment by the President of a junior over his senior officer is a permanent official injury, one that holds him up as a target for the contempt of his brother officers, and renders his commission almost without value . . ."[1]

Bonneville's anguished letter appears to have brought no reply from the lame duck President. Lee, however, was reassigned and Twiggs was summoned back to his command. Surgeon White stated that though "the Colonel's habits are exemplary in respect to temperance" he was "so low that there was doubt that he would recover, that in any case, he would not be able to resume his duties in less than a year." Conceding, Bonneville applied for a sick leave, as advised, and while he waited for a reply there were new developments in Texas. Years later, in a letter, he remembered the sequence of events: While Twiggs "was under orders to be relieved, McCullough (of the Texas militia) grabbed San Antonio and the stores of the Department. Col. Waite, the officer assigned to relieve General Twiggs, found the Department in rebel hands . . . I had been dangerously sick, had applied for sick leave; this I received as Col. Waite arrived. I wrote to him that if he did not recognize the surrender, I would remain and assist him; he replied that he would carry out the arrangement made by General Twiggs. Then I told him I accepted my sick leave."[2]

Twiggs' arrangement included turning over all federal property to the state of Texas. Then and later, Secretary of War John B. Floyd was accused of having assigned key posts to Southerners, making it easy for forces of the rebellion to seize supplies and installations. However the "American Military History and Department of the Army Manual" disputes "the charges that [Jefferson] Davis and Floyd purposely hamstrung the Army." Though Floyd departed "with his accounts in a mess," the charges "derived from some of his foolish and untruthful boasts after he joined the Confederate Army," the Manual states.[3]

Twiggs had ordered all Army units to evacuate their posts. Major Oliver L. Shepherd, left by Bonneville in command at Fort Clark, defied an admonition from Texans that he march his troops unobtrusively around San Antonio because of anti-Union sentiment there. Instead, he stopped outside of town to unpack dress uniforms, and the Third Infantry marched through the heart of San Antonio with "colors flying, band playing, drum major nearly turning himself inside out with his baton, and every officer as fine as brass and bullion could make him."[4] It is a pity their departed Colonel did not see them.

Sick Leave to Pennsylvania and St. Louis

Bonneville's homecoming was to Delaware County, Pennsylvania, where Ann and Mary lived in the autumn of 1860, perhaps at the home of Ann's sister, Mary Leiper. "Ann Bonneville" is said to be scratched on a window pane at "Avendale," the Leiper home. From the harsh military scene, Bonneville stepped into a tranquil setting, and in this sheltered world, his health improved. Mary had been thirteen years old when he left. Now, at eighteen, she was the pride of the old man's heart, an observer wrote. There had been changes in Ann's family. Her widowed sister Agnes Elizabeth Campbell had married Edward Stiles, a distant relative. The Campbell son and daughter Robert and Mary G. spent considerable time with their aunts, Mary Leiper and Ann Bonneville. Word from Cousin William Irvine, operating Grandfather Irvine's faraway Warren county estate, announced the exciting discovery nearby of petroleum.

As soon as he was able, Bonneville endeavored to get on with his life. "Proceeded to St. Louis . . . " he wrote later. With Ann and Mary, and Aunt Betsy, he may have resided in his duplex on Sixth Street. A family letter mentions, with some coolness, that Bonneville "had a home of his own choosing."[5] He owned other property in St. Louis, some of it portions of the original Chouteau holdings. Apparently he had chosen St. Louis for his retirement home. A circle of French families lived there; business man and civic leader Amadee Valle was his own special friend. Here also were Army and ex-Army personnel, among others, Ethan Allan Hitchcock who had resigned in 1855 in a dispute with Jefferson Davis. Now, appalled at the mounting dissension in the nation, Hitchcock wrote letters to editors urging peaceable solutions. He also warned of the danger of an attack on the St. Louis Arsenal.

Many fur-trade veterans called St. Louis their home. Some still sent caravans to the mountains, while others had established fur-related businesses. For Bonneville the charm of St. Louis was partly that it had been the scene of the launching of his earlier wonderful plan to explore the West. That the United States had prevailed in the Pacific Northwest was due to the efforts of many, but Bonneville could rightly feel a glow of pride in his own vision, even if most citizens did not associate Irving's dashing Captain Bonneville with the pudgy infantry colonel sagging from years of Army drudgery.

The Civil War Begins

But no one, least of all Bonneville, was thinking of retirement in 1861. After Lincoln was elected and South Carolina made good the threat to secede, other Southern states dropped from the Union like dominoes. The catch-phrase "states rights" evolved into the notion that this struggle was somehow akin to the War for Independence, at least in the eyes of the South. Some wanted to compromise and let the slave states go their way in peace. But Abraham Lincoln "left the South no alternative but to return to the Union, or else fight to stay out," historian John D. Hicks has written.[6] In that bitter and divisive season, few realized the enormity of the conflict shaping up. On April 12, 1861, the former United States Secretary of War Jefferson Davis ordered troops commanded by former Superintendent of the Military Academy P. G. T. Beauregard to fire on Fort Sumter.

Army officers could not enjoy the luxury of indecision. They controlled the weapons of war. Each had sworn to protect and defend the government, but each was also the fruit of his nurturing. General Scott pleaded with all the officers to stay loyal, but one-third chose to go with the South. Bonneville remained faithful to the Union and waited out his sick leave in St. Louis.

Virginia, uncommitted for a season, seceded. Nebraska and California leaned to the Union; Arkansas and Tennessee voted secession. Abandoning the naval yards at Norfolk, Virginia, Union forces burned facilities and ships as President Lincoln announced blockades of Southern harbors. Confederates courted and won most of the prairie Indians. In the West, the sudden absence of federal troops brought defiance and bloodshed.

Calls went out for militia. Many responded, some scrambling for positions of authority, some eager for adventure, and all mesmerized with their individual versions of loyalty. In both North and South, politicians and civic notables vied with military men for commissions. Most of the bright young officers of the Mexican War became brigadier generals or better. George B. McClellan, tapped to organize and train a huge "Army of the Potomac," was thirty-four years old. After his service with I. I. Stevens' railroad survey his rise had been rapid. Ulysses S. Grant, Bonneville's Fourth Infantry quartermaster, fared well. A civilian for a number of years, he became a Brigadier General; it was said to be an accidental honor, bestowed by a congressman who had it to give.

St. Louis, always a heady mixture of rowdiness and gentility, seethed in divided loyalties. Ties of family and tradition bound many to the South. Ambitious Yankee newcomers aggressively sought leadership in state and local governments; European immigrants had swelled the population. These new citizens, working people, were strangers to the plantation system, and viewed forced free labor as competitive to them in job markets.

On May 10, 1861, Bonneville saw war come to St. Louis. State militiamen, flaunting their allegiance to the Confederacy, had encamped in Lindell Grove. The nearby Arsenal was a tempting target, the largest repository of arms and ammunition in the Mississippi valley. Apprehensive, Arsenal Commander Nathaniel Lyon raided the grove and arrested the rebel troops. Pro-South supporters were livid; their militia included young men of the best families, while Lyon's troops were augmented by Yankee merchants plus German and Irish working men not too long from the old country. Crowds gathered; mob fury exploded. Gangs rampaged through the streets. Over three dozen people died.

During the last week in July, John C. Fremont came to St. Louis to take command of the Western Department. With his customary good luck, he had arrived from a European trip at precisely the right time to receive the important assignment. Fremont worked to assemble and fit out a viable army, but critics complained he was high-handed and conceited. He made errors of judgment: popular General Lyon died in the Battle of Wilson Creek near Springfield; he had asked Fremont in vain for reinforcements. Fremont was soon reassigned.

It was not a good summer for the Union. In July, against counsel from General Scott for better preparation, President Lincoln dispatched thirty thousand men to capture Richmond, the Confederate capitol. But at Bull Run, near Manassas, Virginia, Union forces were stunned by Confederates led by Generals Beauregard and Joseph E. Johnston. It was to be a longer conflict than some had supposed.

Bonneville's Appeal for a Military Assignment

In September, before his year's sick leave came to an end, Bonneville presented himself before the "Board for Retiring Disabled Officers" in Washington, D. C. An extract of the proceedings begins, "Col. Bonneville made a long verbal statement . . . the import being that his general health was so much restored that he considered himself as able to do military service as any man his age." While admitting that he "had been very sick in Texas . . . legs had been swollen . . . had some weakness in the knees," Bonneville asked to be restored to duty. Dr. W. J. H. White, asked if he believed the Colonel would be capable of active service in the field at the present or if he would ever be, answered "No . . . the attack . . . in a person of the Colonel's age would have a tendency to recur and my opinion is that exposure to the vicissitudes of camp life would bring it on at any time."

"The board was then closed for deliberation and . . . find that Colonel Bonneville of the 3rd Infantry is incapacitated for active service and incapable of ever performing the duties of his office, and that said incapacity results from long and faithful service, and from sickness and exposure in the line of duty."[7]

Washington mocked the disappointed Bonneville. The streets were filled with marching troops, and bands playing. In the first flush of optimism for a quick victory, three-month-volunteers were welcomed. After the disaster at Bull Run, the call went out for men willing to serve for three years. Every man would be needed, posters proclaimed, but sixty-five-year-old colonels were not in demand. Bonneville wasted no time nursing his chagrin. Shortly, he was listed as "Superintendent of Recruiting Service" and "Chief Mustering and Disbursing Officer of Missouri" with headquarters in St. Louis.

The miraculous telegraph blanketed the eastern half of the nation. Accounts of battles flashed to the newspapers in unbelievable time. Word of mouth reports flew in profusion as well, apprising those on the fringes of the action—like Bonneville—of victories and defeats. Near Leesburg, Virginia, Confederate troops routed Union forces in the Battle of Ball's Bluff. One of the triumphant rebel generals was Theophilus Holmes, Bonneville's long-time friend. The North applauded a sea expedition which netted installations on the North Carolina coast. Union naval forces tightened the blockade of southern ports, where owners set fire to their own bales of cotton on the docks; if the cotton could not be exported to England the Yankees would not get it either.

Ailing seventy-five-year-old General Scott retired. He had given astute advice which was not often followed. George B. McClellan emerged as Commander in Chief of the Army. Randolph B. Marcy, his father-in-law, drew the position of chief of staff. Actions on many fronts filled the newspapers. Brigadier General Ulysses S. Grant captured Fort Henry on the Tennessee River and moved on to Fort Donelson on the Cumberland. Union gunboats shelled the well-fortified work, and after fierce fighting Grant took possession. The Confederate commanders, Gideon Pillow and John B. Floyd, departed secretly by boat. Left to surrender the mighty fort's fifteen thousand men was Simon Bolivar Buckner, who had fought with Bonneville and Grant in Mexico, and, it was said, loaned down-at-the-heels Grant money to get home after his Army career had collapsed in California.

Assigned as Commander of Benton Barracks in St. Louis

In St. Louis, Col. Bonneville took command of Benton Barracks in March, 1862. The sprawling camp, a city in itself, was the creation of John C. Fremont, who had envisioned a training facility for twenty thousand volunteers. On Fairgrounds Park and property west of it, hundreds of workers had built barracks, storehouses and stables, and graded the grounds for parade and drill. Near the western exit, a two-story commandant's headquarters building and residence had been dedicated with military ceremonies. To no one's surprise, Fremont named the post for his famous father-in-law.

When Bonneville took command, Benton Barracks had already turned out dozens of companies of volunteers. Over twenty-three thousand would-be soldiers had spent a miserable winter in the encampment, with appalling conditions of mud, stench, fever and measles, according to a visitor. Bonneville worked hard to meet this new challenge, for conditions improved, order came out of confusion, and Benton Barracks became a showplace where civilians came to share the excitement of the times. Bonneville commanded Benton Barracks for the remainder of the war.

Most of the raw recruits were incredibly young, fresh from farms or small towns. Militia officers had little military training. The task at Benton Barracks was to clothe this throng of young men in the trappings of their new trade and to teach them how to use their deadly tools. Under specifications of the times, they must learn to march, wheel, and form the lines from which they would sight their guns and fire, not at squirrels or birds, but at young men very much like themselves. If this thought was uncomfortable, there were bands playing stirring marches, the sounds of staccato commands from drill officers, and the creaking and shouting of the supply and ordnance details to distract them. Officers from the regular Army assigned to novice units helped bring order.

Buildings within the fairgrounds were used for hospitals, for soon hundreds of the young men who had swaggered off came back wounded. Digestive ailments and contagious diseases took a massive toll. It was a price no one expected to pay, and with disease totals added to the grim statistics from each battle and skirmish, it became apparent that the ultimate sacrifice of life itself was given by all too many.

Sidelined officers like Bonneville, though working to exhaustion, could only agonize over accounts in the press. Missouri, with long stretches of two great rivers, suffered unending raids and guerilla attacks. At Shiloh, in southern Tennessee, the great armies of Albert Sidney Johnston and U. S. Grant battled to a standstill. Johnston was killed. Both sides claimed victory; death won most as each side counted casualties—almost one-fifth of the Union forces and one-fourth of the Confederate. In New Mexico, Texas Confederates completed a sweep up the Rio Grande to Santa Fe but were turned back by volunteers and Union regulars. The Union captured southern seacoast forts and cleared the Mississippi for water travel, but the South conceded nothing. Armies maneuvered, probed and planned, while the great adventure lost luster for many.

It was a season for carping: the South's brilliant Thomas J. Jackson, fondly known as Stonewall, came in for criticism. P. T. G. Beauregard, at odds with many, was replaced by Braxton Bragg. On the Union side, John Charles Fremont, given a field command in western Virginia, resigned rather than serve under John Pope. President Lincoln trimmed McClellan's duties and appointed Henry Halleck Commander in Chief. Curiously, in this early part of the war, socials, balls and theatricals flourished in the circles of the wealthy and important. The McClellans entertained lavishly at their home in Washington. A Union raid broke up a stylish house party at Robert E. Lee's Virginia home, Arlington. Lee had been courted by both North and South. He chose the Confederacy.

Death of His Daughter and Wife

In St. Louis, Bonneville had his family with him. He and Ann had been married twenty years, but their time together could be counted in months. Most of Bonneville's assignments had been to uncertain frontiers; Ann's fragile health and Mary's education were reasons enough for them to remain in the safer family circles in Pennsylvania. Perhaps that very isolation left them more vulnerable to the searing summer heat of St. Louis, and the diseases which continually swept through Benton Barracks.

Mary died. It was yellow fever, some accounts say. The "Missouri Republican" of August 5, 1862, carried the death notice: "On the 4th inst. at Benton Barracks, St. Louis County, Mary, daughter of Col. B. L. E. Bonneville, aged 18 years, 11 months and 10 days. The funeral will take place at 9 o'clock on Tuesday morning the 5th inst. from the residence of Amadee

Valle, Esq. south side of Chouteau Avenue. The friends of the family are respectfully invited to attend." After the funeral at the Valle home, Mary was buried in Bellefontaine cemetery, north of the city. Eleven days later, tragedy struck again.

"Died at Benton Barracks, aged 51 years, Mrs. A. C. de Bonneville." Services were at the Valle home, and Ann was buried beside her daughter.

For Bonneville, it must have seemed as if his world had stopped. This precious wife and daughter who had come to him so late in his life "in a few days left me alone in the world" he wrote to a friend, and added bleakly, "That I have survived them is a wonder to me, for they were my joy, and my hope of the future."[8]

Bonneville ordered his mother's burial casket moved from Calvary Cemetery to his lot in Bellefontaine. Epitaphs on the stones are almost obliterated in the 20th century, but read, in part:

"To my mother, Margaret B., wife of Nicolas De Bonneville, depute of 1789 France . . ."

"To our daughter Mary I De Bonneville . . . Come, dear mama, come. I'm waiting that we may come into paradise together . . ."

"My Wife Ann C. De Bonneville . . . My husband, I follow our Precious daughter . . . yet a little while you will also be among us . . . Oh where is our little angel boy . . ."

A few months later, Bonneville had the body of his baby son Nicolas moved from Carlisle to Bellefontaine in St. Louis.[9]

The War Continues

On September 12, Bonneville was back at his work. It was a time of gloom, for the war ground on. The pace at Benton Barracks remained constant with incoming novice and outgoing presumably trained soldiers, while the makeshift hospitals in the fairgrounds buildings bulged with ill and wounded. Disappointing news arrived daily.

Confederate guerrillas captured Independence, Missouri, and Gallatin, Tennessee. Pope's forces suffered a humiliating defeat in the Second Battle of Bull Run. Stonewall Jackson captured Harper's Ferry, where Dixon S. Miles and twelve thousand Union troops guarded quantities of stores. Miles was mortally wounded and died there. I. I. Stevens, late the Governor of Washington Territory, died while leading a Union charge at Chantilly. On Antietam Creek, fifty miles from Washington, Lee's and McClellan's armies clashed in what Civil War historian Bruce Catton has called "the most murderous single day of the entire war."

President Abraham Lincoln issued a "Preliminary Emancipation Proclamation" declaring that all slaves would be free on January 1, 1863, and proposed that Congress authorize compensation to the slave owners. Southerners were outraged, though three-fourths of the South's citizens owned no slaves. To many, slavery was a separate issue: the question was states' rights as opposed to federal authority. In this country, not yet a century old, it had been a bitter year. The conflict of ideas, so brashly and confidently begun, had turned into a bloody and ugly season of hatred among fellow Americans, with no end of the tragedy in sight.

It had been a bleak year for Bonneville as well. Facing the empty years without his family, he knew the sorrow of many of his countrymen, but also, perhaps more than most, mourned the "might have beens" forever lost. Ann's sister Agnes Elizabeth offered Bonneville assistance and sympathy at the time the double blow had wiped out his family. "Elizabeth was always fond of the Major," Aunt Rebecca Fayssoux wrote in February, 1863. Mentioning that her "poor old sister," Aunt Betsy, had gone to live with another relative because of Ann's death, she continued in her letter, "I think though the poor old man was afflicted in the loss of wife and child, it was not . . . so deep a sorrow as though their lives had been passed together . . . but as I do not know everything, perhaps Elizabeth was right; he is a lonely old man; it is time he should have some human sympathy."[10] It was true the family had been little together. Bonneville's life was the Army, and he had served faithfully. His lot now was mundane and grinding, but he did not scorn it. Those who grieve learn that for others the clock still ticks. Tasks must be done; there are still needs. It is life which calls, and somehow, one must accept it.

In spite of the war, loyal citizens like Bonneville could note with pride that the United States was still growing and ambitious. Two railroad companies launched plans for transcontinental lines, spurred by generous land grants from the government. Congress passed a "Homestead Act" enabling any person, male or female, to claim one hundred sixty acres of land merely by living on it. States were given generous tracts to sell for school needs. Congress created and President Lincoln endorsed the Territory of Idaho, carved out of Dakota, Washington and Oregon. Idaho included Bonneville's haunts on Snake River, Wind River, Salmon River and Green River, as well as the area which would become Montana. The Territory of New Mexico was divided, not horizontally, as had been projected, but vertically, to form the Territory of Arizona. The sturdily independent western half of Virginia, adopting a constitution calling for gradual emancipation of slaves, became West Virginia, the 35th state of the Union.

The Army of the Potomac lost to Confederate forces at Fredericksville and at Chancellorville, with thousands killed and wounded. Grant captured Vicksburg, the rebel stronghold on the Mississippi. Richard Ewell and Jeb Stuart raided Carlisle, Pennsylvania, and burned the Barracks.

A three-day slaughter of young Americans would go down in history as the most important battle of the Civil War. Robert E. Lee's and Geo. Gordon Meade's great armies converged in southern Pennsylvania. Divisions poured in and both sides scrambled to control the high spots. Bloody charges and counter-charges left dead and wounded on the green slopes. Batteries mowed down infantrymen. In close-quarter fighting soldiers fired into each others' faces and fought with bayonets and pistols until there were literally heaps of dead men. The Union position held and the July 3, 1863 Battle of Gettysburg was over;. Lee loaded up his wounded and began his retreat. Meade did not pursue him.

Bonneville received a new staff member at Benton Barracks—Randolph B. Marcy, lately Brevet Brigadier General with the title "Chief of Staff" for his lately demoted son-in-law George B. McClellan. Now he was Colonel Marcy; if his present assignment "Inspector of Volunteers" seemed contrived, Marcy accepted it, and continued to shuttle from one obscure post to another for the remainder of his career. Bonneville's business of turning raw young men into soldiers continued at Benton Barracks. Generous bounties enticed so many enlistees that the draft was little used. Some companies returned for mustering out, but many veterans reenlisted. Excitement had given way to the matter-of-fact conviction that the job was not yet finished and must be done.

Ann's sister, Agnes Elizabeth, the lady mentioned as "always being fond of the Major," was in St. Louis in early 1864. Her son, Robert Campbell, now in his early twenties, may also have been at Benton Barracks, for he later made his home with Bonneville. On March 23, 1864, Elizabeth, too, died at the post. Her marker, on Bonneville's Bellefontaine plot reads: "Mrs. A. E. D. Stiles . . . Place of Birth, Virginia; Late Residence, Benton Barracks; Age 49 years." Elizabeth's second husband, Edward Stiles, had resigned from the U. S. Navy to serve in the Confederacy. According to Civil War records, he spent considerable time in Europe seeking naval support for the South.[10]

Immigrants still poured into the United States in spite of the war. Many traveled to the West, some to claim land, and some to evade the draft, for they shunned old-country conscription. Booming from new mining discoveries, Nevada became the 36th state of the Union, while gold-rich Montana Territory was created from a segment of Idaho. In New Mexico, a somber chapter unfolded for the Navahos. Compounding earlier blunders, officials commissioned Kit Carson to uproot the tribes from their traditional homeland and force the cruel "Long Walk" to a bleak tract at Bosque Redondo. Carson burned crops and houses, destroyed orchards, and herded the luckless Navahos three hundred miles to the internment camp. Resisters were shot; the others were ravaged by starvation and disease during the coming years. Obliterated were past efforts to encourage peaceful co-existence and self reliance as advocated by commanders like Bonneville and Indian agents like Henry Dodge and Michael Steck.

Congress created the title Lieutenant General for Ulysses S. Grant and made him Commander in Chief. Now the war would be brought to a finish, many thought, and few realized the sacrifices yet to be exacted. Grant began a campaign into Virginia, where bitter and frustrating engagements netted hundreds of casualties for both sides. But the Union could replace their fallen men, while the South was running out of manpower, food and fighting tools. William Tecumseh Sherman marched from Chattanooga into Georgia, destroying property, burning buildings and wrecking railroads as he went. Joseph E. Johnston fought delaying and defensive action to little avail; Sherman burned Atlanta.

The U. S. Navy took Charleston harbor. Sherman's army cut a swath sixty miles wide and three hundred long to Savannah, then trampled a wide trail up through the Carolinas. The pillaging troops poured out extra measures of venom on the people of South Carolina, calling them the culprits who had started all the trouble. Columbia went up in flames.

Under Grant's siege, Lee abandoned Richmond. But Grant's ponderous, bulldog grip expanded just fast enough to close the route of escape. At Appomattox on April 9, 1865, Robert E. Lee surrendered to Ulysses S. Grant. When the totals were added, over half a million young Americans had died of wounds and disease, with another half million or more wounded in body or in spirit, or both.

President Lincoln's Assasination

President Lincoln asked the vanquished to lay down their arms and go back to being citizens of the United States. He urged that the government pay the slave owners for their property so that black people could go free. But dissidents on both sides howled with rage; some called Lincoln a "baboon." Within a week, Lincoln lay dead, shot by a frenzied actor who is said to have shouted "The South is avenged!"

At Benton Barracks, Bonneville supervised the mustering out of hundreds of tired soldiers. The excitement, the bravado, had vanished. Dirty uniforms and unkempt bodies reflected the weariness and lost innocence these hardened men-so-lately-boys were feeling. The nation had been preserved, but regret and hatred clouded the triumph. Sorrow for the killed and wounded touched both North and South, but ties of kinship and friendship seemed forever broken.

Commissioned a Brigadier General

Benton Barracks was officially closed September 1, 1865. Bonneville concluded the arrangements during the fall. He recommended his chief surgeon, Ebenezer Swift, for brevet promotion for exceptional service. Bonneville received a commission as Brigadier General on December 2. The promotion had been recommended by General U. S. Grant and signed by President Abraham Lincoln the preceding March.

Events After War's End

Command of Jefferson Barracks was Bonneville's new assignment. The facility had been used for the wounded during the war. Under Bonneville's command, Jefferson Barracks once again served as the departure point for companies ordered to Western assignments. A handsome house near the river served as quarters for the commanding officer.

"Soon after our arrival at Jefferson Barracks we received a call from the post commander, General Benjamin Bonneville," a young officer's wife, Elizabeth Burt, wrote in her diary in early 1866. "He was host at the first dinner party I attended in the army, filling the position delightfully, with the assistance of his charming nieces, Mrs. Crittenden and Miss Bacon. The dismal picture that had been drawn for me before I started West, of eating from tin plates, was dispelled when we gathered around that beautiful table with its faultless napery, silver, glass, delicate china and flowers."[11]

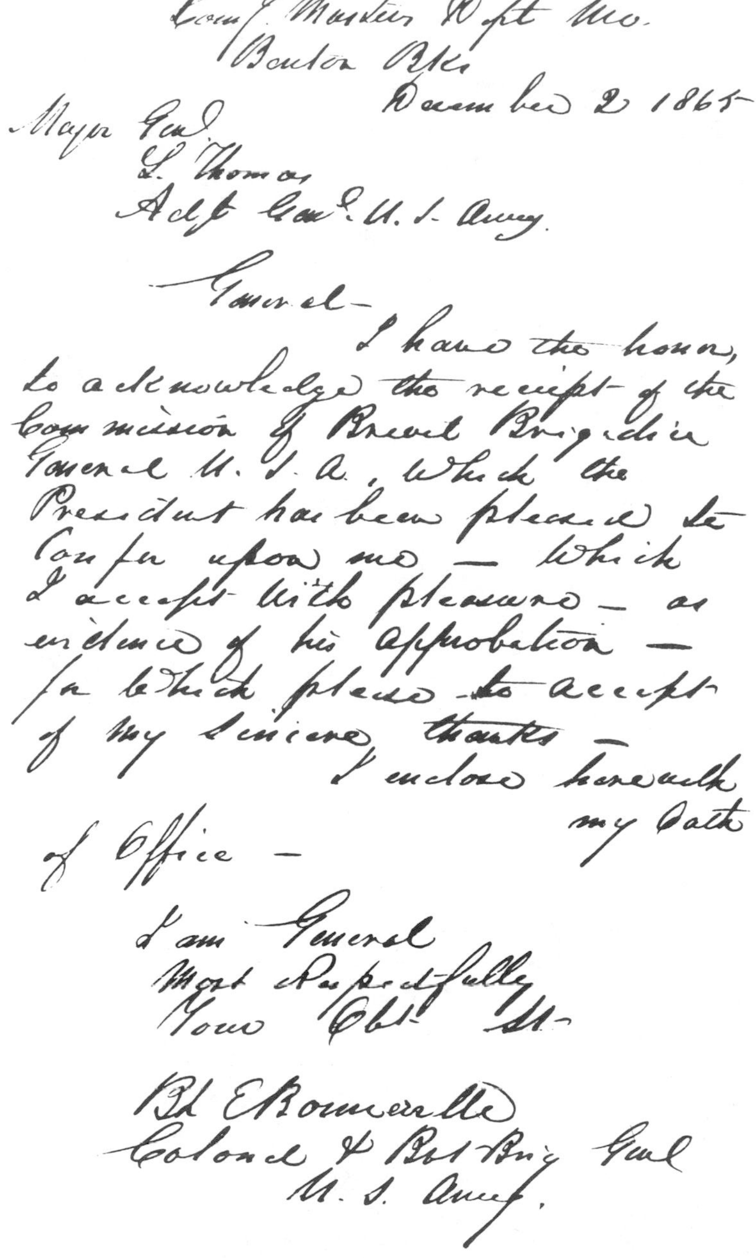
Comy. Muster Dept Mo.
Benton Bks
December 2 1865

Major Genl
L. Thomas
Adjt Genl U.S. Army.

General—
I have the honor, to acknowledge the receipt of the Commission of Brevet Brigadier General U.S.A., which the President has been pleased to Confer upon me — which I accept with pleasure — as evidence of his approbation — for which please to accept of my sincere thanks —
I enclose herewith my Oath of Office —

I am General
Most Respectfully
Your Obt. St.

B L E Bonneville
Colonel & Bvt Brig Genl
U.S. Army.

This is Bonneville's letter acknowledging his commission as Bvt. Brigadier General. The commission is dated April 3, 1865, and signed by Abraham Lincoln, President, and U.S. Grant, Commander in Chief, though Bonneville did not receive it until December.

The table appointments were undoubtedly Ann's; some may have borne the monogram "I" for Irvine. One fancy which has appeared in print is that Bonneville fell heir to Washington Irving's linens and silver. Bonneville had no known association with the writer after selling his notes to him. The identity of the nieces is uncertain. Ann's brother, Callender Lewis, had married Annie Bacon. They were the parents of a daughter, Alice, who could have been "Mrs. Crittenden," and it is possible "Miss Bacon" was a relative. Or the two may have been daughters of other associates. Like Lafayette, who had called him "son," Bonneville liked young people.

If Elizabeth Burt saw the poignancy of Bonneville's situation, she did not record it. He had attained the position for which he had toiled fifty wearisome Army years: the title General and a pleasant post near the city where lived many of his closest friends. Though he had lost Ann, who would have stood beside him as a gracious companion, and Mary, his "hope of the future" he was striving to fill his role as benign host, even if he had to find substitute hostesses.

Tree-shaded and spacious, Jefferson Barracks spread westward from the Mississippi on gentle bluffs. General Henry Atkinson had chosen the spot in 1824 at the south end of Broadway to replace the earlier post on the northern end of that venerable St. Louis street. Stephen Watts Kearny had constructed the first buildings, and two dozen years later came back from his stormy Mexican War assignment with the fevers which took his life. In the interim, Henry Leavenworth had set out from Jefferson Barracks on the exploration which claimed his life, also from disease. Other ghosts, too, lurked in the shadows of the bridle-paths and may have hovered, listening, when the officers sat on the piazzas and smoked their pipes at dusk. The Atkinsons had begun a tradition of balls and galas attended by St. Louis luminaries—the Governor William Clarks, the Senator Thomas Bentons and the old French families, Chouteaus, Valles, Cerres, and others. Washington Irving and artists George Catlin and Alfred Jacob Miller visited. Zachary Taylor, William Jenkins Worth, Newman S. Clarke, Albert Sidney Johnston and Dixon S. Miles had been stationed there.

Other sojourners still lived, though their military careers had crumbled: Jefferson Davis, Robert E. Lee, Joseph E. Johnston and Braxton Bragg. Like Bonneville, some of the officers—William S. Harney, Ethan Allan Hitchcock and others—had trudged about as far along military paths as their aging bodies could carry them. Hitchcock maintained a home in St. Louis. Like Bonneville, he had served in the management of volunteer forces in the late war. His gloomy and mostly correct comments on the progress of the war had been brushed aside, as was the advice of his mentor, Winfield Scott. General Scott died in May, 1866. Philip St. George Cooke, a little younger but with a long beard which gave him a patriarchal look, visited Bonneville at Jefferson Barracks in 1866 on his way to a prairie assignment. The war had hurt him deeply; his son and two sons-in-law chose the Confederacy. His son still would not speak to him, and son-in-law Jeb Stuart had lost his life.

There were fairer memories of the post. Phil Kearny met and married Henry Atkinson's sister-in-law. John Charles Fremont met Jessie Benton, and Ulysses S. Grant met Julia Dent.

The summer of 1866 was hot and troubled. Europe's great cholera epidemics spread to the United States. Smallpox, typhus and yellow fever also took their toll. The war's end malaise grew more virulent too, as the vindictive and the forgiving battled to control government affairs. It had been thought that Tennessean Andrew Johnson, succeeding Abraham Lincoln, would agree to stern measures against the South but as President, Johnson extended, as Lincoln had done, more compassion than punishment. Andrew Johnson had risen from poverty and illiteracy and his views were hard-won. To muster support he toured cities with General U. S. Grant. His enemies moved with him and his speeches were interrupted by noisy protests. St. Louis was no exception, though his supporters tried to do him honor, hailing his arrival on the presidential steamer with fitting fanfare.

Retirement

Bonneville's career in the United States Army came to a close on October 15, 1866. He moved to Yeatman Flats, 1120 Olive Street, and later to 1106 Chouteau. For well over fifty years, he had served the length and breadth of the country in mostly disagreeable and unrewarding situations. A harsh taskmaster, the military; it demanded armed presence at whatever trouble spot contemporary political judgment willed. Family and permanence placed second. Without a doubt, the non-heroes of the late war found retirement lonely. In this period of his life, Bonneville was reported as devoting time to "arranging his maps and collecting his notes with a view of leaving behind much important information omitted by Mr. Irving . . . he was not communicative, and seldom spoke of his remarkable adventures in the Rocky Mountain region, and very rarely of his early days or his family history, only occasionally with a small circle of friends," according to one writer.[12]

A new generation of adventurers tramped over Bonneville's Rocky Mountain trails. The "St. Louis Dispatch" advertised an excursion "To Idaho and the Gold Mines: to Fort Benton, Helena, Virginia and Bannack Cities," though these diggings were now in Montana Territory. Idaho had gold mines too, including rich fields on the Salmon and Boise Rivers, where Bonneville had looked for furs and information. The Army had built a post, Boise Barracks, to control the Indians, and a town was thriving there, complete with a newspaper. St. Louis newspapers carried bulletins from the "Idaho Statesman" by the magic of transcontinental telegraph. Gold, it was apparent, was now the word for the West, and few cared about the fur-trade days in the mountains.

The "St. Louis Dispatch" printed news from Europe as well as items about steamboat disasters and the progress of the Atlantic-to-Pacific railroad. A cure for cancer had been discovered, the newspaper noted, and a Swedish engineer named Alfred Bernhard Nobel had developed a new explosive called dynamite which was said to be better than black powder. The news columns carried full quotas of national political discontent. President Johnson could please no one, apparently. One action which brought only small notice and was labelled "folly" was the government's purchase of "Russian America," a vast northern tract which was renamed Alaska. It was cheap enough, less than two cents an acre, and said to command valuable fishing territory.

In October, 1867, Bonneville and nephew Robert Campbell traveled to Pennsylvania for the marriage of Robert's sister Mary Gill Campbell to Dr. Thomas Reed. A cousin described the wedding at Avendale in Delaware County at the home of the bride's aunt, Mary Leiper. "Yesterday, the Girls arranged the rooms very beautiful with flowers and green vines along the staircase and windows. All agree that the wedding passed off charmingly . . . General DeBonneville came on with Robert Campbell & is much pleased with Dr. Reed and enjoys the lively girls."[13]

The quarrels in Washington D. C. boiled over in 1868. President Johnson fired Secretary of War Stanton and in return faced impeachment in Congress on charges brought by Stanton's supporters. He escaped dismissal by one vote. Commander in Chief of the Army Ulysses S. Grant, having put distance between himself and Johnson, gained the heady position of Republican nominee for President. He campaigned little, as if somewhat surprised by the notion. Associates from earlier days in the Army were astounded. But they had been equally nonplussed that their quiet brother-in-arms had somehow managed to be in the right place at the right time—and make the right moves—in the late war. Now, once again, Grant was lucky. America was ready for a war-hero President.

"I am packing my trunk to start for Irvine, and for Philadelphia, Pa., where relatives have made me promise to go and pay them a visit," Bonneville wrote to a friend in September, 1868. "So I go—and will be back in a month or two."[14] Ann's cousin, Dr. William Irvine, lived at the Warren County estate of Grandfather Irvine of Revolutionary War fame. Nephew Robert Campbell may have been with Bonneville, and perhaps also nephew Callender Lewis, whose father Callender senior had died in 1863. In a letter a few months later, Bonneville wrote, "Mrs. Lewis, my sister-in-law is still in Frankfort Kentucky. Her son Callender, however, is with me."[15]

Dr. William Irvine had promising new ventures afoot. Pennsylvania oil discoveries had brought prosperity to the area, and he too had oil tracts. Bonneville also invested in oil—the Charles W. Fork Oil Company and the Great Western Petroleum Company on Pit Hole Creek, according to a letter he wrote from St. Louis in March, 1869 to "My Dear Sir" name unspecified. Not specified, either, is the state in which the oil prospects were located. Bonneville asked advice on "how best to work this up as you understand the ropes . . . Robert Campbell, my nephew, has charge of the business to sell, work, or anything he may think best . . . give us your advice, and the names of men able to counsel us in case of a pinch . . ."

The 1869 letter reveals other thoughts Bonneville had at this time. Of U. S. Grant's presidency: "All I can say the Republican party is in power, and I hope they may use it to make the country prosperous and happy . . . The west and northern portion of the state is filling up quite rapidly and I am glad to say with northern men. I see that great exertions are being made to establish a Grand Trunk to the Pacific . . . over the 35th parallel. This of course would run through Arkansas up the Canadian through Albuquerque &c &c to San Francisco, and with the Rail Road through Indian Territory, with their suffrage accorded them as the constitutional amendment proposes would make these Cherokees, Choctaws, Creeks, &c &c a great and prosperous people."[16]

Bonneville's thoughts had turned to Arkansas, and he went there in the spring of 1869 for an extended visit. He had written to Major T. J. Eckerson, his Vancouver colleague now stationed at Little Rock, "I expect to go by water, and of course shall see my friend Eckerson and his good wife . . . and others." Presumably he renewed these friendships, and paid a visit to W. E. Woodruff, retired now from the "Arkansas Gazette." The long-time editor counted other successes: politics, real estate, and eleven children. A son had become editor, and had fought bitter verbal battles with carpetbaggers from the north. Initially Confederate, Arkansas had changed hands during the war, and Union officers who occupied W. E. Woodruff's home had permitted the destruction of many of his papers.

There were bruised feelings in Fort Smith, too. Property had been confiscated by each side in its turn, with no courtesy shown by either. Toward the end of the conflict, looters roamed the countryside, pretending to be either Union or Rebel as the occasion indicated. At one point, Arkansas' governor suggested that all of the states west of the Mississippi should secede from the Confederacy.[17] In Arkansas as in other areas, disgust with the ways of war would be a long time mending.

Like Bonneville himself, the post at Fort Smith was now an anachronism, an aging monument of blended glories and failures of the past. Because John Roger's hotel had burned down some time previously and the "Father of Fort Smith" had died, Bonneville found lodgings at a popular boarding house on Second Street. The proprietors were Anton and Catherine Neiss, natives of Alsace, France. Their oldest daughter Susan was twenty-three years old when Bonneville returned to Fort Smith. She was said to be tall, and of proud carriage; one contemporary remembered that she portrayed "Miss Liberty" in a Fort Smith pageant. The father, Anton, ran a butcher-shop. Some Fort Smith residents are said to have sneered at Anton as a "cattle-killer" and likewise disapproved of the inn-keeping labor of the mother, Catherine. Perhaps they were a bit jealous, one Fort Smith historian explained. Bonneville found warm welcome with them.

One story of that time, from D. B. Johnson, daughter of Bonneville contemporary, B. T. Duval, concerns a little girl from Alsace brought by her older sister to the Neiss home. "After she landed here, no one, not even her sister paid much attention to her. One of the happiest of her experiences were those times when General Bonneville would pull her up to him on the sofa, in the parlor of the Neiss home, and talk to her in French. He told her of fighting Indians, and of his trip out west. Of all the stories I've heard or read about Bonneville, I like best this one of him comforting that lonely little French girl."[18]

Bonneville was back in St. Louis in December, 1870, for he replied from there to an inquiry from a Professor Brewer about John Charles Fremont's ascent of a Wind River peak. Though he stated that his own maps were sometimes credited to Fremont, Bonneville was non-judgmental of his former fellow-officer, perhaps concluding that Fremont needed no criticism.[19] Once a millionaire, the multi-ambitioned "Pathfinder," as some called him, had lost his fortune in railroad ventures. His political career had died a-borning, and his former substantial contributions of maps and journals weighed poorly against the record of his Civil War assignments.

A St. Louis columnist wrote, "General Bonneville lives here almost within sound of the locomotive which could whisk him to Astoria in a week. He is a hale old man, one of the finest examples left to our times of the 'antique courtesy' of which Irving loved to write. The spirit of the old soldier seems still equal to the command of perilous expeditions, mingled with the easy competance and honor of his age. He has but one grievance; he never can quite understand why he should have been retired from the service of the country to which he has given so many honorable years."[20]

Bonneville Remarries

The "hale old man" was not as elderly as the reporter supposed, for he was soon back in Fort Smith looking after his interests which included the Neiss family. Before coming to the United States, Catherine Neiss had two children by a previous marriage. Their father had died in 1869, and Catherine wanted to go to Alsace in hopes of obtaining inheritance for the two children, now grown. Bonneville paid her expenses for the trip.

"She was worried at the time about the possibility of her young daughter Sue marrying the old general," according to D. B. Johnson, "and she came back to Fort Smith in the same year she went over and the marriage took place soon after her return."

The bride was twenty-five and Bonneville was seventy-five, a gap of fifty years. The wedding was on November 30, 1871. "It was a marriage in the European style," one writer later decided, meaning, perhaps, that Sue would care for her husband in his old age in return for his estate. But was it?

"The general was crazy about Susie and made her very happy," W. L. Euper wrote. "She loved him, and wasn't ever interested in other men . . ."

It was the biggest wedding Fort Smith had ever seen, guests reported, a spectacular mix of military pomp and frontier celebration. To the strains of "Here the Conquering Hero Comes" the Fort Smith brass band escorted

Bonneville and Sue from the Neiss home to the Catholic church. Rev. Father Lawrence Smythe officiated.

"The responses of both bride and groom were prompt and clear . . . the general looked as manly, vigorous and modest as a youth of 25 and every inch the veteran of many hard fought battles, while the lovely bride in her elegant attire appeared serene and happy." From the church, the band piped the wedding party nine blocks to a reception at Adelaide Hall on Garrison Avenue. Bonneville wore his full-dress brigadier-general's uniform, Susan a magnificent gown of white uncut Spanish velvet trimmed with satin and fringe. "The veil encircled with orange blossoms, like the lovely bride, looked as pure and beautiful as the white snow which covered Mother Earth outside." The guests, "a full representation of the gallantry and beauty of Fort Smith," danced until 1 a.m. when the band led a grand march to an "elegant supper." The dancing resumed and "all went merrily till four o'clock when the last dance was announced to the regret of all . . . it was evident that each wished that weddings like the General's came around oftener than once or twice a lifetime."[21]

Bonneville and his Sue made their home in the duplex at 730 South Sixth in St. Louis. The rapport with Ann's family appeared a little strained at this point: one relative announced to another, "Did I write about Col. de Bonneville—I hear he is going to marry a child of sixteen. Rob Campbell has left his roof, seeing that there is no prospect of his being 'My Uncle's heir.' "[22] Later, the relationship was patched up, at least as concerned Robert Campbell. Bonneville transferred St. Louis property and other assets to Sue "for love and affection"; at the top of one list, he wrote in his firm hand "I owe no man."

The fiction of Sue being only sixteen was but one of the legends which surfaced then and later. Newspaper accounts of the marriage asserted that the ceremony was performed "fifty years to the hour and the day" of Bonneville's first marriage. In truth, he was on a troop ship on the Mississippi on November 30, 1821, and his first marriage was to Ann Callender Lewis in December 1842. Bonneville stories continued to be printed for decades. One account stated that both Washington Irving and John Jacques Audubon accompanied him on his western expedition, and another recorded that Robert E. Lee carried him off the battlefield when he was wounded in Mexico.

St. Louis bustled with new enterprise. Factories, flour mills, breweries and shops reflected the bounteous crops and blossoming inventiveness throughout the land. James B. Eads' arched steel bridge across the Mississippi neared completion, plagued by a few tragedies and a great deal of scoffing. There was a public school system, and colleges and academies. There were libraries, art exhibits, theatre and musical presentations. Shaw's Botanical Gardens had grown Eden-like. Lafayette Park held two new statues, one of George Washington, and the other, a bronze work cast in Germany of the late Thomas Hart Benton. His daughter Jessie Fremont had unveiled it.

Bonneville's roster of friends and associates had thinned. David Adams still hoped to put together a journal of his mountain experience. Amadee Valle's home was on Lucas; Robert Campbell—the fur trader—lived in a handsome brick house on Locust Street.

Ulysses S. Grant had proved to be a disappointing president, allowing opportunists to flourish. Nevertheless, he was reelected. The Fifteenth Amendment to the Constitution had been ratified guaranteeing citizens' rights to vote despite "race, color or previous condition of servitude," but when Susan B. Anthony and her friends tried to vote they were arrested. France, still struggling for liberty, fraternity and equality now essayed a Third Republic, having sacked several monarchs. France's liberators, as always, could not agree among themselves, and in the latest maneuvers had lost Alsace and Lorraine provinces to Germany.

A New Home in Arkansas

At about this time, Bonneville and his Alsatian bride decided to go back to the tranquillity of Arkansas and build a home. "A large crew of men spent months in chopping the finest logs available, and they were transported to Fort Smith by ox teams from Waldron," one account states. The finished "Mansion," a mile or so east of town, was spacious and square, with wide verandas encircling each of the two stories. It was painted pale sunshine yellow. A wide driveway led up the slope, for the home stood on a commanding eminence 200 feet above the surrounding prairie in a grove of cedars. Outbuildings included a stone smoke house; some have speculated that small buildings with barred windows were slave cabins, but Bonneville did not at any time own slaves and in the 1870s, slavery was no more. Furniture was purchased in Philadelphia, the walnut woodwork custom-fashioned in Little Rock. A large ballroom was designed with raised seats on the sides, and huge fireplaces on each end.

"This was the setting on many scenes of splendor and gayety when the General entertained . . . He is pictured as a most noble host; the charming old explorer would sit at one end of the fireplaces and chat with the passing couples of young dancers," J. H. Daily wrote.

R. C. Bollinger reminisced, "We had three violins, double bass, guitar, piccolo and flute. We used to play at the dances out at Bonnevilles and he was generous—he paid us three or four dollars apiece for a dance, maybe once a month or so. They danced mostly square dances, some waltzes, polkas and a few could schottische and varsouviene. We played 'Old Dan Tucker', 'Arkansas Traveler', 'Turkey in the Straw' and 'Mocking Bird'. The general danced once in a while but not often. He always wore a collar with wide points, a long-tailed black coat and a cut away black vest with a stiff pleated bosom. He was smooth shaven except for a few side burns. I do not remember ever seeing the general take a drink, or never heard of his doing so."

Another contemporary wrote, "The General was courteous to everyone, no matter who they were or what they did. He was always so polite to Susie, at all times." Maggie Walker recalled, many years later, of riding out on her pony to see "the wonderful new home of the Bonnevilles. I remember his sweet courtesy, his gallant manner and his sophisticated French ways. The general took me all through the house, showing me all of the things and telling me what they were and where they came from."

In the 1930s, J. H. Daily, whose family knew the Bonnevilles, wrote an essay about Bonneville and saw the keepsakes then extant. They included a pistol which the General carried in the Mexican War, the sword presented to Thomas Bonneville for his service on the "Wasp" when it sank the British "Reindeer" in 1814, and a sword which Lafayette gave to the General. Articles which had belonged to Nicolas Bonneville included his volume of poetry dated 1786, documents of the French National Assembly and other papers, as well as "the famous ivoryheaded cane, once the property of an Eastern potentate, who presented it to Louis Sixteenth who gave it to Nicolas." Another source says the cane was carved from an elephant's tusk, and was given by Louis Sixteenth to Bonneville's grandfather, perhaps M. Brazier, Margaret's father, the "grand chamberlain in the Palace of Versailles."

"On one page of Bonneville's scrap book are strands of hair from the heads of his mother, father, brother and daughter, and a pressed rose or flower from the grave of his first wife," Mr. Daily wrote. "There is also a bag containing several hundred garnets, some of considerable size that Bonneville mined while in the Rocky Mountains. On the outside of the bag is written 'Mary Bonneville' and a Philadelphia address. Only three of these gems were ever cut. These three were given to the writer's grandmother who had them made into a ring." Also mentioned are the Bonneville family record book, Bonneville's military documents, Lafayette letters, and linen designated as from Washington Irving, which no doubt were Irvine heirlooms.

Church-goers remembered Bonneville as being "a short but very dignified man who attended services every Sunday. He would speak pleasantly." Mrs. J. H. Krone remembered as a child she "always watched General Bonneville at the door of the church. He wore a wig, and at the door, often took out a small comb from his pocket and smoothed his hair down in back."

Sue Bonneville lived until 1910, and Fort Smith residents remembered her as a warm and gracious lady, "immensely popular." She did not remarry after Bonneville's death, but made a home for a number of orphaned nieces and nephews.

"Scribner's Magazine" for June, 1873, carried an account of an ascent of the Grand Teton peak in the Territory of Wyoming by members of a government survey party. Nathaniel P. Langford, the author, wrote to Bonneville and sent him a copy of the publication. In his letter of reply, Bonneville thanked him for the "complimentary letter" and commented:

"Climbing high mountain peaks is no child's play; but once the ascent is made, what a rich reward presents itself to view a world below us. This wonderfully tumbled up mass around us, the frightful gashes in the mountain sides force imagination to wander far away into the region of space, and indeed, theories of the wildest nature."

In that vein, he speculated that a "star, passing through our solar system might in its monstrous convulsions form huge mountain ranges; water receding carry debris from the Torrid to the Polar Regions." At the heights, Bonneville suggested, "Man thinks himself something extra . . . when on the plain again, a mere atom of creation."

The Snake River plain still intrigued Bonneville; he wondered if the surrounding mountains had once been continuous before the advent of the great lava flows. He also wrote the "Fire Hole . . . some day may become a place of public resort," as it did, shortly, as Yellowstone National Park with N. P. Langford appointed first superintendent. The Territory of Montana had launched a historical society, and in reply to an inquiry, Bonneville wrote "Reciprocating your very kind and complimentary letter and circular, I would remark, with every disposition to assist you in preserving interesting data respecting our Far West in early days, after an absence of near half a century

I must decline to review or attempt any addition to my journal. You ask me if I knew of the thermal springs and geysers. Not personally, but my men knew about them, and called the location the "Fire Hole."

Answering a number of questions the writer had asked, Bonneville described various trapping ventures not included in Irving's published version of his explorations. He touched on several incidents in his Army career, including some that had hurt. "Half a century is a long time to look back, and I do so doubting myself. I have to thank the government for many favors granted me at different times...I came here and opened a farm on lands I purchased in 1837, where I am now, in my old age, a farmer, my family with me."[23]

America's centennial birthday drew near. It was a time to be proud and even a little boastful. Other nations had staged World's Fairs, and it was fitting that the United States essayed the continent's first one at Philadelphia, site of the signing of the Declaration of Independence. Railroad companies promoted the "Centennial Exposition" by offering special excursions. Bonneville and Sue attended.

At Fairmont Park, two hundred exhibit buildings held "Arts, Manufactures, Products of the Soil and Mines" from twenty-six states and three dozen nations. In the main hall, touted as the "largest structure in the world," twenty-nine-year-old Alexander Graham Bell demonstrated his "talking telegraph" which could transmit a human voice over a wire. One scoffer called it a toy because the user could speak or listen, but not both at once. F. Remington and Sons Fire Arms Company showed their mechanical typewriter, which made only capital letters. Most impressive to many was Machinery Hall, dominated by a massive Corliss Steam Engine, called the "symbol of the age." Another engine used crude petroleum as fuel, but produced minimal power, and the assembled inventors noted that German machinists were working with four-cycle gasoline engines.

En route from Philadelphia, the Bonnevilles stopped to visit friends in St. Louis. A reporter sought Bonneville for an interview and "found him at Planter's Hotel, entertaining visitors . . . General Bonneville was then 80 years of age but he looked ten years younger."

"Reviewing his military career, the General mentioned the Mexican War and was said to have an immense fund of anecdotes to relate of Generals Wool and Taylor.

"When the General was asked if he thought that education had made the Indian any more loyal to the United States, replied: 'I knew a Choctaw Indian who often said that he did not know how much he was wronged by the United States until the United States had educated him.' "[24]

This was Bonneville's last visit to St. Louis, for the time was approaching when Sue would bring his body here to lie beside the family he loved. After the people of Fort Smith had paid their respects, Sue with nephew Robert Campbell and others would bring the metallic casket with silver-plated handles and silver name-plate to the home of Amadee Valle at 1516 Lucas Place. Old Army friends, Union and Confederate, plus aging Robert Campbell of the fur trade and the faithful Valle would act as pallbearers for the last rites at St. John's Church. But this was in the future. Benjamin Louis Eulalie Bonneville's death was on June 12, 1878.

In 1876, Bonneville was still in good health, and not yet finished with the gentle warmth of an Indian summer season of life. Did he think of the might-have-beens? He had been too young for the War of 1812 and too old for the Civil War for military fame. In the Mexican War, the old heroes of 1812 held the positions of command and surrounded themselves with young hotspurs, while the laborious troop advances, battle lines and occupation fell to the middle-aged officers whose promotions had come so slowly. Bonneville had seen much of the contentious jockeying that prevailed in his profession but the years had put it in some perspective.

There were fairer memories of the Army: the bugled summons to greet the morning, the smartness of company drills, the forays and bivouacs into remote places, the map-making, the planning and building of posts and roads, the assembling of troops and supplies for campaigns, and finally the honor paid to the title "General." True, Bonneville was only a Brigadier General, but he had paid in full for every rung of the ladder. The Army had given him good times and bad, friends, enemies and years of toil, but as he had written in 1835, it was his very life. His years of service were, in some measure, his gift to his country.

Readers still enjoy *The Adventures of Captain Bonneville*, and in spite of what Bonneville regretted as omissions and errors, Washington Irving captured the essence of his personality in the word "bonhommie." The image endures of an earnest, friendly, courteous man whose persistent faith in every human being's right to a decent, orderly place on earth was equaled only by his appreciation of nature's boundless wonders.

Life's work draws to a close. Some are bitter that the world is not much changed for all one's best efforts. But Bonneville's interests were wide, his personal contacts warm, his life full. And of all the good memories left to him in his old age, perhaps the best were of his years in the fur-trade and Indian world of the Rockies, living with ambition and eagerness and a splendid dream.

Like many of his time, Bonneville wore a wig in his later years. He may have looked like this when the Indians called him "the bald chief."—Pen stetch by Kathryn Jenson.

The Bonneville monument in Bellefontaine Cemetery, St. Louis.

Notes

Chapter One

In the 1930s, J. S. Daily of Fort Smith, Arkansas, saw and wrote about the Bonneville family record book which is in private hands.

Appreciation goes to Elizabeth Hoskyns and Margaret Wing for translation assistance, to Van Wyck Brooks and John A. Kouwenhoven for breathing life into early New York City and its people, and to Ernest Dupuy for lore of early West Point.

Thomas Paine biographies are in oversupply; Moncure D. Conway's century-old work has been of most value in this endeavor.

1. Le Harivel, Phillippe, "Nicolas de Bonneville, Pre-Romantique et Revolutionaire," 3.
2. Baldensperger, Fernand, "Legion d'Honneur" V. XLV #4, 270, 271.
3. Le Harivel, 6.
4. Le Harivel, 10.
5. Conway, Moncure D., "The Life of Thomas Paine" 446, 447. Conway used the papers of William Cobbett, who had obtained notes and information from Marguerite Bonneville. Her quotations are from this source.
6. Thomas Paine Historical Society
7. Conway, 335.
8. Conway, 351.
9. Conway, 448.
10. Le Harivel, appendix.
11. Conway, 449.
12. Conway, 451, 453, 456.
13. Paine's will is printed in Volume X of William Van der Weyde's "The Life and Works of Thomas Paine," 291.
14. Letter, New York Historical Society.
15. Information and "The Speech of Counsellor Sampson, Trial of James Cheetham, Esq., for a libel on Mrs. Margaret Brazier Bonneville . . ." New York Historical Society.
16. Conway 403, 452 f.
17. Le Harivel, 13.

18. Typescript and letter to author from Captain F. Kent Loomis, Assistant Director of Naval History, Department of Navy.
19. Morgan Seacord, letter to author.
20. Conway, 430, 431, 451.
21. Le Harivel, 15, 16.
22. Bonneville to G. W. Cullum, 1860, Bonneville File.

Chapter Two

The "Arkansas Gazette" published continuously from 1820, recording both small-town progress and the history of the nation. "Territorial Papers of the United States" furnish flavor of the times: the troubles, endeavors, quarrels and successes as shown in unedited correspondence and official pronouncements. Post Returns military records pinpoint locale attendance.

Historian Grant Foreman's writings of pioneer days and Indian problems in Arkansas and Oklahoma are full and authentic, as also those of Brad Agnew, Ed Bearss and Arrell M. Gibson.

Travelers James Fenimore Cooper, Washington Irving and others describe France in the 1820s.

1. Holman, Hamilton, "Zachary Taylor", 65-67.
2. Doss, Richard B., "Andrew Jackson, Road Builder", in *Journal of Mississippi History*, Vol. XVI, No. 1.
3. Bonneville to T. J. Eckerson, 1868, Oregon Historical Society.
4. Ford, Anne E., "Some Adventures of Captain Bonneville," *Chronicles of Oklahoma*, V. VI, No. 2., 129-128.
5. Morgan Seacord letter to author.
6. Cullum, G. W., letter from Bonneville, 1860.
7. Le Harivel, Philippe, "Nicolas de Bonneville . . .," 15.
8. Maryland Historical Society holds some of the original invitations.
9. Prucha, Francis Paul, "Army Life on the Western Frontier," 137.
10. Le Harivel, 16.
11. James, Marquis, *The Raven*, 110.
12. Wisehart, M. K., "Sam Houston, American Giant," 56.
13. NA Sec. of War, Unregistered Series, Micro 222, Roll 25. LR
14. James, 159.
15. Arkansas Territorial Papers, XXI, 200.
16. Foreman, Grant, "An Unpublished Report by Captain Bonneville," *Chronicles of Oklahoma,* V. XI, 326-330.

Chapter Three

Think not that we would rewrite Irving. *The Adventures of Captain Bonneville* is most worthy of reading it its entirety. The goal in this work is to put Bonneville's expedition into its official context as evidenced by extant government records, and to add dimension from contemporary accounts and later studies.

Fur trade literature bulges with books of diverse authenticity. Works of Dale Morgan, David Lavender and Bernard DeVoto are most solid. *Mountain Men and the Fur Trade* in ten volumes, edited by Leroy R. Hafen and written by many enhances fur-trade lore.

Outdoorsmen-historians enjoy tracing Bonneville's footsteps. Orrin H. Bonney's conclusions concerning Wind River country are dependable. John Stricker knows Big Horn Canyon well. T. S. Easton, John L. Rogers, T. F. Lathrop, John A. Himmelwright, J. H. Horner and J. F. Winnefred differ only slightly about Hells' Canyon and Wallowa mountains routes. Alvin A. Josephy's knowledge of Nez Perce people and villages are most valuable. Others have claimed camps and travels in many spots, and who knows? Bonneville tramped the mountains for three years, and part of his enduring charm is the elusive notion that all of his story's not yet been told.

1. Bonneville File, NA RG 94 AGO 2742-ACP 1878, contains the letters and reports of the Rocky Mountain expedition.
2. Dunbar, Seymour, *History of Travel in America*, 1200.
3. House Executive Document 104, 22 Cong. 2 Sess.
4. Irving, Washington, *Adventures of Captain Bonneville*, Edgeley Todd, ed., LI.
5. Goetzmann, Wm. H., *Exploration and Empire*, 49.
6. Meany, Edmond S., *History of the State of Washington*, 59.
7. Lavender, David, *Westward Vision*, 229.
8. "Darby's Recollections," 233, Missouri Historical Society.
9. Gilbert, Bil, *Westering Man, The Life of Joe Walker*, 7, 299, 300.
10. Dr. J. Nielson Barry wrote of his successful search for the long-missing "Report" in *Annals of Wyoming*, April, 1932.
11. Gilbert believes that Bonneville was in the east making preparations during the winter, and that he made the request in person. Gilbert, 125, 306. Walker presented the passport, No. 2567, in California, according to Leroy Hafen in *Old Spanish Trail*, 242.
12. David Adams papers, Missouri Historical Society.

13. Ferris, Warren Angus, *Life in the Rocky Mountains*, 164, 165. A civil engineer, Ferris came west in 1830 and kept a journal during his six years in the mountains.
14. Edgeley Todd, editing a 1961 edition of *Adventures of Captain Bonneville*, 49, quotes a 1954 letter from Jenkins describing the rotted ends of the pickets, bits of metal, and traces of an underground runway to the river.
15. Report.
16. David Adams papers.
17. Bonneville letter in "Contributions," V. 1, No. 1, Montana Historical Society.
18. Lorraine and Orrin H. Bonney, in *Guide to Wyoming Mountains and Wilderness Areas*, 36, 37, quote from W. O. Owen's papers, held by the University of Wyoming.
19. Report.
20. Bonneville's view of Pierre's Hole and Snake River Valley places his crossing of the mountains south of a later Teton Pass highway, probably near later sheep trails of Fogg Hill.
21. Ferris, 147-149. The site is five miles downstream from Salmon, Idaho.
22. Report. "Comanche" was used by newcomers for "Camas" or "Quamash," a blue-flowered edible-bulb plant.
23. Report. These rivers begin in the Sawtooth Range.
24. Report.
25. Wyeth, Nathaniel, "Correspondence and Journals," 115-126, 260, 261.
26. Orrin and Lorraine Bonney trace the trapper trails.
27. Rich, E. E., "HBC Governor Geo. Simpson's Journal," Oct. 26, 1824.
28. *Adventures of Zenas Leonard, Fur Trader*, John C. Ewers, ed., 64, 65.
29. DeVoto, Bernard, *Across the Wide Missouri*, 58, 59, 110.
30. Report.
31. Bonneville File. The report is also printed in full in *Adventures of Captain Bonneville*, edited by Edgeley Todd.
32. Bonney, 81, 109.
33. Josephy, Alvin Jr., "The Nez Perce and the Opening of the West"; Barry papers, Boise State University, and Kuykendall papers, Washington State University.

34. Kuykendall papers, Washington State University.
35. Powers, Alfred, ed., Klickitat edition, *Adventures of Captain Bonneville*, foreword.
36. Bonneville to Secretary of War, Sept. 30, 1835.
37. Ewers, John C., ed., *Adventures of Zenas Leonard*; Ellison, Wm. H., *The Life and Adventures of George Nidever*; Victor, Frances Fuller, *River of the West*, 143-158, (Joe Meek); Jonesborough, Tenn., *Sentinel*, March 1837. (Stephen Meek); Beall, Thomas J., *Recollections of William Craig*, Lewiston, Idaho "Morning Tribune," March 3, 1918.
38. Leonard, 70, 72.
39. "Exploration of the Sierra Nevada," California Historical Society. Some believe Walker ascended the Sierras by a tributary of Carson or Walker rivers. Frances P. Farquhar suggests he reached Tioga Pass into Yosemite.
40. Victor, 150, 151.
41. Leonard, 131.
42. Victor, 152-157.
43. Bonneville letter, "Contributions," V. 1, No. 1.
44. Bonneville letter to War Department, Sept. 30, 1835.
45. Leonard, 135. Antonio Montero received a draft from American Fur which he sent with Cerre, apparently transferring his services to Bonneville at this time.
46. Townsend, John Kirk, *Narratives of a Journey Across the Rocky Mountains*, 271-273.
47. Wyeth, 198, 199.
48. Russell, Osborne, *Journal of a Trapper*, 8.
49. Wislizenus, Frederick A., *Journey to the Rocky Mountains*, 126.
50. Leonard, 138, 156. An erroneous reading of a Fort Hall account book places Walker at Wyeth's Portneuf post during the winter. The Fort Hall sojourner was John, not Joseph Walker.
51. Leonard, 160.
52. Washington Irving's Introduction *Adventures of Captain Bonneville.*
53. NA RG 94 File 2742 ACP 1978, (Bonneville File) contains the letters pertaining to the reinstatement actions.
54. DuPuy, R. Ernest, *Men of West Point*, 2729. Symons, Thos. W., U.S. Army Chief Engineer, Dept of the Columbia, to the 47th Congress, 1882, Exec. Doc. 186.
55. Meany, 98, 99.
56. Lee File, AGO LR RG 94, NA.

57. McDermott, John Francis, "Washington Irving and Bonneville's Journal," *Mississippi Valley Historical Review*, Dec. 1951.
58. Warren, G. K., "Exploring Expeditions, 1800-1857," *Annals of Wyoming*, July, 1943.
59. Irving to Hook, March 27, 1836, Bixby Collection, Missouri Historical Society. Irving, Pierre, "Life and Letters of Washington Irving," 114.
60. Morgan, Dale L. and Harris, Eleanor Towles, eds., *The Rocky Mountain Journals of William Marshall Anderson*, 257

Chapter Four

Mention of "Irvine" in Oregon Historical Society's Bonneville-to-Eckerson 1868 letter led to Pennsylvania Historical Society's Nicholas Wainwright and at his direction to Elissa Jones of Vinings, Georgia. That gracious historian of Irvine, Lewis, Fayssoux and Callender families has shared information and personal letters, bringing to life Bonneville's Ann Callender Lewis.

1. Bonneville File, NA RG 94 AGO 2742ACP 1878.
2. Darby, John, "Recollections," 233, Missouri Historical Society.
3. "St. Louis Observer," Aug. 15, 1836.
4. Bonneville letter, "Contributions," Vol. 1, No. 1, Montana Historical Society.
5. David Adams File, Missouri Historical Society.
6. Davenport, Odessa, and Porter, Mae Reed, "Scotsman in Buckskin," 109-111.
7. Drury, Clifford, "First White Women Over the Rockies," 67.
8. "New York Review," Vol. 1, Oct. 1837.
9. Foreman, Grant, "Advancing the Frontier," 155, 156.
10. Mahon, John K., *History of the Second Seminole War*, 216.
11. Foreman, 86, 89, 91.
12. Agnew, Brad, *Fort Gibson*, 179. No accompanying report is found.
13. Bonneville letter, "Contributions," Vol. 1, No. 1.
14. Douglas, Marjory Stoneman, *The Everglades*, 227, 228.
15. Mahon, 263.
16. RG 94 Doc. File 39 NA.
17. John T. Sprague wrote *Origin, Progress and Conclusion of the Florida War*, the only first-hand account.
18. Bonneville to John Rogers, Pennsylvania Historical Society.

19. The money involved sale of property, according to Elsa Vaught, in *John Rogers, the Father of Fort Smith.*
20. Elissa Jones; Wainwright, Nicholas B., *The Irvine Story.*
21. Sunder, Wm., *Bill Sublette, Mountain Man*, 200.
22. Bonneville to Rogers, Pennsylvania Historical Society.
23. Prucha, Francis Paul, *Army Life on the Western Frontier*, 130.
24. Goetzmann, Wm. H., *Army Explorations in the American West*, 117, 118.
25. Elsa Vaught.
26. Elissa Jones.

Chapter Five

Credit is due in this chapter to Justin Harvey Smith, Albert Ramsey, Robert Selph Henry and Alfred Hoyt Bill for their accounts of the Mexican War. Mexican War diaries and records reveal harsh aspects of the military profession—searing ambition, ruthless maneuvering and abrasive disagreement among some in officers' circles.

1. Sen. Doc. 32, 31st Cong. 1 Sess. records Wool's march into Mexico. Josiah Gregg's *Diary and Letters* adds interest.
2. Grant, U.S., *Personal Memoirs,* 123.
3. Grant, 132.
4. Henry, Robert Selph, *Story of the Mexican War,* 291.
5. Exec. Doc. 60, H. R. 30 Cong. 1 Sess., 994, 995.
6. Ramsey, Albert C., *The Other Side of the Mexican War,* 221-226.
7. Smith, Justin Harvey, *The War With Mexico,* 71.
8. Bill, Alfred Hoyt, *Rehearsal for Conflict,* 265.
9. Exec. Doc. 1, 30 Cong. 1 Sess., 310, 316, 338.
10. Bill, 278, 279.
11. Verbatim quotations are from NA RG 153, Bonneville Court Martial.
12. Ramirez, Jose Fernando, *Mexico During the War with the United States,* 152.
13. Calderon de la Barca, Fanny, *Life in Mexico During a Residence of Two Years,* 96.
14. Smith, E. Kirby, *To Mexico With Scott,* 216.
15. Exec. Doc. 1, 30 Cong. 1 Sess., 354-356, 361-375, Appendix 134-164.
16. Exec. Doc. 1, Sen. 30 Cong. 1 Sess., 414-416, 418, Appendix 180, 184, 185.
17. Hoffman to AG, Dec. 18, 1847, printed in HEH 6, 30 Cong, 1 Sess.

Chapter Six

Ronald Shaw, Walter Havighurst and Fred Landon picture the world of early canal and Great Lakes travel and tradition. John Easter Minter, Bayard Taylor and David Howarth describe Panama's scenes, its dark history and charm.

1. Gregg, Josiah, *Diary and Letters*, 178.
2. Henry, Robert Selph, *Story of the Mexican War*, 376, 377.
3. Foreman, Grant, *Advancing the Frontier*, 71.
4. Bonneville to G. W. Cullum, Bonneville File.
5. West Virginia WPA Guide, 429.
6. "Fort Smith Herald," Nov. 22, 1848.
7. Bonneville to Cullum. Oakley, Francile B., "Arkansas' Golden Army of '49," Arkansas Historical Quarterly, V.6, No. 1.
8. "Fort Smith Herald," Mar. 21, 1849; reprinted in other papers.
9. Settle, Raymond W., *March of the Mounted Riflemen*, 60, 302. Fort Kearny has been authentically rebuilt. Some of the trees growing there are said to have been planted in 1849.
10. Stansbury, Howard, *Exploration and Survey of the Great Salt Lake Valley of Utah*, 199.
11. Woodward, W. E., *Meet General Grant*, 103.
12. Kellogg, Louise P., Old Fort Howard," in *Wisconsin Magazine of History.* V. 18, Dec. 1934, 125-140.
13. Swekersky, Wm. G., *Old Public Buildings of St. Louis*.
14. Grant, U. S., *Memoirs*, 195.
15. "Sheffield Reminiscenses," *Washington Historical Quarterly*, XV, 1924, 50, 52.
16. Grant, 195.
17. Taylor, Bayard, *El Dorado*, 14.
18. Sheffield, 55, 56; Grant, 197.
19. Newspaper clippings courtesy of California State Library.
20. Sheffield, 52, 59.
21. Grant, 203.
22. Nichols, Leona, *Mantle of Elias*, 285.
23. *Pacific Northwest Letters of George Gibbs*, 32, 35.
24. Warner, Ted J., "Peter Skene Ogden," 213, in V. 3, *Mountain Men and the Fur Trade*.
25. Meany, Edmond S., *History of Washington State*, 62.

26. T. C. Elliott discusses Ogden's memoirs in Oregon Historical Quarterly, July, 1910.
27. Fuller, Geo. W., *History of the Pacific Northwest*, 218.
28. Sheffield, 61.
29. "Portland Journal," Jan. 6, 1946.
30. Maddux, Percy, *City on the Willamette*, 31, 47.
31. Sheffield, 60, 62.
32. Nichols, 86; Hussey, John A., *History of Fort Vancouver*, 211.
33. Frazer, Robt., ed., *Mansfield on the Condition of Western Forts*, 174, 175.
34. Bonneville to Eckerson, Oregon Historical Society.
35. Victoria L. Ransom, Fort Vancouver Historical Society.
36. Meany, 62.
37. Bird, A. L., "Thomas McKay," *Oregon Historical Quarterly*, March 1939.
38. Stevens to Bonneville, Fort Vancouver Historical Society.
39. Tripler, Eunice, *Some Notes of Her Personal Recollections*.
40. Dale Morgan letter to author.

Chapter Seven

Bonneville appreciated the scenes and history of the Southwest as much as did contemporary journal-keepers John Russell Bartlett, W. W. H. Davis and the Abbe Domenich. To Bonneville, however, fell a burden of mediating and policing, and of meting out justice to fellow men of diverse intentions and culture, some of them guilty only of existing.

1. Bonneville to Eckerson, 1855, Oregon Historical Society.
2. Bennett, James A., *Forts and Forays, A Dragoon in New Mexico*, 77.
3. Emmett, Chris, *Fort Union and the Winning of the West*, 189.
4. Davis, W. W. H., *El Gringo*, 216; Bennett, 65.
5. Domenich, Abbe, *Deserts of North America*, 189; Davis, 61-63.
6. Davis, 44.
7. Reeve, Frank D., "The Federal Indian Policy in New Mexico," *New Mexico Historical Review*, V. 12, 1937, 218-225.
8. Hammond, Geo. P., ed., "The Journal and Letters of Col. John Van Deusen Du Bois," and Reeve, Frank, D., ed., "Puritan and Apache: a Diary" (Henry Lazelle), *New Mexico Historical Review*, Oct., 1948, Jan. 1949.

9. Lazelle, 297.
10. Secretary of War Report, 35 Cong. 1 Sess. SED 2, V. ii, 135-141; f. 306; SED 35 Cong. 2 Sess. No. 1, pt 2, 279-280. *New Mexico Historical Review*: Bender, A. B., "Frontier Defense of New Mexico," V. 9, 354-360. Reeve, F. D., "Federal Indian Policy in New Mexico," V. 13, 1938, 280-283. Ogle, Ralph, H., "Federal Control of Western Apaches, 1848-1886," *New Mexico Historical Review*, V. 14, 1939, 346-350. Du Bois' quotations are from his "Journal," 6, 14, 21, 23, 25, 29, 33, 41.
11. Warren, G. K., "Exploring Expeditions 1800-1857," *Annals of Wyoming*, July, 1943, 220-224.
12. 35 Cong. 1 Sess. HED, No. 2, V. II, pt. ii, 135-141.
13. 35 Cong. 2 Sess. SED 5, No. 1, pt. 2, 279-280.
14. McNitt, Frank, *Navaho Wars*, 310, 313 f, 314 f.
15. Denver to Collins, NA, NMS 21-23. Garland to Brooks, NA RAC RG 393, LS, July 26, 1858.
16. McNitt, 334. Orders, letters and reports of this Navaho campaign appear in Secretary of War Report, 35 Cong. 2 Sess. SED V. 2, No. 1, pt. 2, 35, 309-326.
17. McNitt, 343, 347.
18. McNitt, 349.
19. Backus' map, drawn by Lts. Lazelle and Wm. Bell, is printed in McNitt, 244.
20. Du Bois, 86.
21. Bonneville to AG NA RAC RG 393 LS 2/27/59.
22. Bonneville to AG NA RAC RG 393 LS 4/30/59.
23. Report, Bonneville to General in Chief, NA RAC RG 393, LS 7/15/59.
24. Bonneville to AG NA RAC RG 393 LS 8/9/59.
25. McNitt, 366.
26. Du Bois, 102.
27. Bonneville to G. W. Cullum, Bonneville File.
28. McNitt, 379, 416.

Chapter Eight

Bruce Catton's voluminous writings etch the nation's Civil War agony in sharpness. E. B. Long's "Civil War Day by Day" adds dimension.

Bonneville spent most of his retirement years in Fort Smith, Arkansas. Rella Looney of Oklahoma Historical Society, and Arkansas historians Ed

Louise Ballman, J. S. Daily, Elsa Vaught, Zoe Ellen Cobb, Helen M. Johnson, Susan Swinburn, Maude Sengal and others have shared a treasury of stories, notes and clippings of Bonneville's last years.

1. Bonneville to Buchanan, copy, Montana Historical Society.
2. Bonneville letter, "Contributions," Vol. 1, No. 1, Montana Historical Society.
3. *American Military History and Department of the Army Manual*, 188.
4. Utley, Robt., *Frontiersmen in Blue*, 211, 212 quoting Wm. Bell.
5. Elissa Jones.
6. Hicks, John D., *The Federal Union*, 615.
7. Bonneville File.
8. Bonneville to Eckerson, 1868, Oregon Historical Society.
9. Bellefontaine Cemetery Records.
10. Elissa Jones.
11. Mattes, Merrill J., *Indians, Infants and Infantry*, 23.
12. "Every Saturday," Oct. 14, 1871, Missouri Historical Society.
13. Elissa Jones.
14. Bonneville to Eckerson, 1868.
15. Elissa Jones.
16. Bonneville to "My Dear Sir," 1869, Montana Historical Society.
17. Ashmore, Harry, *Arkansas*, 86.
18. Zoe Ellen Cobb and other Arkansas historians.
19. Bonneville to Brewer, Yale University.
20. Clipping, Kay Reading Lewis, Missouri Historical Society.
21. "New Era" and other 1871 clippings, courtesy of Ed Louise Ballman.
22. Elissa Jones.
23. *Contributions*: Vol. 1, No. 1, Montana Historical Society.
24. *Old Folks and Facts* clipping, Rella Looney, Oklahoma Historical Society.

Bibliography

Books

Agnew, Brad, *Fort Gibson, Terminal of the Trail of Tears*, Norman: University of Oklahoma Press, 1980.

Aldridge, Alfred Owen, *Man of Reason*, N.Y.: Lippincott, 1959. Ashmore, Harry, Arkansas, N.Y.: Norton, 1978.

Bandel, Eugene, *Frontier Life in the Army*, Glendale: Arthur H. Clark Company, 1932.

Bartlett, John Russell, *Personal Narrative of Exploration and Incidents*, Chicago: Rio Grande Press, 1965.

Bearss, Ed, and Gibson, Arrell M., Fort Smith, *Little Gibralter on the Arkansas*, Norman: University of Oklahoma Press, 1969.

Bennett, James A., Forts and Forays, *A Dragoon in New Mexico*, Albuquerque: University of New Mexico Press, 1948.

Bill, Alfred Hoyt, *Rehearsal for Conflict, N.Y.*: Alfred A. Knopf, 1947.

Bonney, Lorraine and Orrin H., *Guide to the Wyoming Mountains and Wilderness Areas*, Denver: Sage Books, 1965.

Brooks, Van Wyck, *The World of Washington Irving, N.Y.*: E. P. Dutton and Company, 1944.

Calderon de la Barca, Fanny, *Life in Mexico During a Residence of Two Years*, N.Y.: E. P. Dutton and Company, 1931.

Carter, Clarence E., ed., *Territorial Papers of the United States*, Vols. XVIII through XXVI, g.p.

Caughey, John W., *Hubert Howe Bancroft, Historian of the West*, Berkeley: Russell and Russell, 1970.

Catton, Bruce, *The Centennial History of the Civil War*, Garden City: Doubleday & Co. Inc, 1965.

Conway, Moncure D., *The Life of Thomas Paine*, 2 vols., N.Y.: G. P. Putnam's Sons, 1892.

Cooke, Philip St. George, *Scenes and Adventures in the Army*, Philadelphia: Lindsey and Blakiston, 1857.

Cooper, James Fenimore, *Gleanings in Europe*, N.Y.: Oxford University Press, 1928.

Cullum, G. W., *Biographical Register of Officers and Graduates of West Point*, N.Y.: g.p., 1879.

Daniels, Jonathan, *The Devil's Backbone*, N.Y.: McGrawHill Book Company, 1962.

Davenport, Odessa, and Porter, Mae Reed, *Scotsman in Buckskin*, N.Y.: Hastings House, 1963.

Davis, W. W. H., *El Gringo: New Mexico and Her People*, Santa Fe: Arno Press, 1973.

De Voto, Bernard, *The Year of Decision, 1846*, Boston: Houghton Mifflin Company, 1943. *Across the Wide Missouri*, Boston: Houghton-Mifflin Company, 1947.

Domenich, Abbe Emmanuel, *Seven Years Residence in the Deserts of North America*, London: Longman, Green and Co., 1869.

Douglas, Marjory Stoneman, *The Everglades*, N.Y.: Rinehart, 1947.

Drury, Clifford, *First White Women Over the Rockies*, Glendale: Arthur H. Clark Company, 1966.

Du Bois, J. Van D., *Campaigns in the West*, Tucson: Arizona Pioneers Historical Society, 1949.

Dunbar, Seymour, *A History of Travel in America*, N.Y.: Tudor Publishing Co., 1937.

Dunshee, Keneth Holcomb, *As You Pass By*, N.Y.: Hastings House, 1952.

Dupuy, R. Ernest, *Where They Have Trod*, N.Y.: Stokes, 1940. *Men of West Point*, N.Y.: Sloane, 1951.

Elliott, Charles Winslow, *Winfield Scott, the Soldier and the Man*, N.Y.: Macmillan Company, 1937.

Ellison, Wm. Henry, *Life and Adventures of George Nidever*, Berkeley: University of California, 1937.

Emmett, Chris, *Fort Union and the Winning of the Southwest*, Norman: University of Oklahoma Press, 1965.

Ewers, John C., *Adventures of Zenas Leonard*, Norman: University of Oklahoma Press, 1959.

Faulk, Odie B., *Destiny Road*, N.Y.: Oxford University Press, 1973.

Fayel, Wm., *Encyclopedia of History of St. Louis*, St. Louis: 1899.

Federal Writers Project Guides: Arkansas, New Mexico, Oregon, Washington, Wyoming, West Virginia.

Ferris, Warren Angus, *Life in the Rocky Mountains*, Denver: Old West Publishing Co., 1940.

Foreman, Grant, *Pioneer Days in the Early Southwest*, Cleveland: Arthur H. Clark Company, 1926. *Advancing the Frontier*, Norman: University of Oklahoma Press, 1933.

Frazer, Robt., ed., *Mansfield on the Condition of Western Forts*, Norman: University of Oklahoma Press, 1963.

Freeman, Douglas Southal, *Robert E. Lee*, a Biography, N.Y.: Charles Scribner's Sons, 1934.

Fuller, Geo. W., *A History of the Pacific Northwest*, N.Y.: Alfred A. Knopf, 1966.

Fulton, M. G., ed., *Diary and Letters of Josiah Gregg*, Norman: University of Oklahoma Press, 1941.

Ganoe, Wm. Addleman, *History of the United States Army*, N.Y.: D. Appleton and Co., 1924.

Gilbert, Bil, *Westering Man, the Life of Joe Walker*, N.Y.: Atheneum, 1983.

Goetzmann, Wm. H., *Army Exploration in the American West 1803-1863*, New Haven: Yale University Press, 1955. *Exploration and Empire*, N.Y.: Alfred A. Knopf, 1966.

Grant, Ulysses, *Personal Memoirs*, N.Y.: C. L. Webster & Co., 1885.

Gregg, Josiah, *Diary and Letters of Josiah Gregg*, Norman: University of Oklahoma Press, 1941.

Hafen, LeRoy R., *Mountain Men and the Fur Trade*, 10 vols., Glendale: Arthur H. Clark Company, 1965-1972.

Hamilton, Holman, *Zachary Taylor*, N.Y.: Bobbs-Merrill Company, 1941.

Hammersly, Thos. H. S., *Complete Regular Army Register of the United States*, Washington: g.p., 1881.

Havighurst, Walter, *The Long Ships Passing*, N.Y.: Macmillan Company, 1942.

Headquarters of the Army, *American Military History*, Washington: g.p., 1959.

Heitman, Francis B., *Historical Register and Dictionary of the U. S. Army*, Washington: g.p., 1903.

Henry, Robert Selph, *The Story of the Mexican War*, N.Y.: Bobbs-Merrill Company, 1950.

Hicks, John D., *The Federal Union*, Cambridge: Houghton-Mifflin Company, 1937.

Hitchcock, Ethan Allan, *Fifty Years in Camp and Field*, N.Y.: G. P. Putnam's Sons, 1909.

Howarth, David, *Panama*, N.Y.: McGrawHill Book Company, 1966.

Hussey, John W., *History of Fort Vancouver*, Vancouver: Washington State Historical Society, 1957.

Irving, Washington, *The Rocky Mountains or Scenes, Incidents and Adventures in the Far West, digested from the Journal of Captain B. L. E. Bonneville, U.S.A.* . . . , Philadelphia: Carey Lea and Blanchard, 1837 and subse quent editions.

Jackson, W. Turrentine, *Wagon Roads West*, New Haven: Yale University Press, 1952.

James, Marquis, *The Raven*, N.Y.: Bobbs-Merrill Company, 1929.

Josephy, Alvin Jr., *The Nez Perce and the Opening of the Northwest*, Lincoln: University of Nebraska Press, 1971.

Kouwenhoven, J. A., *The Columbia Historical Portrait of New York*, N.Y.: Doubleday & Co. Inc., 1953.

Landon, Fred, *Lake Huron*, N.Y.: Bobbs-Merrill Company, 1944.

Lavender, David, *Westward Vision*, N.Y.: McGrawHill Book Company, 1963.

LeHarivel, Philippe, *Nicolas de Bonneville, Pre-Romantique et Revolu tionaire*, Paris: 1923.

Leonard, Zenas, *The Adventures of Zenas Leonard, Fur Trader and Trapper*, Cleveland: Burrows Brothers Company, 1904.

Long, Everette B., *The Civil War Day by Day*, Garden City: Doubleday & Co. Inc., 1971.

McNitt, Frank, *Navaho Wars*, Albuquerque: University of New Mexico Press, 1972.

Maddux, Percy, *City on the Willamette*, Portland: Binfords and Mort, 1952.

Mahon, John K., *History of the Second Seminole War*, Gainesville: University of Florida Press, 1967.

Mattes, Merrill J., *Indians, Infants and Infantry, Denver: Old West Publishing Co., 1960.*

Meany, Edmond S., *History of Washington State*, N.Y.: Macmillan Company, 1942.

Meriwether, David, *My Life in the Mountains and Plains*, Norman: University of Oklahoma Press, 1965.

Miller, Helen Markley, *Benjamin Bonneville: Soldier-Explorer*, N.Y.: Julian Messner, 1957.

Minter, John Easter, *The Chagres: River of Westward Passage*, N.Y.: Rinehart, 1948.

Morgan, Dale L. and Harris, Eleanor Towles, eds., *The Rocky Mountain Journals of William Marshall Anderson*, San Marino: Huntington Library, 1967.

Nevins, Allen, *John Charles Fremont, Narratives of Exploration and Adventure*, N.Y.: Longmans, Green, 1956.

Newell, Robert, *Robert Newell's Memoranda*, Portland: Oregon Historical Society, 1959.

Nichols, Leona M., *The Mantle of Elias*, Portland: Binfords and Mort, 1941.

Ogg, F. A., *The Reign of Andrew Jackson*, New Haven: Yale University Press, 1919.

Payette, B. C., *Oregon Country Under the Union Jack*, Montreal: Privately printed, 1961.

Prucha, Francis Paul, *Guide to the Military Posts of the U. S.*, Madison: State Historical Society of Wisconsin, 1964.

Ramirez, Jose Fernando, *Mexico During the War With the United States*, St. Louis: University of Missouri, 1950.

Ramsey, Albert C., *The Other Side of the Mexican War*, N.Y.: B. Franklin, 1850.

Rich, E. E., *Hudson's Bay Company Records*, Vol 2, London: Hudson's Bay Record Society, 1941.

Ross, Ishbel, *The General's Wife*, N.Y.: DoddMead and Company, 1959.

Russell, Osborne, *Journal of a Trapper*, Lincoln: University of Nebraska Press, 1955.

Saxon, Lyle, *Old Louisiana*, N.Y.: Century Co., 1929.

Semmes, Raphael, *Service Afloat and Ashore During the Mexican War*, Cincinnati: Kelly, Piet Co., 1851.

Settle, Raymond, *March of the Mounted Riflemen*, Glendale: Arthur H. Clark Company, 1940.

Shaw, Ronald E., *Erie Water West*, Lexington: University of Kentucky, 1966.

Simmons, Marc, *New Mexico*, N.Y.: Norton, 1977.

Smith, E. Kirby, *To Mexico with Scott*, Cambridge: Harvard University Press, 1917.

Smith, Justin Harvey, *The War with Mexico*, N.Y.: Macmillan Company, 1919.

Spaulding, Oliver Lyman, *The United States Army in War and Peace*, N.Y.: G. P. Putnam's Sons, 1937.

Sprague, John T., Origin, *Progress and Conclusion of the Florida War*, N.Y.: D. Appleton and Co., 1848.

Stansbury, Capt. H., *Exploration and Survey of the Great Salt Lake Valley of Utah*, Washington: g.p., 1853.

Stevens, Hazard, *The Life of General I. I. Stevens*, N.Y.: Houghton-Mifflin Company, 1901.

Stewart, Geo. R., *The California Trail*, N.Y.: McGraw Hill Book Company, 1963.

Stryker, Lloyd Paul, *Andrew Johnson, a Study in Courage*, N.Y.: Macmillan Company, 1929.

Sunder, Wm., *Bill Sublette, Mountain Man*, Norman: University of Oklahoma Press, 1959.

Taylor, Bayard, *Eldorado*, Palo Alto: Osborne, 1968.

Terrell, John Upton, *Furs by Astor*, N.Y.: Morrow, 1963.

Thomlinson, M. H., *The Garrison at Fort Bliss*, El Paso: Hertzog and Resler, 1945.

Tousey, Thomas G., *Military History of Carlisle and Carlisle Barracks*, Richmond: Dietz Press, 1939.

Townsend, John Kirk, *Narratives of a Journey Across the Rocky Mountains*, Philadelphia: Henry Perkins, 1839.

Tripler, Eunice, *Some Notes of Her Personal Recollections*, N.Y.: privately printed, 1910.

Utley, Robert M., *Frontiersmen in Blue*, N.Y.: Macmillan Company, 1967.

Van Brough, Charles Hill, *Historic Homes*, Little Rock: 1906.

Van der Weyde, Wm., *The Life and Works of Thomas Paine*, 10 vols, New Rochelle: Thomas Paine National Historical Association, 1925.

Victor, Frances Fuller, *River of the West*, Oakland: Brooks-Sterling, 1974.

Wallace, Edw. S., *General William Jenkins Worth*, Dallas: Southern Methodist University Press, 1953.

Warren, G. K., *Memoir . . . Pacific Railroad Survey*, Washington: g.p., 1859.

Wheat, Carl I., *Mapping the American West*, San Francisco: Institute of Historical Cartography, 1958.

Whitlock, Brand, *La Fayette*, N.Y.: D. Appleton and Co., 1929.

Wisehart, M. K., *Sam Houston, American Giant*, Washington: B. R. Luce, 1962.

Wyeth, Nathaniel J., *Correspondence and Journals*, Eugene, Oregon: University Press, 1899.

Young, Otis E., *The West of Philip St. George Cooke*, Glendale: Arthur H. Clark Company, 1955.

Booklets

Carstensen, Vernon, ed., The Pacific Northwest Letters of George Gibbs, Portland: Oregon Historical Society, 1954.

Exploration of the Sierra Nevada, California Historical Society, n.d.

Gilbert, G. K., *Lake Bonneville*, U.S. Geological Survey, Monograph I, Washington: g.p., 1890.

Swekersky, Wm G., *Old Public Buildings of St. Louis*, Missouri Historical Society, n.d.

Vaught, Elsa, *Captain John Rogers, Father of Fort Smith*, Van Buren: privately printed, 1959.

Wainwright, Nicholas B., The Irvine Story, Philadelphia: The Historical Society of Pennsylvania, 1964.

Periodicals

Annals of Wyoming

Barry, J. Nielson, "Bonneville," July 1932. Warren, G. K., "Exploring Expeditions 1800-1857," July 1943.

Arkansas Historical Quarterly

Oakley, Francile B., "Arkansas' Golden Army of '49," Vol. 6, No. 1, 1947.

Chronicles of Oklahoma

Ford, Anne E., "Some Adventures of Captain Bonneville," Vol. VI, No. 2. Foreman, Grant, "An Unpublished Report by Captain Bonneville," No. XI.

Contributions, Montana Historical Society

"Correspondence from B.L.E. Bonneville," Vol. 1, No. 1.

Legion d Honneur, Baldensperger, Fernand, "Nicolas de Bonneville," XLV, No. 4.

Journal of Mississippi History, Doss, Richard B., "Andrew Jackson, Road Builder," V. 17, No. 1.

Mississippi Valley Historical Review, Mc Dermott, John Francis, "Washington Irving and Bonneville's Journal," Dec. 1951.

New York Review, Vol 1, Oct. 1837.

New Mexico Historical Review

Bender, A. B., "Frontier Defense of New Mexico," Vol. 9. Myers, J. W., "Military Establishments," Vol. 43, No. 1. Ogle, Ralph H., "Federal Control of Western Apaches, 1848-66," Vol. 14. Reeve, Frank D., ed., "Puritan and Apache: a Diary," Vol. 23, Oct. 1848, Jan. 1949. Webb, Henry B., "Sketch of Jefferson Barracks," Vol. 34, July 1946.

Oregon Historical Quarterly

Bird, Annie Laurie, "Thomas McKay," March 1939. Clark, Robert Carlton, "Military History of Oregon, 1849-1859," March 1935. Elliott, T. C., "Peter Skene Ogden," July 1910.

Washington Historical Quarterly

"Sheffield Reminiscenses," Vol. 15, 1924. Abel-Henderson, Annie, "General B.L.E. Bonneville Documents," Vol. 18, No. 1, No. 3, 1927.

Wisconsin Magazine of History, Kellogg, Louise P., *Old Fort Howard*, Vol. 18, Dec. 1934.

Newspapers

Arkansas Gazette, Arkansas Intelligencer, Alta California, Fort Smith Herald, Idaho Statesman, Niles Register, Missouri Republican, Oregon Statesman, Portland Oregonian, Portland Journal, Sacramento Union, St. Louis Argus, St. Louis Beacon, Santa Fe Gazette.

National Archives

22 Cong. 2 Sess. House Executive Document 104.
30 Cong. 1 Sess. House Executive Document 6.
30 Cong. 1 Sess. House Executive Document 60.
30 Cong. 1 Sess. Executive Doc. 1.
31 Cong. 1 Sess. Senate Document 32.
35 Cong. 1 Sess. Sec. of War Report. SED 2, v. ii.
35 Cong. 2 Sess. SED 1, pt ii.
35 Cong. 1 Sess. HED 2, v. II, pt ii.
35 Cong. 2 Sess. SED 5, No. 1, pt 2.
35 Cong. 2 Sess. SED v.2, No. 1, pt 2, Sec. of War Report.
NA NMRA 181 (2136) Bonneville personal file.
NA RG 94 Adjutant General's Office, 2742-ACP '78. Bonneville File.

NA RG 94 AGO LR Richard Bland Lee File.

NA RG 94 Doc. File 39.

NA RG 98 Vol. 10. Department of New Mexico, letters.

NA RG 153 N. 797 (10846) Court Martial Proceedings.

NA RG 393 Record of Army Commands LS 2/27/59-8/9/59. 7/26/58.

RG 94 Micro 222, Roll 25, LR; Micro 562 Roll 11, LS; Micro 565, Rolls 16, 17, 18, 19. LS; Micro 566, Roll 136, LR; Micro 567, Rolls 85, 136, 260 458. LS; Micro 617 Post Returns, Rolls 13, 128, 145, 187, 366, 404, 405, 489, 507, 545, 722, 843, 1066, 1456, 1531.

Index